WOMAN
New Dimensions

WOMAN
New Dimensions

edited by
Walter J. Burghardt, S.J.

Contributors

Constantina Safilios-Rothschild

Elisabeth Schüssler Fiorenza

Margaret A. Farley, R.S.M.

Rosemary Radford Ruether

Elizabeth Carroll, R.S.M.

Raymond E. Brown, S.S.

George H. Tavard

Mary Aquin O'Neill, R.S.M.

Anne E. Patrick, S.N.J.M.

PAULIST PRESS
New York/Ramsey/Toronto

261. 835

Cover Photos: Rick Smolan, John Glaser, Don Doll

Library of Congress
Catalog Card Number: 76-50969

ISBN: 0-8091-2011-9

Published by Paulist Press
Editorial Office: 1865 Broadway, N.Y., N.Y. 10023
Business Office: 545 Island Road, Ramsey, N.J. 07446

Printed and bound in the
United States of America

CONTENTS

PREFACE

Woman: New Dimensions is the product of a fruitful collaboration between the editors of the scholarly journal *Theological Studies* and staff members of the Center of Concern, an independent public-interest group located in Washington, D.C., and engaged in analysis and advocacy of global social-justice issues. In initial meetings of the two groups at the beginning of 1975, the many and complex facets of the topic were discussed with complete frankness. These sessions and broader consultations brought about an agreement on the areas to be covered and the experts to be approached. A special meeting with most of the prospective authors delineated even more sharply the issues that called for specific treatment, divided the material in such fashion that duplication would be avoided, and arranged for the submission of preliminary, provisional texts. With the cooperation of the nine authors, the final versions of all the articles were in my hands by mid-August, and the symposium appeared as a special theme issue of *Theological Studies* in December 1975.

This effort to insert theology into woman's struggle for freedom, equality, and personhood has not been a simple task; for the "new dimensions" are multiple, history and cultures are integral background, age-old traditions come under attack, scholarship turns passionate. And yet the issues must be explored, broadly and profoundly, in interdisciplinary fashion, with special contributions from woman's own perspectives. What we offer here is not an end but a beginning, not so much solutions as approaches.

More than a year has passed since these contributions first came off the press; and so the knowledgeable reader may note in the present volume the need for some updating, perhaps even revision. But such deficiencies seem minor when set against the need to offer these striking essays to a wider public than those who purchased all 8800 copies of them upon their original appearance. The legitimate aspirations of the world's women, their yearning not only to grow interiorly but to leaven each land with their God-given gifts, to contribute their rich potential

to the world's redemption, depend for their realization on the extent
to which men and women become aware of the issues involved, grasp
the genesis of the pertinent problems, relive woman's history, re-
evaluate the traditions and stereotypes that keep woman "in her place,"
and learn to discriminate between what is profoundly valid and what is
superficially seductive in today's outcry and argumentation. It is largely
to these ends that this volume has been fashioned.

Walter J. Burghardt, S.J.

I

THE CURRENT STATUS OF WOMEN CROSS-CULTURALLY: CHANGES AND PERSISTING BARRIERS

CONSTANTINA SAFILIOS-ROTHSCHILD

Wayne State University

THE PROCLAMATION by the United Nations of 1975 as the International Women's Year has helped focus attention on women and sex discrimination around the world. The very fact, however, that there is need for an International Women's Year to foster awareness about women's condition and stimulate interest and action to improve their status underlines the subordinate position of women. While women are discriminated against in all societies and life sectors, some changes have already occurred that represent tangible improvements in some aspects of their status. These changes are uneven because, due to different combinations of cultural, socioeconomic, political, and historical factors, existing sociopsychological and structural barriers have been overcome more or less easily in different societies and social classes. In addition, the "status" of women is not a unidimensional concept but a configuration of statuses in different life sectors (education, occupation, politics, family, etc.) which are not necessarily interrelated. Thus changes and improvements in one indicator of the status of women are not necessarily related to a proportionate improvement in other indicators. There is evidence that (a) the equalization of men's and women's educational options is not necessarily related to the equalization of employment options,[1] (b) the equalization of men's and women's educational or/and occupational options is not related to the equalization of familial and social-mobility options,[2] and (c) the equalization of educational and occupational options is not related to the equalization of political options.[3] Thus, even when significant advances are made in the over-all educational achievements of women, this does not necessarily signify that women will have the option to work when they are wives and mothers, as much as similarly educated men. Prevailing values and sex-role stereotypes may allow women to become educated, but may not

[1] Constantina Safilios-Rothschild, "The Options of Greek Men and Women," *Sociological Focus* 5 (1972) 71-83.

[2] *Ibid.*; also Constantina Safilios-Rothschild, *Women and Social Policy* (Englewood Cliffs, N.J., 1974).

[3] *Id.*, "Social Indicators of the Status of Women," paper commissioned by the United Nations Secretariat for the International Women's Year, 1975; *The Status of Women in Canada*, Report of the Royal Commission on the Status of Women in Canada, Ottawa, Sept. 28, 1970.

allow them to work when they are mothers. Recent data from a transitional society like Greece indicate, e.g., that while the principle of equal educational opportunities for men and women is widely accepted, married women's employment option is still accepted primarily by a minority of middle-class and upper-middle-class men and women.[4] Nor do significant advances in women's educational and occupational achievements necessarily open the same political options to women as is true for men.

Because the different indicators of the status of women are not highly interrelated, it is necessary to examine the changes in the status of women as well as the persisting barriers separately in each life sector. It must be noted that while during the last decade a variety of social indicators of social development were developed and used in collecting information, these indicators have seldom tapped the status of women. Thus, even when a social indicator (e.g., life expectancy or literacy rates) could have been quite useful if broken down by sex, the lack of this breakdown renders it inadequate for measuring either the status of women or the degree of social development. Consequently, the analysis that follows concerning the status of women in different life sectors will often suffer from lack of information with regard to crucial indicators.[5]

It must also be noted that many of the available social indicators have limitations due to male and middle-class biases. They tend to concentrate on and to tap dimensions which are more relevant for urban or/and middle-class males than for the rest of the population, these biases being more striking in the area of economic contributions as well as political participation. Thus, particularly the economic contributions of the majority of women around the world (as well as of low-income men in developing societies) are mostly unassessed and unrecognized. Hence women are not recorded as having advanced in status until they cross over to the male (and middle-class, urban) model of economic roles and thus can be included in social indicators and compared with men's achievements.

The status of women will be examined in the following five crucial life sectors: (1) educational and vocational training, (2) employment and other economic roles, (3) marriage and the family, (4) power and political participation, (5) health and nutrition.

Before starting the examination of the status of women in each life sector, it is important to note that women do not uniformly represent half of the population in all societies. At the one extreme, women represent less than one third (31.58%) of the population in Luxembourg, a little

---

[4] *Id.*, "Options" (n. 1 above).
[5] *Id.*, "Social Indicators" (n. 3 above).

over one third (38.14%) in the United Arab Emirates, and approximately 45% in the Central African Republic, French Guiana, Brunei, Iran, Kuwait, and Equitorian Guinea. At the other extreme, in Lesotho 56.8% of the population are women, 54% in the Congo, the U.S.S.R., and the German Democratic Republic, and 53% in Gabon.[6] These large variations in the man/woman ratio are at least partially due to migratory sex selectivity and sex differentials in mortality due to wars, revolutions, and national uprisings as well as childbearing. Of course, the man/woman ratio varies also widely from age group to age group.

EDUCATIONAL AND VOCATIONAL TRAINING

The most basic indicator of the status of women is the rate of illiteracy. The most recent data provided by UNESCO indicate that while female illiteracy by 1970 was practically eradicated in the developed countries, where only 4.3% of all illiterates are women, it is still plaguing developing countries, in which 60.2% of all illiterates are women.[7] Women's illiteracy rates continue to be high, especially in Africa and to a somewhat lesser extent in Asia. In 1960, only 12% of the female population 15 years and over in Africa was literate and 16% in 1970, while 37% of the female population 15 years and over in Asia was literate in 1960 and 43% in 1970. Thus, despite meager advances in African and Asian women's literacy during the last decade, the majority of them are still illiterate and the discrepancies between men's and women's extent of literacy are large. In 1970, more than two times as many African men as women were literate, and 20% more Asian men than women. Also, the rate of improvement in men's literacy in Africa and Asia is respectively 2.5 and 1.5 higher than the rate of improvement in women's literacy. Hence it is clear that unless specific compensatory mechanisms are instituted to diminish the gap between men and women and improve the women's status with regard to this elementary indicator, several decades will pass before the majority of adult Asian and African women have become literate. Latin American women seem to have a better status with regard to literacy: 63% of them were literate in 1960 and 73% in 1970. Furthermore, women's access to literacy nears equality with men, since 72% of men in 1960 and 80% in 1970 were literate, indicating the smallest gap existing between men's and women's literacy in the Third World.[8]

Of course, these over-all rates by continents cover up considerable

[6] *Statistical Yearbook, 1973* (United Nations Publications, Sales No. E/F.74.XVII.1) Table 18, pp. 67–79.

[7] UNESCO, *Statistical Yearbook, 1971*, Table 1.3.

[8] UNESCO, "Report on Women and Education and Training" (United Nations Publication, E/CONF. 66/BP11, 1975).

variations from country to country, from rural to urban context, and from social class to social class. Thus, while 56.2% of Ceylonese women were literate already in 1963,[9] only 18.72% of Indian women were literate in 1971, in contrast to 39.45% of men.[10] Furthermore, the situation for Indian women was worse in rural areas, where only 13.17% of women in contrast to 33.76% of the men were literate, while in urban areas 42.26% of the women were literate and 61.28% of the men.[11] And in general, in most developing societies the percentage of illiterate rural women is considerably larger than the percentage of illiterate urban women. In Turkey, e.g., while in 1969 only 32.7% of all women were literate, 55.1% of urban women were literate.[12] Also, there is evidence that low-income urban women living in slums have consistently much higher illiteracy rates than other urban women. Thus, only 21% of the women living in the Madras slums were literate, while 48% of all Madras women were literate[13] and the corresponding figures for Delhi were 20 and 36%.[14]

Furthermore, there are usually tremendous variations among different age groups: the younger the age group, the greater the percentage of literate women. These trends do reflect the increasing tendency to educate girls even in societies in which still a large portion of the feminine population is illiterate.[15]

The UNESCO statistics with regard to women's participation in literacy courses in 44 countries show that in 16 countries women are still underrepresented, comprising less than 35% of the students.[16] Thus it is important to underline the fact that the status of the majority of women in the developing countries, particularly of Africa and Asia, is quite low as measured by such a basic indicator as literacy. And it must also be underlined that no improvement in the status of these women can be expected before illiteracy has been practically eradicated and literacy combined with basic skills for a variety of economic and productive roles.

The reasons for which women's illiteracy persists in developing nations will become clear as we discuss the obstacles to girls' enrollment and the

[9] Subadra Siriwardena, "The Education of Girls and Women in Ceylon," *International Review of Education* 19, 1 (1973; Special Issue: The Education of Women) 115-20.

[10] S. Anandalakshmy, "Introductory Statement on the Subject of the Status of Women as a Factor Influencing Fertility" (United Nations Publication, ESA/SDHA/AC.2/11, June 21, 1973).

[11] *Ibid.*

[12] *Census of Population, 1965. Social and Economic Characteristics of Population* (Ankara, Turkey, 1969).

[13] P. K. Nambiar, "Slums of Madras City," in A. R. Desai and S. D. Pillai, eds., *Slums and Modernization* (Bombay, 1970) pp. 179-80.

[14] A. R. Desai and S. D. Pillai, "Slums of Old Delhi," in Desai-Pillai, *op. cit.*, p. 203.

[15] Nadia Haggag Youssef, *Women and Work in Developing Societies* (Population Monograph Series 15, University of California, Berkeley, 1974) pp. 42-49.

[16] UNESCO, "Equality of Access of Women to Literacy" (ED/MD/14, 1970) p. 14.

reasons for their high dropout rates. Educational statistics are usually enrollment rather than graduation statistics, despite the fact that the latter type of statistics provides more salient information in determining the status of women. The available enrollment figures for 1971 show that despite moderate gains African and Asian women are the least enrolled women at all levels and particularly at the secondary and college level, while Latin American women are almost as often enrolled as women in developed countries. Furthermore, female enrollment at all levels is much lower in rural areas than in urban areas and in low-income than in middle- or high-income urban districts.[17] In Amman, for example, in the slum districts female enrollment at the elementary-school level ranges from 47–49, while in higher-income districts it ranges from 64–65.[18] In developed countries, on the other hand, female enrollment at the elementary-school level was equalized already in 1960 with male enrollment, and at the secondary-school level in 1970.

Female college and university enrollment, despite a considerable upward change, still lagged behind male enrollment.[19] However, women's enrollment at the college and university level in some developing nations is at present as high as or higher than in developed countries. In Ceylon, e.g., already in 1966, 37% of university students were women, while at that time 38% of the university students in the United Kingdom and 40% of the students in the United States were women.[20]

The situation, however, appears even less optimistic for women's educational chances in developing countries when the school dropout rates are examined. In 1970, only 54% of the girls 6–11 years old enrolled in schools in developing nations remain in school six years later (the corresponding figure for boys being 60).[21] This over-all figure again masks considerable variation in the school dropout rates of girls in developing countries by rural-urban residence, social class, and society. Thus, in general the dropout rates for rural girls are much higher than those of urban girls, and the dropout rates of urban low-income girls much higher than those of middle- or upper-class urban girls.[22] Obsta-

[17] Constantina Safilios-Rothschild and the UNICEF Secretariat, *Children and Adolescents in Slums and Shanty-Towns in Developing Countries* (United Nations Publication, E/ICEF/L.1277/Add. 1, 1971) pp. 58–59.

[18] *Social Survey of Amman, 1966* (Ministry of Social Affairs and Labor, Hashemite Kingdom of Jordan, in co-operation with the United Nations Economic and Social Office in Beirut, March, 1969).

[19] UNESCO, "Report on Women and Education and Training" (n. 8 above).

[20] Siriwardena, *art. cit.*

[21] UNESCO, "Report on Women and Education and Training" (n. 8 above).

[22] Nambiar, *art. cit.*; Marie Eliou, "Scolarisation et promotion féminines en Afrique francophone (Côte-d'Ivoire, Haute Volta, Senegal)," *International Review of Education* 19, 1 (1973) 30–46.

cles to greater female enrollment as well as to girls' dropout and failure rates in developing nations are most often: the lack of schools; the preference of boys over girls in the available school facilities; the scarcity of rural schools that require rural girls to walk long distances and to be exposed to various dangers; the need for the baby-sitting and housekeeping services that a young (even a six-year-old) girl can provide; the scarcity of financial resources that often dictate only one child can go to school, and boys are then preferentially treated; religious beliefs that dictate that the teachers of young girls can be only women, combined, in some societies, with a relatively low number of women teachers; and cultural and religious beliefs that de-emphasize the importance of education for women.[23] Probably the following two sets of factors could be singled out as those that contribute most significantly to girls' losing interest in schoolwork and school attendance: (a) their having to help with household tasks, farm tasks, and child care that interferes considerably with their ability to study and follow the pace in schoolwork; and (b) teachers' open, direct, or occasionally more subtle discriminatory behaviors, their low expectations from girls, and their beliefs that education is wasted on women.

According to a UNESCO report prepared in collaboration with ILO that examined the vocational training received in 1964 by women in 46 countries, women's access to technical and employment-geared training is quite low in both developed and developing nations. The report indicates that the discrepancies between men and women are particularly striking with regard to access to training at the level of technician that prepares for employment in jobs and trades requiring a high level of qualification.[24] More recent UNESCO statistics provide information concerning the percentage of women in vocational and technical education in 1971 ranging from 2% in Niger, to 6% in Afghanistan, to 18 in Morocco and Cuba, 21 in Ghana, 23 in Iraq, 25 in Romania, 26 in Pakistan, 30 in Kenya, 40 in Costa Rica, 48 in France, 50 in West Malaysia, and 51 in Venezuela.[25] These percentages are not, however, very meaningful because of the prevailing sex differentiation in the existing vocational-training programs. In most countries vocational training is differentiated by sex and girls are barred from boys' technical and vocational-training programs. Thus, girls are only trained for "feminine" skills such as home economics, embroidery, sewing, and

[23] *Ibid.;* Desai and Pillai, *op. cit.;* UNESCO, "Report on Women and Education and Training" (n. 8 above); Economic Commission for Africa, "The Role of Women in African Development" (United Nations Publication, E/CONF.66/BP/8, April, 1975).

[24] UNESCO, "Technical and Vocational Training" (ED/MD/3) pp. 27, 94.

[25] UNESCO, *Statistical Yearbook, 1973,* pp. 166 and 188.

handicrafts, i.e., largely nonemployment-geared skills.[26] The available African data, e.g., show that domestic science constitutes more than 50% of the training offered to women. Subjects like animal husbandry, kitchen gardening, or poultry-keeping are occasionally included, while agriculture and co-operative education are only seldom included, despite the fact that women are responsible for more than 70% of the agricultural labor.[27] In developed societies the situation is often similar. In the progressive province of Hesse, West Germany, e.g., the number of apprenticeships for different skills and trades was found to be three times larger for men than for women,[28] and women are often precluded in many countries from "masculine" skills and trades.

The results of acute sex discrimination in the area of technical and vocational training hits hard exactly the groups of women who most badly need employment or must improve their knowledge in order to increase food productivity, i.e., low-income urban and rural women in developing nations. Thus, while food production in many countries of the Third World is in the hands of women, the absurdity of sex discrimination deprives them of agricultural training and in this way contributes to lower yields and to famine.[29] Similarly, because urban low-income women have no access to salable skills, they have to work as unskilled workers at very low salaries and under poor working conditions; or they become prostitutes; or they try to earn an income through illegal activities such as brewing; or through baking, hawking, or some other type of small home-industry.[30]

The reasons often advanced for the existing sex differentiation in the technical and vocational training offered to men and women are: (a) women are not interested in and have no aptitude for other than the traditional feminine skills compatible with their lives as housewives and mothers; and (b) women do not wish to and do not actually work in industry and "masculine" jobs for which technical and industrial skills are needed.[31]

There is evidence from developing countries, however, that when

[26] Safilios-Rothschild and UNICEF Secretariat (n. 17 above); and ECA, "The Role of Women in African Development" (n. 23 above).

[27] ECA, "The Role of Women in African Development."

[28] Alice H. Cook, *The Working Mother: A Survey of Problems and Programs in Nine Countries* (New York State School of Industrial and Labor Relations, Cornell University, 1975) pp. 18–21.

[29] Eliou, *art. cit.*; Solomon Odia, "Rural Education and Training in Tanzania," *International Labor Review* 103 (1971) 13–28.

[30] Safilios-Rothschild and UNICEF Secretariat (n. 17 above); ECA, "The Role of Women in African Development" (n. 23 above).

[31] Safilios-Rothschild and UNICEF Secretariat (n. 17 above).

"masculine" technical and vocational-training programs are open to women, they are attended by women. For example, at the regional technological institute at Ciudad Maders in Mexico, where technical studies at the secondary level are offered, 14 out of the 44 student electricians are women, 10 out of 27 mechanical engineering students, and one third of the trainees in industrial chemistry.[32] Also, in Ghana, where all government vocational-training schools and centers are coeducational, a growing number of women take the courses offered. At the Accra Polytechnic commercial studies, e.g., 24 women and 22 men were enrolled in 1965/66, and 67 women and 49 men in 1969/70.[33] It seems, therefore, that the availability of vocational-training programs rather than the girls' aptitude and interest determines the extent of their enrollment in these programs.

The second argument mentioned above is not valid either, since about one third of workers in manufacturing industries, clothing and footwear industries, chemical industry, electrical engineering, and paper industry are women in several Latin American countries.[34] But due to their lack of skills, these women workers have to work at the lowest, unskilled level without any chance to ever escape from it.

We could conclude, therefore, that the status of the large majority of women in most developing countries, especially in Africa and Asia, with regard to education is quite low, since they are still plagued by illiteracy and lack of employable technical and vocational skills, including agricultural. Furthermore, the educational status of African and Asian women is particularly low in rural and low-income urban sectors in which the large majority of women live. Urban upper-class, upper-middle-class, and increasingly also middle-class women graduate from secondary school and attend the university, but they represent only a small percentage of the female population and thus they accentuate the class differentials in women's educational options that further compound the existing sex differentials.

In developed societies, in which men's and women's access to (but not necessarily graduation from) primary and secondary school have been over-all equalized, women's educational status can be differentiated on the basis of the range of educational options available to women in each society in terms of professional, semiprofessional, and vocational careers. Unfortunately, at this point only information concerning the range of professional fields is consistently available to allow cross-cultural com-

[32] "Youth and Work in Latin America, II: Youth Employment Prospects," *International Labor Review* 90 (1964) 150–79.

[33] Miranda Greenstreet, "Employment of Women in Ghana," *International Labor Review* 103 (1971) 117–29.

[34] "Youth and Work in Latin America" (n. 32 above).

parisons and conclusions. Data from the middle and late 60's show that Poland, Czechoslovakia, Hungary, the U.S.S.R., and Finland provide the widest range of educational levels, with Argentina, Austria, Greece, and Japan following. In countries in which women have a wide range of educational options at the university level, the "masculine" occupations which are most often redefined as "feminine" are pharmacy and dentistry, while occupations such as chemistry and medicine most often become equally open to men and women and lose a sex-specific label. Fields like law and architecture seldom become "feminine" fields (with the exception of Greece, where architecture became a "feminine" field) but women enter them in considerable numbers. Finally, "technical" fields like engineering, aeronautics, or agriculture tend to remain "hardcore" masculine occupations.[35]

Despite considerable progress, therefore, women's education is still lagging behind. Even the elementary goal of literacy has not yet been achieved for the majority of women in Africa and Asia. While the present generation of women has a much better chance for literacy in all countries, probably universal literacy will not have been achieved for the next 2-3 generations. Despite the fact that the barriers to women's literacy and education are known, little concerted effort is made to eradicate them. Furthermore, the exclusion of women from technical and vocational training, including agricultural training, seriously discriminates against women in all societies and contributes to the underdevelopment of the Third World. But even in the case of most advanced societies, women's educational options must be considerably enlarged before educational equality is reached. Recent changes in the United States, stimulated by the Women's Liberation Movement, have already enlarged women's educational options at the university level, by women's admittance to masculine fields such as medicine and law, but the advances are not as yet spectacular or even throughout all masculine fields.

EMPLOYMENT AND OTHER ECONOMIC ROLES

The available statistics concerning women's employment are besieged by several methodological shortcomings discussed in detail elsewhere.[36] Here it suffices to mention that statistics concerning the labor-force participation of women are inadequate and of little validity, because

[35] Constantina Safilios-Rothschild, "A Cross-Cultural Examination of Women's Marital, Educational and Occupational Options," *Acta sociologica* 14 (1971) 96–113.

[36] Safilios-Rothschild, "Social Indicators of the Status of Women" (n. 3 above); *id.*, "Methodological Problems Involved in the Cross-Cultural Examination of Indicators Related to the Status of Women," paper presented at the American Population Association Meetings, Toronto, Canada, April 1972.

they do not reflect accurately the extent of women's employment and give no indication concerning marital status and extent of employment participation (part-time or full-time). Statistics concerning women's participation in the labor force are particularly misleading in countries of high unemployment and thus of lesser value in the case of developing societies. In general, the best indicators of women's employment are (a) the percentage of women employed of all women in the working ages, (b) the percentage of married women working of all working women, and (c) the percentage of women working full time.[37] Information with regard to all three indicators is not available for all societies, and even when it is available, there are serious comparability problems. The census definitions of employment for women in different countries are not the same, because women unpaid family workers in rural or urban areas are included in some censuses and excluded from others.[38] Actually, information concerning the percentage of women in the category "unpaid family workers" is useful, since it indicates the extent to which women can work outside the home and the extent to which they have a right to remuneration for their work. In Pakistan, e.g., the over-all low status of women is reflected in the fact that 68.3% of employed women are unpaid family workers.[39]

Furthermore, it is difficult to assess the economic contributions of women, especially in developing countries, because three sets of indicators of economic activity are usually missing: (a) indicators that assess the extent to which rural and urban low-income women (and men) play economic roles (in other ways than by means of conventional employment) and participate in local development efforts such as community development programs, different types of co-operatives (e.g., consumer, marketing, health, credit) or self-help projects; (b) indicators that allow the assessment of women's productivity in rural areas not only in terms of food production but also in terms of food preservation as well as marked participation in different types and levels of markets; (c) special social indicators tapping and assessing the contributions of housewives to the economy through the performance of household tasks, child care, and a variety of services rendered to the husband and the entire family.[40]

The recent compilation of information concerning the economic roles of African women by the Women's Programme Unit at the Economic Commission for Africa represents a pioneer effort that illustrates the serious underestimation of women's economic roles in the absence of the

[37] Ibid.
[38] Lee L. Bean, "Utilization of Human Resources: The Case of Women in Pakistan," International Labor Review 98 (1967) 391–410.
[39] Ibid.
[40] Safilios-Rothschild, "Social Indicators of the Status of Women" (n. 3 above).

above three sets of indicators. They estimate that 60–80% of agricultural labor in Africa is carried out by women. More specifically, they estimate that 70% of food production is done by women, 50% of domestic food storage, 100% of food processing, 50% of the responsibility for animal husbandry, 60% of marketing, 90% of brewing, 90% of the labor involved in securing water supply, and 80% of the labor involved in securing fuel supply; 70% of self-help projects are undertaken by women. In Kenya, e.g., it is estimated that women provide 80% of the self-help labor involved in building roads, schools, village centers, etc.[41] Because, however, these important economic roles played by women cannot be classified under the traditionally defined regular gainful employment, the census of many African countries omits them altogether or seriously underestimates them.

Keeping all these limitations in mind, we can turn now to examine whatever cross-cultural employment data are available and the trends they indicate. The ILO *Yearbooks of Labour Statistics* for 1971, 1973, and 1974 indicate that the lowest percentage of economically active female population can be found in all Arab countries, Iran, and Pakistan, in which the percentage varies from 1.8 in Algeria to 8.0 in Morocco and 8.3 in Iran.[42] Women in these countries, therefore, have in fact a very low status, since it is only a tiny minority of the female population that is literate (little over 1/10) and economically active (around 1/20).

The Central American countries come in second lowest (closely followed by the Latin American countries), with the economically active female population ranging from 8.2 in Guatemala and 10.4 in Mexico to 11.4 in Nicaragua, 17.7 in Panama, and 21.5 in El Salvador. Four European countries, Spain, Italy, Netherlands, and Malta, have less than 20% of economically active female population, while in the remaining European countries percentages vary from 26.2 in Belgium to 48.1 in Romania.[43]

Finally, countries with over half the female population economically active are predominantly in East, West, and Central Africa: Lesotho, Madagascar, Upper Volta, Burundi, and Guinea Bissau. In addition, many of the countries with over two fifths of the female population economically active are also situated in Africa in such countries as Botswana, Chad, Ivory Coast, United Republic of Tanzania, and Gabon.[44] Thus African women, despite their very low educational status, are not inhibited from playing economic roles, although much of their economic activity is limited to agriculture and their economic roles may

[41] ECA, "The Role of Women in African Development" (n. 23 above).
[42] ILO, *Yearbook of Labor Statistics*, 1971, 1973, and 1974, Table 1 in each.
[43] *Ibid.*
[44] ECA, "The Role of Women in African Development" (n. 23 above).

not often fit traditional Western employment models. This is a case in which educational and employment indicators for women are poorly interrelated.

When the percentage of women in the labor force is calculated over the base of female population in the working ages, as has been done for selected European countries, the picture changes considerably and the highest percentages of working women can be found in East Germany and the U.S.S.R. (80%), followed by Sweden (53.7), West Germany (47), and the lowest in Norway (23.8), Netherlands (22.6), and Belgium (25.8).[45] While this type of indicator is clearly more accurate for developed societies, it may tend to underestimate women's economic activity in developing societies, unless the working age is extended considerably at both ends.

Other indicators concerning the employment of women which are sensitive in tapping ongoing social changes and in accurately reflecting the status of women in this area of employment are (a) percentage of women employed who are married with husband present and children younger than three years old; (b) percentage of women employed by specific type of occupation; (c) degree of discrepancy between men's and women's wages and salaries, controlling for level and type of position, level of employee's skill, and length of service; and (d) percentage of women in top administrative, managerial, and executive positions.[46] While all four indicators are extremely important for the more refined measurement of the status of women in the economic sector, only spotty data are available for a few and mostly for developed societies.

With respect to the first indicator, there is considerable evidence that the extent to which women are integrated into the labor force can be measured by the degree to which married women are working.[47] In addition, the extent to which mothers work, especially mothers of more than one young child, is a further sensitive indicator of women's integration in the labor force.[48] The available evidence indicates that there has been an increase in the labor participation of married women and mothers of young children, especially in North America and in Eastern European and Scandinavian countries.[49] We know that in 1972 in Sweden 53.7 of the women in the labor force were mothers of children

[45] Marjorie Galenson, *Women and Work: An International Comparison* (New York State School of Industrial and Labor Relations, Cornell University, 1973).

[46] Safilios-Rothschild, "Social Indicators of the Status of Women" (n. 3 above).

[47] Jerzy Berent, "Some Demographic Aspects of Female Employment in Eastern Europe and the U.S.S.R.," *International Labor Review* 101 (1970) 175-92.

[48] Galenson, *op. cit.*; Cook, *op. cit.*

[49] Berent, *art cit.*; Cook, *op. cit.*

under 7, while in 1968 this percentage was only 42.1,[50] and that in 1969, 48% of the Swedish working women had children under 3.[51] Similarly, motherhood, when the child is under 6, and working status seem to be most compatible in Finland, East Germany, and Romania and least compatible in Japan, Canada, Denmark, West Germany, Great Britain. and Norway.[52] The greater the extent of this incompatibility and the greater the numbers of women affected, the lower the status of women in the employment sector since work discontinuity affects adversely not only the women directly involved but the over-all image of working women as "temporary" and therefore not seriously committed workers. There is only sporadic information, however, from developing societies concerning the extent to which the mother role is compatible with the working role when the children are very young. It can only be hypothesized that these roles are quite compatible due to the existence of some type of extended family.

With regard to the second indicator, information is most often available concerning women's occupational distribution by broad occupational categories, an indicator that does not reflect accurately the occupational status of women in different societies. since significant variations usually exist within occupational categories. In general, the larger the women's range of educational options, the larger also their range of occupational options. Thus we find that the U.S.S.R., Finland, Poland, Hungary, East Germany, and Bulgaria (as well as the other Eastern European countries), which offer women the widest range of educational choices, also offer them the widest range of occupational choices. Thus, even in a hardcore masculine occupation such as engineering, 25% of engineers in Bulgaria are women, 22 in East Germany, 33 in Hungary, 18 in Poland, and 40 in the U.S.S.R.[53] Other cross-cultural trends in women's occupational distribution are the following:

a) Up to now in most societies women have been allowed to enter only low-prestige and low-pay occupations that are labeled "feminine." While there is nothing "feminine" about occupations labeled feminine, their only characteristic is low prestige and low pay.[54] In all societies and times, the "masculine" label is attached to occupations with higher prestige and pay than "feminine" occupations. The same occupation may be "masculine" in one society and "feminine" in another because of

[50] Cook, *ibid.*
[51] *Women in Sweden in the Light of Statistics* (Stockholm, 1971).
[52] Cook, *op. cit.*
[53] *Ibid.*
[54] Safilios-Rothschild, *Women and Social Policy* (n. 2 above).

its relative standing in comparison to other occupations. Medicine, e.g., a high-prestige and high-pay occupation in the United States, has been an almost exclusively "masculine" occupation. In the U.S.S.R., however, where a physician is paid 110 rubles and the highly skilled blue-collar worker 120 rubles,[55] medicine is a "feminine" occupation. Similarly, when the occupation of secretary or "house servant" carries considerable prestige and a relatively good pay, as has been the case in some African nations, men dominate it. But when other occupational avenues of greater prestige and pay become available, men abandon them, and women are allowed to enter them when they have assumed the characteristics of a "feminine" occupation—that is, lower prestige and pay than male-dominated occupations.[56]

b) Even within "feminme" occupations the minority of men usually occupy the best-paid and most prestigious positions as well as all decision-making and supervisory posts. In the U.S.S.R., e.g., although 4 out of 5 physicians are women, 4 out of 5 physicians of high rank are men.[57] Also, while air hostesses on American (and most other) airlines are women, the few men are pursers, playing a supervisory role and enjoying a greater prestige and pay. The recent breakdown of this sex-differentiated organizational structure in the United States represents an important victory due to its visibility and despite the small number of women involved.

c) Women's entry in a "masculine" field does not tend to decrease the prestige or level of pay attached to an occupation, only when women enter it not because men have abandoned it but because ongoing ideological and other social changes break down structural barriers and women's stereotypic constraints. In several European societies, e.g., pharmacy became equally or predominantly "feminine" without any negative effect upon pharmacists' prestige or remuneration. The same holds true for fields such as dentistry or architecture. Similarly, the recent entry of American women in law and medicine due to the Women's Liberation ideology has not in any way altered the prestige and high pay attached to these occupations.

d) When women manage to enter in considerable proportions a "masculine" field such as dentistry or pharmacy, they are usually able to enter other "masculine" fields as well, such as medicine, law, or architecture, although there may be a time lag before entry in other masculine fields takes place.

In view of the above discussion on women's cross-cultural occupational

[55] Cook, *op. cit.*

[56] Safilios-Rothschild, *Women and Social Policy.*

[57] Norton T. Dodge, *Women in the Soviet Economy* (Baltimore, 1966).

patterns, it becomes clear why available data consistently show that the pay of women is only a fraction of men's pay, ranging from 40 to 80%. The concentration of women in low-pay fields and low-pay positions within any given field accounts for the over-all significantly lower wages and salaries of women. Furthermore, even when women are employed in exactly the same jobs with men, they are usually paid less than men, most often regardless of the type of legislations existing regarding "equal pay for equal work."[58] This is produced by either outright discriminatory practices against women or by means of subtler discriminatory practices that assign slightly different labels and job classifications to women's jobs that render the comparison with men's salaries impossible, since only women are employed in some types of low-paid jobs.[59] Another factor responsible for the lower salaries of white- and blue-collar women workers is their significantly lower degree of unionization and their lesser tendency to strike and fight for their rights.[60] In the United States (and most other countries) slightly over 10% of women workers belong to trade unions.[61] Sweden[62] and Finland[63] represent outstanding exceptions to this trend, with Finnish working women belonging to unions almost as frequently as men. The male domination in union membership, but even more importantly in union leadership, has led to unions' disinterest in women and in helping equalize their salaries.[64] Actually, as things stand now, many union and nonunion shops have different categories for women's and men's jobs that provide men with the more prestigious, responsible, and better-paid jobs—and unions often write separate work agreements covering women's and men's jobs, thus institutionalizing sex discrimination.[65]

The few data available on the degree of discrepancy between men's and women's wages and salaries controlling for all work-related relevant factors show that women are consistently paid less in all societies and

[58] *Ibid.*; Cook, *op. cit.*; ECA, "The Role of Women in African Development" (n. 23 above).

[59] Cook, *op. cit.*; Safilios-Rothschild, *Women and Social Policy*; Nobuko Takahashi, "Women's Wages in Japan and the Question of Equal Pay," *International Labor Review* 106 (1975) 51–68.

[60] Giselle Charzat, *Les françaises: Sont-elles des citoyennes?* (Paris, 1972).

[61] Judy Edelman, "Unions on the Line: Myths vs. Reality," *Up From Under* 1 (1970) 34–37.

[62] Gunnar Qvist, "Landorganisationen (LO) en Suède et les femmes sur le marché du travail, 1898–1973," *Sociologie et sociétés* 6 (1974) 77–91.

[63] Elina Haavio-Mannila et Eeva-Liisa Tuominen, "La situation de la femme au travail en Finlande," *ibid.*, pp. 93–103.

[64] Alice H. Cook, "Women and American Trade Unions," *Annals of the American Academy of Political and Social Science* 375 (1968) 124–32; Lucretia W. Dewey, "Women in Labor Unions," *Monthly Labor Review* 94 (1971) 42–48.

[65] Cook, *ibid.*

continue to be underpaid despite a variety of correcting mechanisms set to work in some developed societies. Thus, data from Poland, the United States, Canada, and Sweden show quite similar trends despite many differences in official policies and the nature of the women's work involvement.[66] Finally, with respect to the last indicator, whatever cross-cultural data exist show an extremely high degree of agreement in that women hold an extremely low percentage of top, decision-making, or policy-making, powerful, prestigious, and highly-paid positions. This trend holds true regardless of the over-all percentage of employed women, the type of occupational distribution, or the nature of existing laws. Thus, this trend has been documented for Poland[67] and the U.S.S.R.[68] as well as the United States,[69] Canada,[70] all African nations,[71] and Australia.[72] It must be noted, however, that in several developing nations such as India, Thailand, or Ceylon, a number of women can be found in top decision-making and policy positions. While such women are quite visible in their positions as prime minister, or minister, or director of a large hospital or a large business undertaking, percentage-wise they are few and their positions do not reflect an improvement in the status of all women. The paradox can be explained in terms of their social-class background. They are usually upper-class or upper-middle-class women who are favored over middle-class men in societies with rigid social stratification systems and a particularistic, familistic orientation.[73]

We can conclude that in both developing and developed societies women are not able to make maximum economic contributions and are excluded from all prestigious and high-paying occupations and positions. But even within the "feminine," low-prestige, and low-pay occupations in which they are allowed to engage, they are paid less than men and cannot attain supervisory and decision-making positions, accessible only to men. In addition, women in the Third World, particularly rural and urban low-income women, play a variety of significant economic and productive roles which are not usually assessed and rewarded.

[66] Magdalena Sokolowska, "Some Reflections on the Different Attitudes of Men and Women toward Work," *International Labor Review* 92 (1965) 35–50; Safilios-Rothschild, *Women and Social Policy* (n. 2 above).

[67] Sokolowska, *ibid.*

[68] G. Barker, "Les femmes en Union soviétique," *Sociologie et sociétés* 4 (1972) 159–91; Claude Alzon, *La femme potiche et la femme bonniche* (Paris, 1973).

[69] Safilios-Rothschild, *Women and Social Policy* (n. 2 above).

[70] *The Status of Women in Canada* (n. 3 above).

[71] ECA, "The Role of Women in African Development" (n. 23 above).

[72] S. Encel, N. Mackenzie, and M. Tebbutt, *Women and Society: An Australian Study* (Melbourne, 1974).

[73] Safilios-Rothschild, *Women and Social Policy.*

MARRIAGE AND THE FAMILY

The status of women in this area can be measured on the basis of several indicators such as (a) age at marriage—legal minimum and actual age, (b) age difference between spouses, (c) women's right to free choice in marriage, (d) women's right to property and divorce, (e) rate of remarriage of widows and divorcees, (f) mean number of children born to married women, (g) percentage of women marrying younger men, (h) type of division of labor within the family, and (i) the extent to which women have a choice as to whether to marry or not, as well as to the age by which they must marry.[74] In addition, many other indicators of familial options would be extremely valuable in assessing women's status in the family, such as the extent to which women can initiate or reject sexual relations with their husbands, but such information is only sporadically available and cross-cultural comparisons are not possible.

Cross-cultural data are available with respect to minimum legal age at marriage and show that at present three countries have 12 as the minimum legal age at marriage for women: Chile, Panama, and Peru; six have 14: Argentina, Mexico, Guyana, Philippines, Hungary, and Italy; and three societies have 15: Mauritius, Turkey, and Costa Rica.[75] In addition, several societies in Africa and Asia either have no minimum legal age at marriage or circumvent the legal minimum in practice. There is evidence, e.g., that in Algeria, despite the minimum legal age at marriage set at 16 for women, girls of 12 or 13 are married secretly and their position is regularized at the marriage registry only when they become 16. Thus, in 1967 more than three quarters of Algerian women were already married by the age of 20.[76] And in India, despite legal provisions against it, girls are wed before puberty and children are engaged to marry.[77] There is no question that the status of women is quite low in societies in which girls are made to marry before 15, and in those sectors of the population within which such early marriages are widely practiced. It is obvious that such early marriages and early motherhood, which usually is the result, interfere with the girls' chances for education and training.

In the 60's, in many developed societies, the actual age at marriage tended to decrease due to a transitional stage in the status of women during which women could get jobs and thus did not have to wait until the man had a well-paying job.[78] This trend has proved detrimental to the status of women, because it interfered with women's chances for

---

[74] Safilios-Rothschild, "Social Indicators of the Status of Women."

[75] United Nations, *Demographic Yearbook, 1972.*

[76] Evelyne Sullerot, *Woman, Society and Change* (New York, 1971).

[77] *Ibid.*

[78] *Ibid.*

college education and for the development of high career commitment
and achievement aspirations. There are some indications, however, that
in the 70's this trend has again started reversing itself. In the United
States, e.g., the age of marriage is going up.[79]

With regard to the age difference between husband and wife, the
available cross-cultural data are poor. In general, it can be assumed that
many marriages in which the husband is considerably older than the wife
indicate a low status of women and unequal exchanges between marital
partners. Because women have no access to income and status, they have
to exchange youth and attractiveness for status and financial security.
Small age differences between spouses, on the other hand, do not
necessarily reflect a higher status of women. They may instead reflect a
higher level of development in which younger men can achieve adequate
status and financial security so that women do not have to marry older
men in order to secure status and financial security. The percentage of
women marrying men five or more years younger than themselves is,
however, a good indicator of the status of women, since the higher this
percentage, the more women are employed and the more they have
achieved sufficient fame, wealth, and status to be fascinating to younger
men and the more they are able to exchange these "scarce and desired
goods" for youth and attractiveness.[80] Actually, it has been found that
there is a good correlation cross-culturally between women's economic
activity and the percentage of women marrying younger men.[81]

Women's legal right to divorce is a very important right that in the 60's
has been granted even in countries such as the Arab states, Iran, and a
Catholic country like Italy (for the first time it was extended to both men
and women in the 70's). In addition to women's legal ability to divorce, it
is important to note that divorce rates have increased throughout the
world for a variety of reasons, one of which is of interest here: women's
increasing ability to support themselves that allows them to divorce
when their marriage is unbearable. Considerable evidence from societies
in which women, due to lack of skills, could not support themselves
except by becoming maids or unskilled workers has shown that women
had to tolerate unhappy and oppressive marriages because they could
not return to their parents and had no other alternatives. Thus, it can be

[79] U. S. Department of Health, Education, and Welfare, National Center for Health
Statistics, *Vital Statistics of the United States, 1970* 3: *Marriage and Divorce* (Rockville,
Md., 1974).

[80] Safilios-Rothschild, "A Cross-Cultural Examination..." (n. 35 above); *id., Women
and Social Policy* (n. 2 above); *id.*, "Dual Linkages between the Occupational and Family
System: A Macro-Sociological Analysis," *Signs: Journal of Women in Culture and Society*,
forthcoming in December 1975.

[81] Safilios-Rothschild, "A Cross-Cultural Examination..." (n. 35 above).

said that the considerable recent increases in divorce rates in the United States, Canada, Hungary, Sweden, Denmark, and Czechoslovakia[82] may be at least partially due to the increasing economic independence and self-sufficiency of women that renders divorce an option to an unhappy marriage.

There are some indications that as long as the status of women is low in society and women are viewed as objects (that become "used" after marriage), the remarriage rates of widows and divorcees are very low, and much lower than the marriage rates of single women of the same age groups. But since few detailed data are available about most societies, it is not possible at present to describe the status of women around the world with regard to this variable.

Coming now to fertility, the evidence is overwhelming that the higher the status of women, the lower is their fertility.[83] There is an especially strong relation between women's education and fertility level, the decline in fertility being associated with even small educational achievements on the part of women when the over-all educational status of women is low. Thus, in societies such as the African societies or India where women's illiteracy is high, women's fertility declines when a woman is literate and has attended a few grades of school. On the other hand, when the over-all educational status of women is higher, declines of fertility are brought about by much higher educational achievements, such as at least some years of high school or high-school graduation.[84] As long as women's status in a society is very low and prospects for future improvement are poor, mothers as well as fathers are anxious to have at least two sons in order to have some financial security in old age, and in search for these sons they end up having a large number of children.[85] Once women's status, especially in terms of education, training and economic independence, improves, there is a decline in fertility, because mothers in increasing numbers work and do not wish to spend their entire lives bearing and rearing children; girls tend to be valued as much as boys by their parents; and parents increasingly have high educational aspirations for their children, including their daughters. Thus fertility reflects the actual status of women as well as prospects for improvement.

An area in which it is important to examine the status of women is the

[82] United Nations, *Demographic Yearbook, 1972.*

[83] United Nations, "Study of the Interrelationship of the Status of Women and Family Planning," Conference background paper, World Population Conference, Bucharest, 1974.

[84] Constantina Safilios-Rothschild, "Socio-Psychological Factors Related to Fertility in Urban Greece," *Journal of Marriage and the Family* 31 (1969) 595-606.

[85] Thomas Poffenberger, *Husband-Wife Communication and Motivational Aspects of Population Control in an Indian Village* (Department of Child Development, M. S. University of Baroda, India, 1968).

degree to which they are free to choose a mate. While forced marriages have drastically declined in most traditional societies, they can still be found in Algeria[86] and other Arab countries as well as among the traditional segments of the population in Latin American, Mediterranean, and Asian societies. It has been found, e.g., that arranged marriages are much more frequent among Greek women living in villages and small towns, and among the low-income urban women who are the least educated and hold the most traditional, stereotypic views concerning the roles of men and women.[87] Among middle-class and upper-middle-class urban women, on the other hand, arranged marriages have practically entirely disappeared. On the other hand, there is some evidence that even women college students in a country like Pakistan or Japan reject only partially the notion of arranged marriages, in that they want to have a definite say as to whether or not they accept men proposed by their parents.[88] But most of them tend to be afraid to shoulder the responsibility entailed in choosing their mate entirely on their own. Furthermore, in urban Japan arranged meetings between boys and girls are used as a sort of guided dating that may or may not lead to marriage.[89] It seems, therefore, that women must have enjoyed for more than one generation high educational and employment status and freedom of movement before they can feel confident to take the choice of a mate in their hands.

An area in which the status of women in the family is reflected quite accurately is the division of labor within the family. The lower the over-all status of women, the more unequal is the division of labor within the family, with women being assigned the responsibility for carrying out all the time-consuming child care, housekeeping, and other family tasks and activities. The more married women are not allowed to work, the more "natural" it becomes for them to carry the entire burden of family responsibilities, since they have more "free" time. Even when in some developed societies husbands *help with* some tasks, their contributions remain peripheral and unreliable. In fact, husbands tend to help mostly during family crises such as the wife's illness, pregnancy, or right after

[86] Fadela M'Rabet, *La femme algérienne et les algériennes* (Paris, 1969).

[87] Constantina Safilios-Rothschild, *The Modern Greek Family* 1: *The Dynamics of the Husband-Wife Relationship* (Athens: National Center of Social Research, forthcoming in 1976); Choong Soon Kim, "The *Yon'jul-hon* or Chain-String Form of Marriage Arrangement in Korea," *Journal of Marriage and the Family* 36 (1974) 575–79.

[88] J. Henry Korson, "Students' Attitudes toward Mate Selection in a Muslim Society, Pakistan," *Journal of Marriage and the Family* 31 (1969) 153–63; Robert O. Blood, Jr., *Love Match and Arranged Marriage: A Tokyo-Detroit Comparison* (New York, 1967) pp. 35–59.

[89] *Ibid.*

the birth of a child. Otherwise they help when they feel like it, mostly during weekends, and with tasks that are not very time-consuming and that they can label "masculine."[90] It is interesting to note at this point that in developed societies such as the United States, in which most people live in houses rather than apartments, there is evidence that despite the availability of a variety of "time-saving" gadgets housewives spend 55 hours per week in housework, as they did 50 years ago. While they now spend less time preparing food and cleaning up after meals, they spend an equal time in housecleaning and more time shopping, performing "managerial tasks," and on child care.[91]

There is considerable evidence that in many societies the improvement of women's status, particularly with respect to the availability of the option to work for married women, does not alter their status in the family. Thus, even when married women work outside the home, in most societies their position in the family is not significantly improved with regard to the division of labor. Their husbands help them more than is true in the case of housewives, but they cannot be relied upon, since they seldom carry out some specific tasks consistently or share a household responsibility with their wives. In Yugoslavia, e.g., only 3.7% of the husbands help their wives when they are housewives, while 11.4% of them help their wives when they are working.[92] Similar trends have been reported for Hungary and the Scandinavian countries.[93] But in a number of developing societies, even when women work, husbands do not help their wives, as is true for India, Greece, and most Latin American, African, and Asian nations.

The "double burden" of women is unbearable unless their income allows them access to hired help, or their mothers or other female relatives can be relied upon for free housekeeping and child-care help. Hence the existence of traditional or "modified" extended families facilitates the work of married women in developing (and developed) societies in which they cannot expect any help from their husbands.

The only exception to the above trends has been Sweden, where in 1971 it was reported that 72% of the husbands *shared* (not helped with)

[90] Alexander Szalai, ed., *The Use of Time: Daily Activities of Urban and Suburban Populations in Twelve Countries* (Paris, 1972).

[91] Joann Vanek, "Time Spent in Housework," *Scientific American* 231 (1974) 116-20.

[92] Zlata Grebo, "La famille dans une société en évolution: Problèmes et responsabilités de ses membres: Yougoslavie," United Nations Interregional Seminar on the "Family in an Evolving Society; Problems and Responsibilities of its Members," London, July 18-31, 1973 (United Nations Publication No. ESA/SDHA/AC.3/Wf.20).

[93] Veronica Stolte-Heiskanen and Elina Haavio-Mannila, "The Position of Women in Society: Formal Ideology vs. Everyday Ethic," *Social Science Information* 6 (1967) 169-88.

washing up with their wives, 66% shared cooking, and 63% shared cleaning.[94] This, however, constitutes an anomaly in the world trends, although there are some indications that increasingly American young couples are replicating the Swedish model.

For the vast majority of working women around the world, therefore, their work role does not lighten their burden of family responsibilities. Thus, despite the fact that working women, at least in developed societies, tend to simplify some housekeeping tasks and to have some help from husbands, children, and mothers, time-budget studies in nine societies have shown the oppression of women within the family. In the U.S.S.R., e.g., it has been found that women work three times as much as men in the house and spend on the average 2.5–4 hours during weekdays and 5 hours during Sundays doing housework and taking care of the children.[95] Here men enjoy 1.9 times more leisure than their wives, in that they travel and study 1.2 times more often than their wives, engage in sports 2.2 times more, etc. Furthermore, another study has shown the dismal picture for Russian women: 52% of the husbands do not help at all or help only one hour per week, despite the fact that most of these husbands were married to working women.[96] Similar data have been reported from other Eastern and Western European societies.[97] The conclusion is clear: working women as well as housewives have a very low status in the family and have little right to leisure time, even in terms of rest and reading. This oppression is even more spectacular in the case of working women who fight continuously with time and who are plagued with fatigue.

The main obstacle to the equalization of men's and women's status in the family and the equalization of familial responsibilities and duties as well as privileges are the traditional sex-role stereotypes that tend to rigidify and differentiate the roles played by men and women according to sex. Social movements such as the Women's Liberation Movement, backed by egalitarian family laws, can help bring about a redefinition of husbands' and wives' roles, as is happening in Sweden.

POWER AND POLITICS

There are indications that the improvement of women's educational and occupational status does not necessarily bring about an improvement in their political status. To some extent the same obstacles which bar women from the top occupations and positions account for women's

---

[94] *Women in Sweden in the Light of Statistics* (n. 51 above).

[95] Alzon, *op. cit.*; Barker, *art. cit.*

[96] Barker, *ibid.*

[97] Szalai (n. 90 above); France Govaerts, *Loisirs des femmes et temps libre* (Brussels, 1969).

low political participation. In addition, politics as well as any other type of decision-making has been defined as a masculine job entailing intrigues and maneuvering considered to be incompatible with the "feminine" personality. Because of these stereotypes and because men want to keep the political monopoly, women are not trained for leadership and are not socialized for political roles, unless they happen to have a politician as father or husband.[98] And because of the prevailing sex-role stereotypes, women are seldom nominated for political office and are seldom elected.

While the right to vote is by now granted to the large majority of women around the world, it has not yet been granted to women in the following nine countries: Bahrain, Kuwait, Liechtenstein, Nigeria (in six states), Oman, Qatar, Saudi Arabia, United Arab Emirates, and Yemen, as well as in two Swiss cantons.[99] Furthermore, women are often indirectly deprived of the right to vote because they do not meet requirements relating to education, economic status, civil capacity, or family status. The literacy requirement is particularly prejudicial to women, especially in societies in which large segments of the female population are illiterate. Thus, a large number of women in the following societies cannot vote because they are illiterates: Afghanistan, Iraq, Kenya, Nicaragua, Philippines, Sri Lanka, Uganda, and Venezuela.[100] In this respect, then, the women's low educational status is highly related to and directly responsible for women's lack of political participation, even by means of voting.

With regard to women's actual participation in political leadership, a general conclusion that applies to most countries is: the higher the level of political leadership, the tinier women's rate of participation. Thus women tend to participate relatively more at the local level, especially in the United States, Canada, the U.S.S.R., Finland, and Australia, about which data are available.[101] For many of the developing nations, no data are available about women's participation in local politics and it is not possible at this time to evaluate whether the above trend also holds true in their case. Furthermore, even in developed countries in which women's participation in local councils, municipal councils, and other

---

[98] Martin Gruberg, *Women in American Politics* (Oshkosh, Wis., 1968); Kirsten Amundsen, *The Silenced Majority: Women and American Democracy* (Englewood Cliffs, N.J., 1971).

[99] "Women in Political Life," background paper prepared by the United Nations for the International Women's Year Conference, Mexico City, May 1975.

[100] *Ibid.*

[101] Sullerot (n. 76 above); *The Status of Women in Canada* (n. 3 above); Encel, Mackenzie, and Tebbutt, *op. cit.* (n. 72 above); and Elina Haavio-Mannila, "Sex Roles in Politics," *Scandinavian Political Studies* 5 (1970) 209–38.

local leadership is higher than at higher levels, it is not as high as it should be, though many of the usual barriers to women's political participation at higher levels are not present.[102] Moreover, women tend to be nominated and elected to local political offices more often in capitals and large cities than in small towns and villages of developed societies, due to the greater degree of adherence to traditional sex-role stereotypes in the latter.[103] In addition, it must be pointed out that while in the case of men local political offices serve as steppingstones to higher-level offices, the same does not hold true for women whose upward political mobility is small or nil.

At higher levels of political leadership, women's level of participation is extremely low in most countries for which information is available, even in the three countries in which the head of government is a woman (Argentina, India, and Ceylon). The only exceptions to this are the Scandinavian and Eastern European countries, where in the 70's the political participation of women at high levels rose considerably. Thus, in 1972, 21.5% of the members of Parliament in Finland were women, and in Sweden 21%.[104] In the U.S.S.R., 31.3% of those elected to the Supreme Soviet in 1974 were women,[105] but in Poland the percentage was only 15 in 1972.[106] In addition, 2,500 judges in the U.S.S.R. were women, while few or any of the judges are women in other developed societies.[107] In other Western societies, the level of women's political participation in national political bodies rarely surpasses 9 or 10%, and it is even poorer in Latin American, Asian, and African countries. An outstanding exception is Guinea, where 27% of the members of the National Assembly and 16% of the Regional Assemblies are women.[108]

We can conclude, therefore, that the political participation of women at all levels is low with the exception of Scandinavian and Eastern European countries and Guinea. Only specific measures aiming to overcome the sociopsychological, structural, and economic obstacles to women's political participation can increase the level of such participation.

[102] Encel, Mackenzie, and Tebbutt.

[103] Haavio-Mannila (n. 101 above).

[104] Herta Kuhrig, *Equal Rights for Women in the German Democratic Republic* (Publication of the Committee for Human Rights, No. 5; Berlin, 1973).

[105] United Nations Seminar on National Machinery to Accelerate the Integration of Women in Development, Country Paper by the U.S.S.R. (ESA/SDHA/AC.6P.14, Ottawa, September 1974).

[106] United Nations, "Implementation of the Declaration on the Elimination of Discrimination against Women: Report of the Secretary-General" (E/CN.6/571/Add. 2) Table 4.

[107] Encel, Mackenzie, and Tebbutt (n. 72 above).

[108] ECA, "The Role of Women in African Development" (n. 23 above).

HEALTH AND NUTRITION

An easy over-all evaluation of women's health and nutritional status can be obtained by examining women's life expectancy in comparison to that of men. In most African countries men and women have a very low life expectancy, ranging from a very low of 25 years for men in Gabon, and 26 years for men and 28 for women in Guinea, to 41 years for Cameroon, Mauritania, Mozambique, Rwanda, and Sierre Leone, for which the life expectancy at birth is not given broken down by sex. In no African country is the life expectancy for women at birth higher than 61.9 years, which is true for Mauritius. At the other extreme, the highest over-all life expectancy for women at birth is found in European countries and especially in the Netherlands (76.7 years), Sweden (76.5), Iceland (76.2), France (76.1), Norway (76.0), and Switzerland (75.0), as well as in Canada (75.2) and the United States (75.3).[109]

While there is a correspondence between women's life expectancy and other social indicators of the status of women, the relationship is by no means perfect. In some societies, such as the Netherlands and Switzerland, women's health and nutrition is good and their life expectancy high, due to a high degree of societal development, without any considerable concomitant improvement of the status of women in other life sectors.

While in most societies women's life expectancy at birth tends to be slightly better than that of men, in the following countries women's life expectancy is lower than that of men: Nigeria (37.2 versus 36.7 years), India (41.9 vs. 40.6 years), Jordan (52.6 vs. 52.0), Khmer Republic (44.2 vs. 43.3), Pakistan (53.7 vs. 48.8), and Sri Lanka (61.9 vs. 61.4).[110]

The lack of more detailed life-expectancy data for women according to working status does not allow us at present to test the hypothesis that women in the same occupations with men who work for a similar length of time and in similar positions will have the same life expectancy as men. Also, the trend found in the United States and some other developed societies for married women to have a lower life expectancy than single women or married men cannot be tested cross-culturally.[111]

Because detailed morbidity statistics broken down by sex are not available for most societies, it is difficult to assess women's health status with regard to specific illnesses. It is, e.g., not possible to test cross-culturally the extent to which the recent trends found in the United States, Sweden, and a few other Western European countries, according to

[109] United Nations, *Demographic Yearbook, 1972.*
[110] *Ibid.*
[111] Walter R. Gove, "Sex, Marital Status, and Mortality," unpublished paper, 1972.

which women's rates of all types of mental illness are twice as high as those of men,[112] hold in other societies and in which ones. It is possible that such high rates of mental illness in women are found only in societies in which women's status is being considerably improved and women experience the strains of the transition to a higher status.

It is important to note that, probably due to prevailing sex-role stereotypes, women's health is most often discussed in terms of prenatal care, child delivery, and diseases of their reproductive systems and very seldom in terms of health care and illnesses unrelated to pregnancy and childbearing. This stereotypic view of women's health needs does in fact influence the type of health care made available to women as a priority, especially in developing nations, as well as medical research concerning the manifestations of different diseases in women.

Finally, with regard to the nutritional status of women, while there are no systematic data, anthropological evidence from several traditional societies indicates that young girls are often given less food than boys, especially when there is a scarcity of food. The available nutritional surveys have consistently shown that adult women and preadolescent girls tend to be malnourished to a greater degree than other family members, particularly in rural areas and urban slums of developing nations. Thus, food-consumption surveys conducted in Asia have shown that children tend to be more malnourished than adults and, among adults, women tend to be more malnourished than men.[113] A nutrition survey conducted in Nigeria in a low-income area in the town of Abeokuta and in a village showed that pregnant and lactating women did not have the required amount of calories and suffered from extreme calcium deficiency during pregnancy, and that adolescent girls were nutritionally disadvantaged with respect to protein, riboflavin, and calcium requirements.[114] Similarly, a high incidence of anemia as well as calcium and thiamine deficiency was found among pregnant slum women in many Asian countries, due to poverty as well as prevalent food taboos, especially during the last months of pregnancy (as is true in parts of Burma, Indonesia, Malaya, and the Philippines).[115]

[112] Walter R. Gove and Jeannette F. Tudor, "Adult Sex Roles and Mental Illness," *American Journal of Sociology* 78 (1973) 812–35.

[113] "Food and Nutrition," in *Problems of Children and Youth* 2: Selections from the Documents of the Conference on Children and Youth in National Planning and Development in Asia (UNICEF, Bangkok, 1966) pp. 48–49.

[114] Aboderim and M. Bello, "Factors Influencing Food Consumption and Health Practices and Attitudes," in *Report of Nutrition Survey and Applied Nutrition Program, Abeokuta, 1968* (Ibadan, 1968) pp. 83–109.

[115] "Food and Nutrition" (n. 113 above).

CONCLUSION

Having examined the available data concerning the different indicators of the status of women, we can conclude that, despite some progress in some areas, the status of women is still quite low. There is still a long way to go and several generations of women must struggle and persist before a woman has the same options and opportunities as a man in all life sectors. If we accept that a society is modern when it "is successful in removing social and structural constraints and in establishing appropriate compensatory mechanisms so that all individuals, regardless of their categorical membership such as age, sex, race, religion, ethnic origin, or social class, can have equal access to a wide range of options in all life sectors,"[116] no society can claim to have achieved modernity. In some societies such as the U.S.S.R., the Eastern European nations, China, and Cuba, political ideologies helped break down many (but not all) barriers to women's educational options, as well as some barriers to women's occupational options. In some Western, developed societies such as the United States, Canada, England, and the Scandinavian countries, a women's liberation ideology promoted by a women's movement or a sex-role debate has led to the removal of some structural and sociopsychological barriers to women's options in education, employment and occupation, political participation, and family life. But even in the latter societies in which wider and more pervasive changes have taken place, sex discrimination has not been eliminated and probably it has not even decreased. It only changed form: from open, direct sex discrimination to subtle, sophisticated sex discrimination, which tends to be more effective and difficult to fight.

The status of the majority of women who live in the Third World is still low and ongoing social changes either do not affect their status or tend to even further deprive them of options and opportunities. Thus, industrialization and the westernization of the markets in many African societies led to a lower status for women, because women were not trained to function at this level of social development.[117] Similarly, the mechanization of agriculture tends to exclude women from agriculture, since no provisions are made to make agricultural training available to women, thus allowing them to continue to play their traditional productive roles more effectively in a changing agriculture. The majority of women in the Third World are still illiterate and lack any type of vocational, technical, or agricultural skills that would allow them to participate in and

[116] Constantina Safilios-Rothschild, "Toward a Cross-Cultural Definition of Family Modernity," *Journal of Comparative Family Studies* 1 (1970) 17–25.

[117] Ester Boserup, *Women's Role in Economic Development* (New York, 1970).

contribute to the social and economic development of their nations. Probably unless the proposition that "The position of women in a society provides an exact measure of the development in that society"[118] is accepted as an axiom, the societal barriers to the improvement of the status of women will not be removed and sex equality will not be achieved.

[118] Gustav Geiger's proposition quoted in Sullerot (n. 76 above).

II

FEMINIST THEOLOGY AS A CRITICAL THEOLOGY OF LIBERATION

ELISABETH SCHÜSSLER FIORENZA
University of Notre Dame

WRITING AN ARTICLE on feminist theology for an established theological journal is as dangerous as navigating between Scylla and Charybdis. Radical feminists might consider such an endeavor as co-operation with the "enemy" or at best as "tokenism." Professional theologians might refuse to take the issue seriously or might emotionally react against it. Even though the women's movement has been with us almost a decade, it is still surrounded by confusion, derision, and outright refusal to listen to its arguments. Yet, since I consider myself a feminist as well as a Christian theologian, I am vitally interested in a mediation between feminism and theology. And good theology always was a risky enterprise.

In the first part of the article I intend to circumscribe the concrete situation in which feminist theology is situated, insofar as I summarize some of the main tenets of the feminist critique of culture and religion and its reception by churchmen and theologians. The second part will present feminist theology as a critical theology. First, I will attempt to point out the feminist critique of the practice of theology by professional theologians and institutions. Then I intend to show how in the tradition, androcentric theology functions to justify the discriminatory praxis of the Church toward women. A final part will deal critically with myths and images of women. Even though the Mary-myth has emancipatory elements, it was not used to promote the liberation of women. Therefore it has to be balanced and replaced by a new myth and images which evolve from a feminist Christian consciousness and praxis. The article concludes with such an example of the feminist search for new liberating myths and images.

FEMINISM AND THEOLOGY

The analyses of the women's liberation movement have uncovered the sexist structures and myth of our culture and society.[1] As racism defines

---

[1] The literature on the women's liberation movement is so extensive that it is impossible here to mention all works from which I have learned. Especially helpful were V. Gornick & B. K. Moran, *Woman in Sexist Society: Studies in Power and Powerlessness* (New York, 1971); J. Hole and E. Levine, *Rebirth of Feminism* (New York, 1971); E. Janeway, *Man's World, Woman's Place: Studies in Social Mythology* (New York, 1971); *Kursbuch 17: Frau, Familie, Gesellschaft* (Frankfurt, 1969); A. Vesel Mander & A. Kent Rush, *Feminism as Therapy* (New York, 1974); B. Roszak and T. Roszak, *Masculine/Feminine: Readings in Sexual Mythology and the Liberation of Women* (New York, 1969); S. Rowbotham, *Woman's Consciousness, Man's World* (London, 1973).

and oppresses black people because of their color, so sexism stereotypes and limits people because of their gender. That women are culturally oppressed people becomes evident when we apply Paulo Freire's definition of oppression to the situation of women:

Any situation in which 'A' objectively exploits 'B' or hinders his [sic] pursuit of self-affirmation as a responsible person is one of oppression. Such a situation in itself constitutes violence, even when sweetened by false generosity, because it interferes with man's [sic] ontological and historical vocation to be more fully human.[2]

In a sexist society woman's predominant role in life is to be man's helpmate, to cook and work for him without being paid, to bear and rear his children, and to guarantee him psychological and sexual satisfaction. Woman's place is in the home, whereas man's place is in the world earning money, running the state, schools, and churches. If woman ventures into the man's world, then her task is subsidiary, as in the home; she holds the lowest-paid jobs, because she supposedly works for pocket money; she remains confined to women's professions and is kept out of high-ranking positions. G. K. Chesterton's ironical quip sums up the struggles and results of the suffrage movement: "Millions of women arose and shouted: No one will ever dictate to us again—and they became typists." In spite of a century of struggle for equality, women have not yet succeeded in getting leading positions and equal opportunity in the public and societal realm. On the contrary, they were incorporated into the economic system and moral values of our sexist culture, which merely organized women's capabilities for its own purposes.[3]

Feminist Critique of Culture and Religion

Whereas the suffrage movement did not so much attempt to change society as mainly to integrate women into it, in the conviction that women would humanize politics and work by virtue of their feminine qualities,[4] the new feminist movement radically criticizes the myth and

[2] P. Freire, *Pedagogy of the Oppressed* (New York, 1970) pp. 40 f.
[3] Cf. the various analyses in *Liberation Now! Writings from the Women's Liberation Movement* (New York, 1971); C. Bird, *Born Female: The High Cost of Keeping Women Down* (New York, 1968); J. Huber, *Changing Woman in a Changing Society* (Chicago, 1974).
[4] B. Wildung Harrison, "Sexism in the Contemporary Church: When Evasion Becomes Complicity," in A. L. Hageman, ed., *Sexist Religion and Women in the Church* (New York, 1974) pp. 195-216, makes the very helpful distinction between "radical" or "hard" feminism and "soft" feminism. See also her article "The Early Feminists and the Clergy: A Case Study in the Dynamics of Secularization," *Review and Expositor* 72 (1975) 41-52. For the documentation and analysis of the first women's movement, cf. E. Flexner, *Century of Struggle: The Woman's Rights Movement in the United States* (Cambridge, 1966); A. S.

structures of a society and culture which keep women down. The women's liberation movement demands a restructuring of societal institutions and a redefinition of cultural images and roles of women *and* men, if women are to become autonomous human persons and achieve economic and political equality.

The feminist critique of culture has pointed out that nature and biology are not the "destiny" of women, but rather sexist culture and its socialization Women are denied the full range of human potentiality; we are socialized to view ourselves as dependent, less intelligent, and derivative from men. From earliest childhood we learn our roles as subservient beings and value ourselves through the eyes of a male culture.[5] We are the "other," socialized into helpmates of men or sex objects for their desire. Journals, advertisements, television, and movies represent us either as dependent little girls (e.g., to address "baby"), as sexy and seductive women, or as self-sacrificing wives and mothers. Teachers, psychologists, philosophers, writers, and preachers define us as derivative, inferior, and subordinate beings who lack the intelligence, courage, and genius of men.

Women in our culture are either denigrated and infantilized or idealized and put on a pedestal, but they are not allowed to be independent and free human persons. They do not live their own lives, but are taught to live vicariously through those of husband and children. They do not exercise their own power, but manipulate men's power. They usually are not supposed to express their own opinion, but to be silent or to voice only that of their fathers, husbands, bosses, or sons. Not only men but women themselves have interiorized this image and understanding of woman as inferior and derivative. Often they themselves most strongly believe and defend the "feminine mystique."[6] Since women have learned to feel inferior and to despise themselves, they do not respect, in fact they even hate, other women. Thus women evidence the typical personality traits of oppressed people who have internalized the images and notions of the oppressor.

In the face of this cultural image and self-understanding of women, feminism first maintains that women are human persons, and it therefore demands free development of full personhood for all, women and men. Secondly, feminism maintains that human rights and talents or weaknesses are not divided by sex. Feminism has pointed out that it is

---

Kraditor, ed., *Up from the Pedestal: Selected Writings in the History of American Feminism* (Chicago, 1968).

[5] This is elucidated from a linguistic point of view by R. Lakoff, *Language and Woman's Place* (New York, 1975).

[6] Cf. the now classic analysis of B. Friedan, *The Feminine Mystique* (Baltimore, 1965).

necessary for women to become independent economically and socially in order to be able to understand and value themselves as free, autonomous, and responsible subjects of their lives. If women's role in society is to change, then women's and men's perceptions and attitudes toward women have to change at the same time.

Feminism has therefore vigorously criticized all institutions which exploit women, stereotype them, and keep them in inferior positions. In this context, feminist analysis points out that Christianity had not only a major influence in the making of Western culture and sexist ideology,[7] but also that the Christian churches and theologies still perpetuate the "feminine mystique" and women's inferiority through their institutional inequalities and theological justifications of women's innate difference from men. Christian ethics has intensified the internalization of the feminine, passive attitudes, e.g., meekness, humility, submission, self-sacrifice, self-denying love, which impede the development of self-assertion and autonomy by women. "The alleged 'voluntarism' of the imposed submission in Christian patriarchy has turned women against themselves more deeply than ever, disguising and reinforcing the internalization process."[8]

Responses to Feminist Critique

As society and culture often respond to the feminist analysis and critique with denial, co-optation, or rejection, so do the Christian churches and theologians in order to neutralize the feminist critics so that the social and ecclesial order remains unchanged.

1) They deny the accuracy and validity of the feminist analysis and critique. They point out that women are in no way inferior and oppressed but superior and privileged; e.g., Pope Paul's various statements on the superior qualities of women thus serve to support the "feminine mystique." Since women have most thoroughly internalized the ideals and values of this mystique, this repudiation is most effectfully carried out by women themselves. Middle-class and middle-aged women who have learned to suppress their own interests, abilities, and wishes in order to support their husbands' egos and careers feel that they become obsolete because of the feminist critique. They sense that the abolition of

---

[7] S. de Beauvoir's analysis is still paradigmatic: *The Second Sex* (New York, 1961); see also the discussion of her position by M. Daly, *The Church and the Second Sex* (London, 1968) pp. 11–31.

[8] M. Daly, *Beyond God the Father: Toward a Philosophy of Women's Liberation* (Boston, 1973) pp. 140 and 98–106. Cf. also G. Kennedy Neville, "Religious Socialization of Women within U.S. Subcultures," in Hageman, *Sexist Religion*, pp. 77–91: N. van Vuuren, *The Subversion of Women as Practiced by Churches, Witch-Hunters and Other Sexists* (Philadelphia, 1973), deals with the "traits due to victimization" from a historical perspective.

gender stereotypes and traditional roles threatens the value and security of their lives. As in the nineteenth century the Beecher sisters glorified domesticity and sang the praises of motherhood,[9] so today some women's groups behind the anti-ERA campaign idolize women's security in marriage and their protection by law. They support their claim by theological references to the divinely ordained order of creation.[10] Theological arguments justify the privileged status of middle-class women. These women do not realize that they are only one man away from public welfare and that even middle-class women's economic status and self-identity is very precarious indeed.

2) Another way of dealing with the feminist critique is to co-opt it by acknowledging some minor points of its analysis. The establishment can adopt those elements of the feminist critique which do not radically question present structures and ideologies. For instance, Paul VI maintains that the Church has already recognized "the contemporary effort to promote 'the advancement of women'" as "a sign of the times" and he demands legislation to protect women's equal rights "to participate in cultural, economic, social, and political life."[11] Yet he maintains that women have to be excluded from hierarchical orders on the grounds of an antiquated and simply false historical exegesis.[12] Similarly, "liberal" Protestant theologians and churches pay lip service to the equal rights of women; for, even though they ordain women, they erect "qualifying standards" and "academic quotas" which effectively keep women out of influential parish or seminary positions.[13] Some theologians participate in this process of co-optation after the feminist movement has become "acceptable" in intellectual circles and in the publishing industry. In writing articles and books on women in the NT or in the Christian tradition, in filling church commissions on "the role of women in the Church," they not only demonstrate they are still in charge but also enhance their professional status. Another way of co-opting the feminist critique is to turn women against women—"religious" women against "lay" women, moderate theologians against radical ones—or to

[9] See G. Kimball, "A Counter Ideology," in J. Plaskow and J. Arnold Romero, *Women and Religion* (Missoula, 1974) pp. 177–87; D. Bass Fraser, "The Feminine Mystique: 1890–1910," *Union Seminary Quarterly Review* 27 (1972) 225–39.

[10] M. H. Micks, "Exodus or Eden? A Battle of Images," *Anglican Theological Review* 55 (1973) 126–39.

[11] Cf. E. Carroll, "Testimony at the Bicentennial Hearings of the Catholic Church, Feb. 4, 1975, on Woman."

[12] See *National Catholic Reporter*, May 2, 1975, p. 17.

[13] Anonymous, "How to Quench the Spirit without Really Trying: An Essay in Institutional Sexism," *Church and Society*, Sept.–Oct. 1972, pp. 25–37; N. Ramsay Jones, "Women in the Ministry," in S. Bentley Doely, *Women's Liberation and the Church: The New Demand for Freedom in the Life of the Christian Church* (New York, 1970) pp. 60–69.

endow certain women with "token status" in order to turn them against their not so "well-educated" or so "well-balanced" sisters.

3) Where co-optation of the feminist critique is not possible, outright rejection and condemnation often takes its place. The reaction is often very violent, because the feminist demand for institutional and theological change is always a demand for far-reaching personal change and giving up of centuries-old privileges. Whereas the "liberal" Christian press and "liberal" Christian theologians in general pay lip service to the goals of the women's movement, they often label it "anti-Christian," because the feminist critique holds, to a great part, Christianity responsible for the "rationalization" of women's inferior status in our culture. In other words, male theologians are accountable for the ideologization of women's image and role in Christian theology. Being male and being male theologians, they no longer can uphold their "liberal" attitude toward the feminist cause, since they are already personally involved. They declare Christian feminism as "anti-male" and "anti-Christian" in order to avoid radical conversion and radical change.

Those of us who are men can not escape the crisis of conscience embodied in that moment [the ordination of Episcopal women] because whatever our politics on the issue, we are as men associates in the systematic violence done to women by the structures of male supremacy. . . .

As men we must support the movement for equality by women, even as it becomes more radical. And, as men, we must examine and repent of our own parts in the sexist mindset that dehumanizes us. . . . [14]

The unwillingness for radical repentance and fundamental change is the Achilles' heel of the liberal male theologian and churchman.

Christian feminists respond to the systematic violence done to women by ecclesial institutions and male representants basically in two different ways. They do not differ so much in their analysis and critique of the cultural and ecclesial establishment and its ideologies, but more in their politics and strategies. Those who advocate an exodus and separation from all institutional religion for the sake of the gospel and the experience of transcendence point, as justification, to the history of Christianity and their own personal histories, proving that the submission of women is absolutely essential to the Church's functioning. In the present Christian structures and theologies women can never be more than marginal beings.[15] Those Christian feminists who hope for the

[14] J. Carroll, "The Philadelphia Ordination," National Catholic Reporter, Aug. 16, 1974, p. 14.
[15] See M. Daly's "autobiographical preface" and her "feminist postchristian introduction" to the paperback edition of The Church and the Second Sex (New York, 1975). Cf. also S. Gearhart, "The Lesbian and God-the-Father," Radical Religion 1 (1974) 19–25.

repentance and radical change of the Christian churches affirm their own prophetical roles and critical mission within organized Christianity. They attempt to bring to bear their feminist analysis and critique in order to set free the traditions of emancipation, equality, and genuine human personhood which they have experienced in their Christian heritage. They do not overlook or cover up the oppression and sin which they have experienced in Christian institutions and traditions, but brand them in order to change them. Aware that not only Christian institutions but also Christian theology operates in a sexist framework and language, they attempt to reconceptualize and to transform Christian theology from a feminist perspective.

FEMINIST THEOLOGY AS A CRITICAL THEOLOGY

Historical studies and hermeneutical discussions have amply demonstrated that theology is a culturally and historically conditioned endeavor. Moreover, historical-critical studies and hermeneutical-theological reflection have shown that not only theology but also the revelation of God in Scripture is expressed in human language and shares culturally conditioned concepts and problems. Revelation and theology are so intertwined that they no longer can be adequately distinguished. This hermeneutical insight is far-reaching when we consider that Scripture as well as theology is rooted in a patriarchal-sexist culture and shares its biases and prejudices. Scripture and theology express truth in sexist language and images and participate in the myth of their patriarchal-sexist society and culture.

The feminist critique of theology and tradition is best summarized by the statement of Simone Weil: "History, therefore, is nothing but a compilation of the depositions made by assassins with respect to their victims and themselves."[16] The hermeneutical discussion has underlined that a value-free, objectivistic historiography is a scholarly fiction. All interpretations of texts depend upon the presuppositions, intellectual concepts, politics, or prejudices of the interpreter and historian. Feminist scholars, therefore, rightly point out that for all too long the Christian tradition was recorded and studied by theologians who consciously or unconsciously understood them from a patriarchal perspective of male dominance. Since this androcentric cultural perspective has determined all writing of theology and of history, their endeavor is correctly called his-story. If women, therefore, want to get in touch with their own roots and tradition, they have to rewrite the Christian tradition and theology in such a way that it becomes not only his-story but as well her-story recorded and analyzed from a feminist point of view.

Yet a hermeneutical revision of Christian theology and tradition is

[16] S. Weil, *The Need for Roots* (New York, 1971) p. 225.

only a partial solution to the problem. Radical Christian feminists, therefore, point out that the Christian past and present, and not only its records, victimized women. A hermeneutics which merely attempts to *understand* the Christian tradition and texts in their historical settings, or a Christian theology which defines itself as "the actualizing continuation of the Christian history of interpretation," does not suffice,[17] since it does not sufficiently take into account that tradition is a source not only of truth but also of untruth, repression, and domination. Critical theory as developed in the Frankfurt school[18] provides a key for a hermeneutic understanding which is not just directed toward an actualizing continuation and a perceptive understanding of history but toward a criticism of history and tradition to the extent that it participates in the repression and domination which are experienced as alienation. Analogously (in order to liberate Christian theologies, symbols, and institutions), critical theology uncovers and criticizes Christian traditions and theologies which stimulated and perpetuated violence, alienation, and oppression. Critical theology thus has as its methodological presupposition the Christian community's constant need for renewal. Christian faith and life are caught in the middle of history and are therefore in constant need of prophetic criticism in order not to lose sight of their eschatological vision. The Christian community finds itself on the way to a greater and more perfect freedom which was initiated in Jesus Christ. Christian theology as a scholarly discipline has to serve and support the Christian community on its way to such eschatological freedom and love.

Toward a Liberated and Liberating Theology

Feminist theology presupposes as well as has for its goal an emancipatory ecclesial and theological praxis. Hence feminists today no longer demand only admission and marginal integration into the traditionally male-dominated hierarchical institutions of the churches and theology; they demand a radical change of these institutions and structures. They do this not only for the sake of "equal rights" within the churches, but because they are convinced that theology and Church have to be liberated and humanized if they are to serve people and not to oppress them.

Although we find numerous critical analyses of hierarchical church structures,[19] we do not find many critical evaluations of the theological

[17] Against E. Schillebeeckx, *The Understanding of Faith* (New York, 1974).

[18] J. Habermas, "Der Universalitätsanspruch der Hermeneutik 1970," in *Kultur and Kritik* (Frankfurt, 1973) pp. 264–301; *id.*, "Stichworte zu einer Theorie der Sozialisation 1968," *ibid.*, pp. 118–94. For a discussion of Habermas and the critical theory, see the Spring-Summer 1970 issue of *Continuum*, which was prepared by Francis P. Fiorenza. Cf. also A. Wellmer, *Critical Theory of Society* (New York, 1974) esp. pp. 41–51.

[19] See, e.g., E. C. Hewitt and S. R. Hiatt, *Women Priests: Yes or No?* (New York, 1973);

profession as such. Most recently, however, liberation theologians have pointed out that theology in an American and European context is "white" theology and, as such, shares in the cultural imperialism of Europe and America.[20] Theology as a discipline is the domain of white clerics and academicians and thus excludes, because of its constituency, many different theological problems and styles within the Christian communities. Whereas in the Middle Ages theology had its home in cloisters and was thus combined with an ascetic life style, today its place is in seminaries, colleges, and universities. This *Sitz im Leben* decisively determines the style and content of theology. Since theology is mainly done in an academic context, its questions and investigations reflect that of the white, middle-class academic community. Competition, prestige, promotion, quantity of publications, and acceptance in professional societies are often primary motivations for the members of the theological guild.

Feminist theology maintains that this analysis of the life-setting of theology does not probe far enough. Christian theology is not only white-middle-class but white-middle-class-male, and shares as such in cultural sexism and patriarchalism. The "maleness" and "sexism" of theology is much more pervasive than the race and class issue. The writers of the OT lived in Palestine, and Augustine in North Africa, but their theology is no less male than Barth's or Rahner's. Today established theologians often feel free to tackle the social, class, and race issue, precisely because they belong as males to the "old boys club," and they themselves are neither poor nor oppressed. They generally do not, however, discuss the challenges of feminist theology, precisely because they refuse to begin "at home" and to analyze their own praxis as men in a sexist profession and culture. Therefore the much-invoked unity between theory and praxis has to remain an ideology.

Since the NT beginnings and the subsequent history of Christianity were immersed in cultural and ecclesial patriarchy, women—whether white or black or brown, whether rich or poor—never could play a

---

C. H. Donnelly, "Women-Priests: Does Philadelphia Have a Message for Rome?," *Commonweal* 102 (1975) 206-10. C. M. Henning, "Canon Law and the Battle of Sexes," in R. Radford Ruether, *Religion and Sexism: Images of Woman in the Jewish and Christian Traditions* (New York, 1974) 267-91; L. M. Russell, "Women and Ministry," in Hageman, *Sexist Religion*, pp. 47-62; cf. the various contributions on ministry in C. Benedicks Fischer, B. Brenneman, and A. McGrew Bennett, *Women in a Strange Land* (Philadelphia, 1975), and the NAWR publication *Women in Ministry* (Chicago, 1972). I find most helpful the collection of articles by R. J. Heyer, *Women and Orders* (New York, 1974).

[20] See F. Herzog, "Liberation Theology Begins at Home," *Christianity and Crisis*, May 13, 1974, and "Liberation Hermeneutics as Ideology Critique?" *Interpretation* 28 (1974) 387-403.

significant rather than marginal role in Christian theology. When women today enter the theological profession, they function mostly as "tokens" who do not disturb the male consciousness and structures, or they are often relegated to "junior colleagues" dependent on the authority of their teachers, to research assistants and secretaries, to mother figures and erotic or sex partners; but they are very rarely taken as theological authorities in their own right. If they demand to be treated as equals, they are often labeled "aggressive," "crazy," or "unscholarly."

How women feel in a sexist profession is vividly illustrated in an experiment which Professor Nelle Morton devised. In a lecture "On Preaching the Word,"[21] she asked her audience to imagine how they would feel and understand themselves and theology if the male-female roles were reversed. Imagine Harvard Divinity School, she proposed, as a school with a long female theological tradition. All the professors except one are women, most of the students are women, and all of the secretaries are men. All language in such an institution has a distinctly feminine character. "Womankind" means all humanity; "women" as generic word includes men (Jesus came to save all women). If a professor announces a course on "the doctrine of women" or speaks about the "motherhood of God," she of course does not want to exclude men. In her course on Christian anthropology, Professor Ann maintains that the Creator herself made the male organs external and exposed, so that man would demand sheltering and protection in the home, whereas she made the female reproductive organs compact and internal so that woman is biologically capable of taking her leadership position in the public domain of womankind.

Once in a while a man gets nerve enough to protest he use of Mother God, saying that it does something to his sense of dignity and integrity. Professor Martha hastens to explain that no one really believes that God is female in a sexual sense. She makes it quite clear that in a matriarchal society the wording of Scripture, of liturgy and theology, could only come out in matriarchal imagery.[22]

This experiment in imagination can be extended to all theological schools or professional societies. Imagine that you are one of the few men at a theological convention, where the female bishop praises the scholarly accomplishments of all the women theologians without noticing that there are some men on the boards of this theological society. Or imagine that one of the Roman Catholic seminarians tells you, who cannot be ordained because you are a man, that (after her ordination) she will be

---

[21] N. Morton, "Preaching the Word," in Hageman, *Sexist Religion*, pp. 29–46, and "The Rising Women Consciousness in a Male Language Structure," in *Women and the Word: Toward a Whole Theology* (Berkeley, 1972) pp. 43–52.

[22] Morton, "Preaching the Word," p. 30.

essentially different from you. If your consciousness is raised and you complain that you are not considered a full human being in your church, then a liberal colleague might answer you that you yourself should protest, since after all it is not her problem but yours. And all this is done to you in the name of Christian sisterhood!

Such an experiment in imagination can demonstrate better than any abstract analysis how damaging the masculine language and patterns of theology are to women. Therefore feminist theology correctly maintains that it is not enough to include some token women in the male-dominated theological and ecclesial structures. What is necessary is the humanization of these structures themselves. In order to move towards a "whole theology," women and men, black and white, privileged and exploited persons, as well as people from all nations and countries, have to be actively involved in the formulation of this new theology, as well as in the institutions devoted to such a "catholic" theologizing.

What, then, could feminists contribute to such a new understanding and doing of theology? Naturally, no definite answer can be given, since feminist theology is an ongoing process which has just begun.[23] I do not think that women will contribute specifically feminine modes to the process of theology.[24] However, I do think that feminist theologians can contribute to the development of a humanized theology, insofar as they can insist that the so-called feminine values,[25] e.g., concreteness, compassion, sensitivity, love, relating to others, and nurturing or community are human and especially central Christian values, which have to define the whole of Christian existence and the practice of the Christian churches. Feminist theology thus can integrate the traditionally separated so-called male-female areas, the intellectual-public, and the personal-emotional. Insofar as it understands the personal plight of women in a sexist society and church through an analysis of cultural,

[23] See P. A. Way, "An Authority of Possibility for Women in the Church," in Doely, *Women's Liberation*, pp. 77-94; also M. A. Doherty and M. Earley, "Women Theologize: Notes from a June 7-18, 1971 Conference," in *Women in Ministry*, pp. 135-59. For a comprehensive statement of what Christian feminist theology is all about, see the working paper of N. Morton, "Toward a Whole Theology," which she gave at the Consultation of the World Council of Churches on "Sexism," May 15-22, 1974, in Berlin.

[24] Here I clearly distance myself from those Christian feminists and authors leaning in the direction of Jungian psychology. The "equal or better but different" slogan is too easily misused to keep women in their traditional place. Nevertheless I appreciate the attempt to arrive at a distinct self-identity and contribution of women based on female experience. For such an attempt, cf. S. D. Collins, *A Different Heaven and Earth* (Valley Forge, 1974).

[25] For philosophical analyses of how these "feminine" values contribute to women's oppression, see J. Farr Tormey, "Exploitation, Oppression and Self-Sacrifice," *Philosophical Forum* 5 (1975) 206-21, and L. Blum, M. Homiak, J. Housman, and N. Scheman, "Altruism and Women's Oppression," *ibid.*, pp. 222-47.

societal, and ecclesial stereotypes and structures, its scope is personal and political at the same time.

Against the so-called objectivity and neutrality of academic theology, feminist theology maintains that theology always serves certain interests and therefore has to reflect and critically evaluate its primary motives and allegiance. Consequently, theology has to abandon its so-called objectivity and has to become partisan. Only when theology is on the side of the outcast and oppressed, as was Jesus, can it become incarnational and Christian. Christian theology, therefore, has to be rooted in emancipatory praxis and solidarity. The means by which feminist theology grounds its theologizing in emancipatory praxis is consciousness-raising and sisterhood. Consciousness-raising makes theologians aware of their own oppression and the oppression of others. Sisterhood provides a community of emancipatory solidarity of those who are oppressed and on the way to liberation. Consciousness-raising not only makes women and men aware of their own situation in a sexist society and church, but also leads them to a new praxis insofar as it reveals to us our possibilities and resources. Expressed in traditional theological language: feminist theology is rooted in conversion and a new vision; it names the realities of sin and grace and it leads to a new mission and community.[26]

As theology rooted in community, feminist theology finds its expression in celebration and liturgy.[27] Feminist theologians maintain that theology has to become again communal and wholistic. Feminist theology expresses itself not only in abstract analysis and intellectual discussion, but it employs the whole range of human expression, e.g., ritual, symbol, drama, music, movement, or pictures. Thus feminist celebrations do not separate the sacral and the profane, the religious and the daily life. On the contrary, the stuff of feminist liturgies is women's experience and women's life. In such liturgies women express their anger, their frustrations, and their experience of oppression, but also their new vision, their hopes for the coming of a "new heaven and earth," and their possibilities for the creation of new persons and new structures.

In conclusion: Since feminist theology deals with theological, ecclesial, and cultural criticism and concerns itself with theological analysis of the myths, mechanisms, systems, and institutions which keep women down,

[26] See *Women Exploring Theology at Grailville*, a packet prepared by Church Women United, 1972, and S. Bentley and C. Randall, "The Spirit Moving: A New Approach to Theologizing," *Christianity and Crisis*, Feb. 4, 1974, pp. 3–7.

[27] Cf. the excellent collection of feminist liturgies by A. Swidler, *Sistercelebrations Nine Worship Experiences* (Philadelphia, 1974), and S. Neufer Emswiler and T. Neufer Emswiler, *Women & Worship: A Guide to Non-Sexist Hymns, Prayers and Liturgies* (New York, 1974).

it shares in the concerns of and expands critical theology. Insofar as it positively brings to word the new freedom of women and men, insofar as it promotes new symbols, myths and life styles, insofar as it raises new questions and opens up different horizons, feminist theology shares in the concerns and goals of liberation theology.[28] But because Christian symbols and thought are deeply embedded in patriarchal traditions and sexist structures, and because women belong to all races, classes, and cultures, its scope is more radical and universal than that of critical and liberation theology. Feminist theology derives its legitimization from the eschatological vision of freedom and salvation, and its radicalism from the realization that the Christian church is not identical with the kingdom of God.

Tension between Christian Vision and Praxis

Christian feminism is fascinated by the vision of equality, wholeness, and freedom expressed in Gal 3:27 ff.: in Christ Jesus "there is neither Jew nor Greek, neither slave nor free, neither male nor female." This magna carta of Christian feminism was officially affirmed by Vatican II in the Constitution on the Church (no. 32): "Hence there is in Christ and in the Church no inequality on the basis of race and nationality, social condition or sex, because there is neither Jew nor Greek . . . (Gal 3:28)." Yet this vision was never completely realized by the Christian Church throughout its history. The context of the conciliar statement reflects this discriminatory praxis of the Church, insofar as it maintains the equality for all Christians only with respect to salvation, hope, and charity, but not with respect to church structures and ecclesial office. The failure of the Church to realize the vision of Gal 3:28-29 in its own institutions and praxis had as consequence a long sexist theology of the Church which attempted to justify the ecclesial praxis of inequality and to suppress the Christian vision and call of freedom and equality within the Church.

A feminist history of the first centuries could demonstrate how difficult it was for the ecclesial establishment to suppress the call and spirit of freedom among Christian women.[29] Against a widespread theological apologetics which argues that the Church could not liberate women because of the culturally inferior position of women in antiquity, it has to be pointed out that the cultural and societal emancipation of

---

[28] L. M. Russell, *Human Liberation in a Feminist Perspective: A Theology* (Philadelphia, 1974); J. O'Connor, "Liberation Theologies and the Women's Movement: Points of Comparison and Contrast," *Horizons* 2 (1975) 103–13.

[29] Cf. my forthcoming article "The Role of Women in the Early Christian Movement," *Concilium* 7 (January 1976).

women had gained considerable ground in the Greco-Roman world. Paul, the post-Paul tradition, and the Church Fathers, therefore, not only attempted to limit or to eliminate the consequences of the actions of Jesus and of the Spirit expressed in Gal 3:28, but also reversed the emancipatory processes of their society.[30] They achieved the elimination of women from ecclesial leadership and theology through women's domestication under male authority in the home or in the monasteries. Those women who did not comply but were active and leading in various Christian movements were eliminated from mainstream Christianity. Hand in hand with the repression and elimination of the emancipatory elements within the Church went a theological justification for such an oppression of women. The androcentric statements of the Fathers and later church theologians are not so much due to a faulty anthropology as they are an ideological justification for the inequality of women in the Christian community. Due to feminist analysis, the androcentric traits of patristic and Scholastic theology are by now well known.[31]

Less known, however, is how strong the women's movement for emancipation was in the various Christian groups. For instance, in Marcionism, Montanism, Gnosticism, Manicheism, Donatism, Priscillianism, Messalianism, and Pelagianism, women had authority and leading positions. They were found among the bishops and priests of the Quintillians (cf. Epiphanius, *Haer.* 49, 2, 3, 5) and were partners in the theological discourses of some church theologians. In the Middle Ages women had considerable powers as abbesses, and they ruled monasteries and church districts that included both men and women.[32] Women flocked to the medieval reform movements and were leading among the Waldenses, the Anabaptists, the Brethren of the Free Spirit, and especially the Beguines. The threat of these movements to the church establishment is mirrored in a statement of an East German bishop, who "complained that these women [the Beguines] were idle, gossiping vagabonds who refused obedience to men under the pretext that God was

[30] See the excellent article by K. Thraede, "Frau," in *Reallexikon für Antike und Christentum* 8 (Stuttgart, 1973) 197–269, with extensive bibliographical references. Cf. also C. Schneider, *Kulturgeschichte des Hellenismus* 1 (Munich, 1967) 87–117, and W. A. Meeks, "The Image of the Androgyne: Some Uses of a Symbol in Earliest Christianity," *History of Religion* 13 (1974) 167–80, who also point out that the emancipation of women in Hellenism provoked in some groups misogynist reactions.

[31] Representative is the work of R. Radford Ruether; see especially her article "Misogynism and Virginal Feminism in the Fathers of the Church," in *Religion and Sexism*, pp. 150–83.

[32] See my book *Der vergessene Partner: Grundlagen, Tatsachen und Möglichkeiten der beruflichen Mitarbeit der Frau in der Heilssorge der Kirche* (Düsseldorf, 1964) pp. 87–91, and J. Morris, *The Lady Was a Bishop: The Hidden History of Women within Clerical Ordination and the Jurisdiction of Bishops* (New York, 1973).

best served in freedom."[33] Such an emancipatory her-story is surfacing in the story of the mystics of the twelfth-to-fourteenth centuries[34] or in that of the witches; in figures like Catherine of Siena, Elizabeth I of England, Teresa of Avila; in groups like the Sisters of the Visitation or the "English Ladies" of Mary Ward, in Quakerism or Christian Scientism.

Feminist theology as critical theology is driven by the impetus to make the vision of Gal 3:28 real within the Christian community. It is based on the conviction that Christian theology and Christian faith are capable of transcending their own ideological sexist forms. Christian feminists still hope against hope that the Church will become an all-inclusive, truly catholic community. A critical analysis of the Christian tradition and history, however, indicates that this hope can only be realized if women are granted not only spiritual but also ecclesial equality. Twelve years ago, in my book on the ministries of women in the Church, I maintained that women have to demand ordination as bishops,[35] and only after they have attained it can they afford to be ordained deacons and priests. Today I would add that the very character of the hierarchical-patriarchal church structure has to be changed if women are to attain their place and full authority within the Church and theology. The Christian churches will only overcome their patriarchal and oppressive past traditions and present theologies if the very base and functions of these traditions and theologies are changed.[36] If there is no longer a need to suppress the Spirit who moves Christian women to fully participate in theology and the Church, then Christian theology and community can become fully liberated and liberating. Church Fathers and theologians who do not respect this Spirit of liberty and freedom deny the Christian community its full catholicity and wholeness. Feminist theologians and Christian feminists will obey this call of the Spirit, be it within or outside established church structures. They do it because of their vision of a Christian and human community where all oppression and sin is overcome by the grace and love of God.

Christian feminists are well aware that this vision cannot be embodied in the "old wineskins" but has to be realized in new theological and

---

[33] N. Cohn, *The Pursuit of the Millennium* (Essential Books, 1957) p. 167.

[34] E. L. McLaughlin, "The Christian Past: Does It Hold a Future for Women?" *Anglican Theological Review* 57 (1975) 36–56.

[35] Schüssler, *Partner*, pp. 93–97.

[36] This is not sufficiently perceived or adequately stressed by G. H. Tavard, *Women in Christian Tradition* (Notre Dame, 1973). See also his statement in his article "Women in the Church: A Theological Problem?" in G. Baum, ed., *Ecumenical Theology No. 2* (New York, 1967) p. 39: "Once a Christian woman knows—not only in her intellect, but in her heart and in her life—that in her mankind is fullfilled, it makes no more difference to her that, in the present circumstances, she cannot be ordained. . . . "

ecclesial structures. If change should occur, a circular move is necessary.[37] Efforts concentrated on bringing women's experience and presence into the Church and theology, into theological language and imagery, will not succeed unless the ecclesial and theological institutions are changed to support and reinforce the new feminist theological understanding and imagery. On the other hand, efforts to change the ecclesial and theological institutions cannot be far-reaching enough if theological language, imagery, and myth serve to maintain women's status as a derivative being in church and theology. Structural change and the evolution of a feminist theology, and nonsexist language, imagery, and myth, have to go hand in hand.

TOWARD NEW SYMBOLS, IMAGES, AND MYTHS

Whereas theology appeals to our rational faculties and intellectual understanding, images and myths provide a world view and give meaning to our lives. They do not uphold abstract ideals and doctrines but rather provide a vision of the basic structure of reality and present a model or prototype to be imitated. They encourage particular forms of behavior and implicitly embody goals and value judgments. Insofar as a myth is a story which provides a common vision, feminists have to find new myths and stories in order to embody their goals and value judgments. In this search for new feminist myths integrating the personal and political, the societal and religious, women are rediscovering the myth of the mother goddess,[38] which was partially absorbed by the Christian myth of Mary, the mother of God.

Yet feminist theologians are aware that myths have also a stabilizing, retarding function insofar as they sanction the existing social order and justify its power structure by providing communal identity and a rationale for societal and ecclesial institutions. Therefore, exactly because feminist theologians value myths and images, they have first to analyze and to "demythologize" the myths of the sexist society and patriarchal religion in order to liberate them.

Feminist Critique of the Mary-Myth

Since the "myth of Mary" is still today a living myth and functions as such in the personal and communal life of many Christian women and men,[39] it is possible to critically analyze its psychological and ecclesial functions. From the outset it can be questioned whether the myth can

[37] This is also pointed out by S. B. Ortner, "Is Female to Male as Nature Is to Culture?" in M. Zimbalist Rosaldo and L. Lamphere, *Woman, Culture and Society* (Stanford, 1974) pp. 67–87.

[38] See, e.g., B. Bruteau, "The Image of the Virgin Mother," in Plaskow and Romero, *Women and Religion*, pp. 93–104; Collins, *A Different Heaven*, pp. 97–136.

[39] A. M. Greeley, "Hail Mary," *New York Times Magazine*, Dec. 15, 1974, pp. 14, 98–100, 104, 108.

give to women a new vision of equality and wholeness, since the myth almost never functioned as symbol or justification of women's equality and leadership in church and leadership in church and society, even though the myth contains elements which could have done so. As the "queen of heaven" and the "mother of God," Mary clearly resembles and integrates aspects of the ancient goddess mythologies, e.g., of Isis or the Magna Mater.[40] Therefore the myth has the tendency to portray Mary as divine and to place her on an equal level with God and Christ. For instance, Epiphanius, Bishop of Salamis, demonstrates this tendency in the sect of the Collyridians, which consisted mostly of women and flourished in Thracia and upper Scythia: "Certain women adorn a chair or a square throne, spread a linen cloth over it, and on a certain day of the year place bread on it and offer it in the name of Mary, and all partake of this bread."[41] Epiphanius refutes this practice on the ground that no women can exercise priestly functions and makes a very clear distinction between the worship of God and Christ and the veneration of Mary. Through the centuries church teachers maintained this distinction, but popular piety did not quite understand it. The countless legends and devotions to Mary prove that people preferred to go to her instead of going to a majestic-authoritarian God.

Yet, although this powerful aspect of the Mary-myth affected the souls and lives of the people, it never had any influence upon the structures and power relationships in the Church. That the Mary-myth could be used to support the leadership function of women in the Church is shown by the example of Bridget of Sweden,[42] who was the foundress of the Order of the Most Holy Savior, a monastery which consisted of nuns and monks. She justifies the leadership and ruling power of the abbess over women and men with reference to Acts 2, where Mary is portrayed in the midst of the apostles. This instance of a woman shaping the Mary-myth for the sake of the leadership and authority of women is, however, the exception in the history of Mariology.

On the whole, the Mary-myth has its roots and development in a male, clerical, and ascetic culture and theology. It has very little to do with the historical woman Mary of Nazareth. Even though the NT writings say very little about Mary and even appear to be critical of her praise as the natural mother of Jesus (Mk 3:31–35),[43] the story of Mary was developed

[40] For a wealth of historical material, cf. H. Graef, *Mary: A History of Doctrine and Devotion* (2 vols.; London, 1963), and C. Miegge, *The Virgin Mary* (Philadelphia, 1955).

[41] Epiphanius, *Panarion* 79. Cf. F. J. Dölger, "Die eigenartige Marienverehrung," *Antike und Christentum* 1 (1929) 107–42.

[42] Schüssler, *Partner*, p. 91.

[43] The interpretation which points out that the fourth Gospel conceives of Mary as the prototype of a disciple overlooks the fact that the scene under the cross defines her as "mother" in relationship to the "Beloved Disciple."

and mythologized very early in the Christian tradition. Even though some aspects of this myth, e.g., the doctrine of her immaculate conception or her bodily assumption into heaven, were only slowly accepted by parts of the Christian Church, we find one tenor in the image of Mary throughout the centuries: Mary is the *virginal* mother. She is seen as the humble "handmaiden" of God who, because of her submissive obedience and her unquestioning acceptance of the will of God, became the "mother of God."[44] In contrast to Eve, she was, and remained, the "pure virgin" who was conceived free from original sin and remained all her life free from sin. She remained virgin before, during, and after the birth of Jesus. This myth of Mary sanctions a double dichotomy in the self-understanding of Catholic women.

First, the myth of the virginal mother justifies the body-soul dualism of the Christian tradition. Whereas man in this tradition is defined by his mind and reason, woman is defined by her "nature," i.e., by her physical capacity to bear children. Motherhood, therefore, is the vocation of every woman regardless of whether or not she is a natural mother.[45] However, since in the ascetic Christian tradition nature and body have to be subordinated to the mind and the spirit, woman because of her nature has to be subordinated to man.[46] This subordination is, in addition, sanctioned with reference to Scripture. The body-spirit dualism of the Christian tradition is thus projected on women and men and contributes to the man-woman dualism of polarity which in modern times was supported not only by theology but also by philosophy and psychology.[47] Moreover, the official stance of the Roman Catholic Church on birth control and abortion demonstrates that woman in distinction from man has to remain dependent on her nature and is not allowed to be in control of her biological processes.[48] According to the present church "fathers,"

[44] This image of Mary led in Roman Catholic thought to the ideologization of womanhood and to the myth of the "eternal woman." Cf. G. von le Fort, *The Eternal Woman* (Milwaukee, 1954), and my critique in *Partner*, pp. 79-83; see also Teilhard de Chardin, "L'Eternel féminin," in *Ecrits du temps de la guerre (1916-1919)* (Paris, 1965) pp. 253-62; H. de Lubac, *L'Eternel féminin: Etude sur un texte du Père Teilhard de Chardin* (Paris, 1968).

[45] G. H. Tavard, *Woman*, p 136: "Pope Paul clearly asserts one basic notion about woman: all her tasks, all her achievements, all her virtues, all her dreams are derived from her call to motherhood. Everything that woman can do is affected by this fundamental orientation of her being and can best be expressed in terms of, and in relation to, motherhood."

[46] V. L. Bullough, *The Subordinate Sex: A History of Attitudes toward Women* (Baltimore, 1974) pp. 97-120.

[47] Numerous analyses of the treatment of women in psychoanalysis and psychotherapy exist; cf., e.g., P. Chesler, *Women and Madness* (New York, 1972).

[48] Cf. the analyses of phallic morality by M. Daly, *Beyond God*, pp. 106-31; J. Raymond, "Beyond Male Morality," in Plaskow and Romero, *Women and Religion*, pp. 115-25; J. MacRae, "A Feminist View of Abortion," *ibid.*, pp. 139-49.

as long as woman enjoys the sexual pleasures of Eve, she has to bear the consequences. Finally, all the psychological qualities which are associated with mothering, e.g., love, nurture, intuition, compassion, patience, sensitivity, emotionality, etc., are now regarded as "feminine" qualities and, as such, privatized. This stereotyping of these *human* qualities led not only to their elimination from public life but also to a privatization of Christian values,[49] which are, according to the NT, concentrated and climaxed in the command to love.

Second, the myth of the virginal mother functions to separate the women within the Roman Catholic community from one another. Since historically woman cannot be both virgin and mother, she has either to fulfil her nature in motherhood or to transcend her nature in virginity. Consequently, Roman Catholic traditional theology has a place for women only as mother or nun. The Mary-myth thus sanctions a deep psychological and institutional split between Catholic women. Since the genuine Christian and human vocation is to transcend one's nature and biology, the true Christian ideal is represented by the actual biological virgin who lives in concrete ecclesial obedience. Only among those who represent the humble handmaiden and ever-virgin Mary is true Christian sisterhood possible. Distinct from women who are still bound to earthly desires and earthly dependencies, the biological virgins in the Church, bound to ecclesial authority, are the true "religious women." As the reform discussions and conflicts of women congregations with Rome indicate, dependency on ecclesial authority is as important as biological virginity.

The most pressing issue within the Catholic Church is, therefore, to create a "new sisterhood" which is not based on sexual stratification. Such a new sisterhood is the *sine qua non* of the movement for ordination within the Roman Catholic community.[50] Otherwise the ordination of some women, who are biological virgins and evidence a great dependency on church authority, not only will lead to a further clericalization and hierarchization of the Church, but also to an unbridgeable metaphysical split between woman and woman.[51]

Traditional Mariology thus demonstrates that the myth of a woman preached to women by men can serve to deter women from becoming fully independent and whole human persons. This observation has

[49] E. Hambrick-Stove, "Liberation: The Gifts and the Fruits of the Spirit," in *Women Exploring Theology at Grailville.*
[50] The issue is correctly perceived by G. Moran, "The Future of Brotherhood in the Catholic Church," *National Catholic Reporter*, July 5, 1974, p. 7, and G. B. Kelly, "Brothers Won't Be Priests Because Priests Won't Be Brothers," *ibid.*, July 18, 1975, p. 9 and 14.
[51] For an exegetical and theological discussion of the notion of priesthood in early Christianity, see my book *Priester für Gott* (Münster, 1972) pp. 4–60.

consequences for our present attempts to emphasize feminine imagery and myth in feminist theology. As long as we do not know the relationship between the myth and its societal functions, we cannot expect, for example, that the myth of the mother goddess in itself will be liberating for women. The myth of the "Mother God"[52] could define, as the myth of the "mother of God" did, woman primarily in her capacity for motherhood and thus reduce woman's possibilities to her biological capacity for motherhood. We have to remain aware that the new evolving myths and images of feminist theology necessarily share the cultural presuppositions and stereotypes of our sexist society and tradition, into which women as much as men are socialized. The absolute precondition of new liberating Christian myths and images is not only the change of individual consciousness but that of societal, ecclesial, and theological structures as well.

Yet, at the same time, feminist theologians have to search for new images[53] and myths which could incarnate the new vision of Christian women and function as prototypes to be imitated. Such a search ought not to single out and absolutize one image and myth but rather put forward a variety of images and stories,[54] which should be critical and liberating at the same time. If I propose in the following to contemplate the image of Mary Magdalene, I do not want to exclude that of Mary of Nazareth, but I intend to open up new traditions and images for Christian women. At the same time, the following meditation on Mary Magdalene might elucidate the task of feminist theology as a critical theology of liberation.

Image of Mary Magdalene, Apostle to the Apostles

Mary of Magdala was indeed a liberated women. Her encounter with Jesus freed her from a sevenfold bondage to destructive powers (Lk 8:3). It transformed her life radically. She followed Jesus.

According to all four Gospels, Mary Magdalene is the primary witness for the fundamental data of the early Christian faith: she witnessed the life and death of Jesus, his burial and his resurrection. She was sent to

[52] This does not mean that we ought not to revise our sexist terminology and imagery in our language about God. It is absolutely necessary, in my opinion, that in a time of transition our vision and understanding of God be expressed in female categories and images, However, I do think we have to be careful not to *equate* God with female imagery, in order that Christian women remain free to transcend the "feminine" images and roles or our culture and church and be able to move to full personhood.

[53] On the relationship of the image to the self, cf. E. Janeway, "Images of Women," *Women and the Arts: Arts in Society* 2 (1974) 9-18.

[54] A creative and brilliant retelling of the biblical aitiological story of the origin of sin is given by J. Plaskow Goldenberg, "The Coming of Lilith," in Ruether, *Religion and Sexism*, pp. 341-43.

the disciples to proclaim the Easter kerygma. Therefore Bernard of Clairvaux correctly calls her "apostle to the apostles."[55] Christian faith is based upon the witness and proclamation of women. As Mary Magdalene was sent to the disciples to proclaim the basic events of Christian faith, so women today may rediscover by contemplating her image the important function and role which they have for the Christian faith and community.

Yet, when we think of Mary Magdalene, we do not think of her first as a Christian apostle and evangelist; rather we have before our eyes the image of Mary as the sinner and the penitent woman. Modern novelists and theological interpreters picture her as having abandoned sexual pleasure and whoring for the pure and romantic love of Jesus the man. This distortion of her image signals deep distortion in the self-understanding of Christian women. If as women we should not have to reject the Christian faith and tradition, we have to reclaim women's contribution and role in it. We must free the image of Mary Magdalene from all distortions and recover her role as apostle.

In her book *A Different Heaven and Earth*, Sheila Collins likens this exorcising of traditions to the process of psychoanalysis. "Just as the neurotic who has internalized the oppressive parent within himself (herself) must go back to the origin of the trouble in his (her) childhood, so the oppressed group, if it is to move from a condition of oppression to one of liberation, or from self-contempt to self-actualization, must go back to its origins in order to free itself from its psychic chain."[56] Just as black people[57] search history for models of identification that indicate the contributions of blacks to culture and history, just as they strive to eliminate racist interpretations of history and culture, so too women and men in the Church must attempt to rewrite Christian history and theology in order to recover aspects that have been neglected or distorted by patriarchal historians and theologians.

A close examination of the Gospel traditions discloses already in the beginning of the tradition a tendency to play down the role of Mary Magdalene and the other women as witnesses and proclaimers of the Easter faith. This tendency is apparent in the Markan tradition, which stresses that the women "said nothing to anyone, for they were afraid" (16:8). It is also evident in the comment of Luke that the words of the women seemed to the Eleven and those with them "an idle tale and they did not believe them" but instead checked them out (24:11). It is,

[55] *Sermones in Cantica*, Serm. 75, 8 (*PL* 183, 1148).

[56] *Op. cit.* p. 93.

[57] For the justification of such a comparison, cf. H. Mayer Hacker, "Women as a Minority Group," in Roszak, *Masculine/Feminine*, pp. 130–48, especially the comparative chart on p. 140 f.

moreover, reflected in the Lukan confessional statement "The Lord has risen indeed and appeared to Simon" (24:34). This Lukan confession corresponds to the pre-Pauline credal tradition quoted in 1 Cor 15:3 ff., which mentions Cephas and the Eleven as the principal Resurrection witnesses, but does not refer to any of the women. This tendency to play down the witness of Mary Magdalene is also apparent in the redaction of the fourth Gospel that takes pains to ensure that the Beloved Disciple, but not Mary Magdalene, is the first believer in the Resurrection (20:1-18).

The apocryphal traditions acknowledge the spiritual authority of Mary Magdalene, but can express her superiority only in analogy to men. They have Jesus saying: "I will make her male that she too may become a living spirit resembling you males. For every woman who makes herself male will enter the kingdom of heaven."[58]

The liturgy and the legend of the Western Church have identified Mary Magdalene with both the sinner in the house of Simon and the woman who anointed Jesus' feet before his death. Modern piety stresses the intimacy and love of the woman Mary for the man Jesus.

In looking at these various interpretations of Mary Magdalene, we find our own situation in the Church mirrored in her distorted image. Women still do not speak up "because they are afraid"; women still are not accepted in theology and the Church in positions of authority but only in junior ranks and special ministries because they are women. The measure of humanity and Christianity is still man even when we stress that the term is generic, for only those women can "make it" who play the male game. Love and service is still mainly the task of women.

Looking at this distorted image of Mary Magdalene and of ourselves, we are discouraged and in danger of trying to avoid suffering. Thus we tend to fall back into the bondage of the "seven evil spirits" of our culture. Let us therefore recall the statement of Bernard: Mary and the other women were chosen to be the "apostles·to the apostles." The first witness of women to the Resurrection—to the new life—is, according to all exegetical criteria of authenticity, a historical fact, for it could not have been derived from Judaism nor invented by the primitive Church. Christian faith and community has its foundation in the message of the "new life" proclaimed first by women.[59]

[58] The Gospel of Thomas, Logion 114. See also the apocryphal writings Pistis Sophia, The Gospel of Mary [Magdalene], and The Great Questions of Mary [Magdalene] in Hennecke-Schneemelcher, New Testament Apocrypha 1 (Philadelphia, 1963) 256 ff., 339, and 342 f.

[59] This meditation was first published in the UTS Journal, April 1975, pp. 22 f. It formed part of a liturgy which was led by women of Union Theological Seminary. I am grateful to the women at Union for the experience of sisterhood. They and the Feminist Scholars in Religion of the New York area helped me to sharpen my thinking on some issues of feminist theology.

III

NEW PATTERNS OF RELATIONSHIP: BEGINNINGS OF A MORAL REVOLUTION

MARGARET A. FARLEY, R.S.M.

Yale University

P ATTERNS OF RELATIONSHIP between women and men are changing. Why they are changing, and how rapidly, are matters of debate. It may be that the chief forces for change are, e.g., economic.[1] Industrialization and the accompanying trend toward smaller, independent families accounts in part for husbands having to share in domestic tasks which stand-in female members of larger, extended families would have assumed. Technological development, which eliminates the requirement of physical strength for many occupations, accounts for the decrease in sex differentiation in portions of the work force. Mass media make feminist ideas accessible to otherwise isolated women, facilitating an unprecedented broadening of the base of challenge from women no longer willing to live within past role definitions. Rising affluence eliminates the need for parents to choose to educate sons in preference to daughters.

It may also be, however, that much of the change in patterns of relationship between men and women is more apparent than real. Some researchers claim, e.g., that despite the seeming loss of authority on the part of fathers, husbands still retain the preponderance of power in the family.[2] Feminist interpreters of life in society and the churches call attention to the fact that since the 1920's women have lost more ground than they have gained in their struggle to share in the public world.[3] Statistics show that in the United States women's growth numerically in the work force has not significantly changed their economic status vis-à-vis men.[4]

Whatever the actual changes already realized in women's and men's social roles, there can be no doubt that there is an important change in

[1] See studies such as Harriet Holter, "Sex Roles and Social Change," in Hans Peter Dreitzel, ed., *Family, Marriage, and the Struggle of the Sexes* (New York, 1972) pp. 153–72. It must also be noted that there are economic causes which reinforce old patterns of relationship. See, e.g., the analysis of the effect of the Industrial Revolution on familial structures in Viola Klein, *The Feminine Character: History of An Ideology* (London, 1971) p. 10.

[2] See D. L. Gillespie, "Who Has the Power? The Marital Struggle," in Dreitzel, pp. 121–50.

[3] See, e.g., Beverly Wildung Harrison, "Sexism and the Contemporary Church: When Evasion Becomes Complicity," in Alice L. Hageman, ed., *Sexist Religion and Women in the Church: No More Silence!* (New York, 1974) pp. 195–216.

[4] Figures in U.S. Bureau of Census Report 1970 show that median income of full-time employed women is half that of men.

persons' assessment of those roles. Sex roles have ceased to be unproblematic, accepted as a given. They are everywhere subject to critical appraisal—whether there is consensus on the critique or not. They have thus at least changed in so far as they have been raised to a level of reflective awareness. Often they have been changed in terms of legal rules, even if they have not yet really altered because of custom or attitude. In any case, for many persons profound conceptual and symbolic shifts have occurred in relation to gender differentiation and sex roles. Indeed, so profound are these changes and so far-reaching their consequences that one is tempted to say that they are to the moral life of persons what the Copernican revolution was to science or what the shift to the subject was to philosophy.

My concern in this essay, however, is less with what has already happened in interpersonal relationships than with what ought to happen. Patterns of relationship, self-understanding, sex roles, and gender differentiations ought to change. They ought to change because over-all they have been inadequate, based on inaccurate understandings of human persons, preventive of individual growth, inhibitive of the common good, conducive to social injustices, and in the Christian community not sufficiently informed by or faithful to the teachings of Christ.

The reasons for past inadequacies and inaccuracies of understanding regarding the relations between men and women are many. It is important to try to understand those reasons, for they help to disclose the need for present and future changes. We may, however, never be able finally to settle questions of, e.g., whether the Judeo-Christian tradition in the past was ultimately responsible for sexism in religion and culture, or whether it only suffered along with other components of human history under limitations imposed by economic, cultural, or psychological factors.[5] What is more important now, given a kind of fulness of time in human history (however prepared for by economic exigencies, technological supports, or whatever else), is to understand the reasons why patterns of relation ought to change.

ROLE FOR THEOLOGY AND ETHICS: FILLING THE HIATUS

Christian theology and ethics have an important role to play in articulating reasons for changes in patterns of relationship and in clarifying what the changes should be. They also have an important role in translating reasons into motives, in providing a climate within which conceptualization and symbolization can facilitate experiences of moral obligation. It is, after all, incumbent upon the Christian community no less than any other group in society (given its fundamental premises,

_____

[5] See Elizabeth Gould Davis, *The First Sex* (Penguin, 1973).

perhaps more so) to consider what is right and just, loving and wise, called for by the gospel regarding human interpersonal relationships. Christian theology is the effort of the Christian community to articulate its faith, and Christian ethics is the effort of the Christian community to understand and articulate how its faith should be lived. But Christian faith does have something to do with relationships between persons, and Christian theological and ethical traditions have offered insights and guidelines, even principles and rules, regarding these relationships. They have done so, in fact, with some degree of specificity regarding sex roles.

Hiatus in the Revolution

We are not now in a situation where Christian theology and ethics must simply provide a Christian commentary on general societal patterns which are questioned and/or in fact changing. We are rather in a situation where, precisely within the Christian community, for whatever reasons, many persons' ideas about sexual identity and gender roles have already changed. To understand the present task of theology, we need to look at the hiatus between past assumptions regarding fundamentally hierarchical patterns for relationship between men and women and today's growing acceptance of egalitarian patterns of relationship.

The "old order" was clearly one in which women were considered inferior to men and in which women's roles were subordinate, carefully circumscribed, and supplementary. Numerous studies have already documented the tendency of Christian theology to undergird this old order by identifying women with evil, by refusing to ascribe to women the fulness of the *imago dei*, and by defining women as derivative from and wholly complementary to men.[6] Beyond this, Christian theological ethics offered theories of justice which systematically excluded the possibility of criticizing sexism. Given the interpretations of women's "nature" as inferior, there was no question of violating the principle of giving "to each her due" when women were placed in subordinate positions or denied rights which were accorded to men. And given a concept of "order" in which one person should hold authority over others, justice was served precisely by the maintenance of a hierarchy—in family, church, or society—in which a male person stood at the head.[7]

---

[6] See, e.g., such studies as Mary Daly, *The Church and the Second Sex* (New York, 1975); George Tavard, *Woman and the Christian Tradition* (Notre Dame, 1973); Rosemary Radford Ruether, ed., *Religion and Sexism* (New York, 1974).

[7] For Aquinas' position in this regard, see, e.g., *Sum. theol.* 1, q. 92, a. 1; q. 93, a. 4; q. 96, a. 3; *On Kingship* 2, 17–20. It is almost superfluous to note here that so-called "pedestalism," whereby women were in some sense exalted as paragons of virtue, etc., served only to finally reinforce their subordination to a woman's "place."

The "new order," however, is based upon a view of women as autonomous human persons, as claimants of the rights which belong to all persons, as capable of filling roles of leadership in both the public·and private spheres, as called to equality and full mutuality in relation to both men and women. It is difficult to exaggerate the radical nature of the shift in the perception of the reality of women and the consequent potential changes in relationships between persons (between men and women, but also between women and women and between men and men). Rilke spoke of a time when woman "will have stripped off the conventions of mere femininity in the mutations of her outward status," when "there will be girls and women whose name will no longer signify merely an opposite of the masculine, but something in itself, something that makes one think, not of any complement and limit, but only of life and existence: the feminine human being."[8] The "new order" is characterized by the belief that such a time has at least begun to be.

Now the hiatus between the old and the new orders is first of all one of understanding. For some Christians the process has been one of awakening, of unfolding, of conversion of thought if not of heart. For others, there has been no process at all. The new order of understanding is tacitly accepted, or at least not actively denied; but its implications are not at all seen. The new order cannot, however, either in logic or in persons' lives, simply be spliced to the old order as if it were another frame in an unwinding film. If there is to be growing clarity regarding social roles and individual identity, Bergson's "between" of process is as important as the beginning and the end. What is at stake is not only a Copernican revolution, where insight may be achieved in the flash of an eye, but a moral revolution wherein the Christian community's first obligation is to try to discern the claims of persons qua persons and the true common good of all persons.

The hiatus is also, of course, a hiatus between thought and reality and a hiatus between persons who behold a new order and those who do not. The gap in these senses is characterized differently in the different Christian traditions, so I shall limit my generalizations to the Roman Catholic tradition.[9] Here new understandings of the nature and role of women have not yet penetrated the pastoral teachings of the Church.[10] Unlike most other Christian traditions, even formal legal barriers to women's fuller participation in the life of the Church still remain. And

[8] Rainer Maria Rilke, *Letters to a Young Poet*, tr. M. D. H. Norton (New York, 1962) p. 59.

[9] Thus far, more efforts have been made to analyze such situations in the Protestant churches than in the Roman Catholic; see Harrison, *art. cit.*

[10] This is eminently visible in even the 1975 statements of Paul VI regarding the International Women's Year.

obviously not all persons in the Church share the new understandings of
social roles and interpersonal relationships or the new experiences of
moral ought which are grounded in these understandings. Even those
who do, readily admit that new patterns of relationship are not fully clear
and that achievement of new self-understandings has not finally been
realized.

Filling the Hiatus

The task of theology has obviously something to do with bridging the
gap. Nowhere is the hiatus more visible, in fact, than in theology itself.
The work of transition from old to new understandings has hardly begun,
and the revolution in thought which it entails cannot come full circle
until the meaning and consequences of the new order are more
adequately probed. What is needed, therefore, is not simply a further
promulgation of new understandings, or a move by the theological
community from tacit to spoken acceptance of new models of interpersonal and social relationships, or even exhortations of the community by
theologians and ethicists. The task of theology is to engage precisely as
theology and as theological ethics in the process whereby new understandings are born and develop.

The most obvious beginning work for theology in this regard is the
self-critical work of disclosing past inaccuracies and distortions in
theological interpretations of, e.g., the nature of woman and the role of
sexuality in human life (a work well begun primarily by some few
feminist theologians).[11] But theology has also a reconstructive task (if
part of the movement in a revolution can be reconstructive as well as
constructive) which will entail, e.g., efforts at a resymbolization of evil
and a further probing of the doctrine of the *imago dei*. The reconstructive
task of Christian ethics is derivative from and dependent upon the fruits
of theological reflection, but it will inevitably involve new efforts to
discern the moral imperatives rising from new understandings of the
indicative regarding relations between persons. It is still the principles of
Christian love and justice which must illuminate and regulate these
relationships. There are, however, crucial considerations to be taken into
account in the elaboration of these principles if they are to be faithful to
Christian revelation as it is received in the concrete experience of the
contemporary Christian community. What I should like to do in the
remainder of this essay is to suggest key ways in which further
considerations precisely of Christian love and justice can aid the process
from old to new understandings of patterns of relationship between
women and men and can thereby inform and give impetus to the moral

[11] See references in n. 6 above.

revolution which now promises to touch and reshape these relationships from the ground up.

ETHICAL RECONSTRUCTION

New Patterns of Relationship: Relevance of Christian Love

At first glance it seems a simple matter to apply the norms of Christian agape to patterns of relationship between persons. If agape means equal regard for all persons, then it requires that women be affirmed no less than men. If agape means a love that is self-sacrificing, then men as well as women are to yield one to the other, to know the meaning of sacrifice and surrender at the heart of their love for God and for human persons. If agape includes mutuality—as the gift it receives, if not the reward it seeks—then some form of equality is assumed in every Christian love.

Yet in the context of male-female relations, there have appeared throughout the centuries countless ambiguities regarding the form of agape when it is for a person precisely as man-person or as woman-person. Among other things, the very notions of equal regard, self-sacrifice, and mutuality become problematic. When agape has been understood as a graced love called forth and measured by the reality of the one loved (as it has been largely in the Roman Catholic tradition), then affirmation of a lesser share in life and in being for women than for men has been justified on the grounds that women are simply inferior to men.[12] When agape has been understood as indifferent to the reality of the one loved, coming forth "unmotivated" from the graced power of the one loving (as it has been in many of the Protestant traditions), then inequality in what is affirmed for women in relation to men has been justified by making love for women as women a "preferential" love, not under the norm of agape.[13] And while Christian love in all persons has indeed always included the notion of self-sacrifice, there have been ways of attributing that element of love especially to women—reinforcing, on the one hand, a sense of subservience in women, and leading, on the other hand, to such strange conclusions as that the woman is the "heart" of the family and the man is the "mind."[14] Finally, the mutuality of love envisioned between men and women has seldom in theory included the full mutuality which is possible only in a relation marked by equality. It has, more often than not, found its analogues in the mutuality of

[12] Sum. theol. 1, q. 92, a. 1, ad 1 and 2.

[13] Such is the conclusion which can be drawn from, e.g., the theories of Kierkegaard or Nygren.

[14] "As he occupies the chief place in ruling, so she may and ought to claim for herself the chief place in love" (Casti connubii, no. 27).

relationships between parent and child, ruler and subject, master and servant.[15]

Many aspects of Christian love could be examined in an effort to reconstruct a Christian ethic which would aid the process to new patterns of relationship between women and men. The notions of equal regard, self-sacrifice, and mutuality offer particularly relevant areas for consideration, however, and it is in these areas that I would like to raise and to consider representative issues.

Equal Regard and Equality of Opportunity

The notion of equal regard as a component of Christian agape has generally meant that all persons are to be loved with Christian love, regardless of their individual differences or their individual merit. They are to be loved, so the Roman Catholic tradition generally holds, because they are lovable precisely as persons (all beloved by God, all objects of the command to love them as we love ourselves).[16] Equal regard has not had sufficient content in the past, however, to save agapeic ethics from sexism; for, as we have seen, it is possible to affirm all persons as persons in a way that maintains a gradation among persons. All are loved as equal before God but not necessarily as equal before one another. When the norm of the objective reality of the person loved is added to the notion of equal regard, then the affirmation of persons as equals depends on the perception of their reality. Now it is just here that Christian ethics has suffered from an inadequate theology of the human person; for as long as the reality of woman is considered to be essentially lesser in being than the reality of man, she can be affirmed as personal but as essentially subordinate to men (in much the same way as children can be loved as persons without love demanding that they be affirmed in all the ways that adults are affirmed).

No one would argue that there are no differences between individual persons or that there are no differences between men and women. The question, of course, for a right love of women as human persons, is whether or not the differences between men and women are relevant in a way that justifies differentiating gender roles and consequent inequality of opportunity for women to participate in the public sphere or to determine the mode of their participation in the private sphere.

[15] These analogous polarities must not be thought to appear only in the Roman Catholic tradition. Reformation views of relationships between men and women did not revolutionize the pattern of hierarchy and subordination. See, e.g., Martin Luther, *Commentary on Galatians* 1535 (*WA* 40, 543); *Commentary on Genesis* 1535–45 (*WA* 44, 704).

[16] For a general analysis of the meaning of "equal regard" see Gene Outka, *Agape: An Ethical Analysis* (New Haven, 1972) chap. 1.

The primary method that theology used in the past to come to conclusions regarding the differences between women and men was a method of extrapolation from biological and sociopsychological data.[17] If theology is today consistent in its method in this regard, it has no choice but to reject its earlier position regarding the nature of woman. Evidence from the biological and behavioral sciences, from history and current practice, is overwhelmingly in contradiction to old claims regarding the intellectual superiority of men, the innate suitableness of women and men for gender-specific social roles, the physiologically determined psychological patterns of women and men, etc.[18] What differences there are between women and men are not differences which justify gender-specific variations in a right to education, to work, to access to occupational spheres, to participation in political life, to just wages, to share in the burdens and responsibilities of family, society, and church. History clearly shows that efforts to restrict social roles on the basis of sex inevitably lead to inequities, to circumscription of persons in a way that limits the possibilities of growth in human and Christian life. A love which abstracts from the fundamental potentialities and needs of persons qua persons (in the name of attending to specific differences among persons) cannot finally be a Christian love which is a love of equal regard.

Self-Sacrifice and Active Receptivity

Self-sacrifice and servanthood go together as important concepts in Christians' understanding of a life of Christian love. In general, there is no difficulty in seeing them as part of the call of every Christian to a love which is like the love of Christ. Yet women have become conscious of the potential falsification of these concepts when they are tied to a pattern of submissiveness to men. As members of the contemporary Christian community, they have thus experienced grave difficulty in sharing the new enthusiasm of men for an understanding of Christian life and ministry in terms of servanthood and surrender. Women have long known their ministry (in home, society, or church) as a ministry of service, but they are painfully aware that for too long they have been primarily the servants of men, subject to the regulations of men, surrendered to the limitations imposed upon them by men. Thus it is that for women theological reflection on servanthood has come to focus

[17] This is not to deny that scriptural exegesis of, e.g., the story of creation has played an important part in theological reflection on the nature of woman. I would argue, however, that such exegesis served until recently proof-text conclusions drawn largely from other sources.

[18] It is, I hope, superfluous to document such an assertion, but it may be helpful to point to such studies as Margaret Mead, *Male and Female* (New York, 1949) and Jean Strouse, ed., *Women and Analysis* (New York, 1974).

importantly on the revelation of service as a form of divine help, a role of privilege and responsibility, never "an indication of inferiority or subordination."[19]

Such clarifications would seem sufficient to restore a needed balance in patterns of relationship and ministry, preserving the fundamental elements of a surrendered and effective, free and whole love. But the ambiguities of sexual identity and culturally conditioned sexual roles are not so easily removed from actual efforts to live lives of Christian love. The process toward a "new order" calls for more careful analysis of the problems and opportunities in integrating sexual identity with agapeic love.

At the root of the difficulty in correcting false emphases in both women's and men's understandings of self-sacrifice, surrender, servanthood, etc., in Christian love, are false notions of receptivity. There is, I suggest, an implicit but direct connection between historical theological interpretations of woman as passive and historical difficulties in interpreting agape as active. In both cases receptivity constitutes a stumbling block.

It is, of course, a favorite theme in traditional interpretations of male-female relations to consider the feminine as passive and the masculine as active, the woman as receptacle and the man as fulfiller, the woman as ground and the man as seed. No other interpretation of the polarity between the sexes has had so long and deep-seated an influence on both men's and women's self-understanding. The source of this interpretation was primarily reflection on the reproductive structures of men and women. These structures served not only as symbols of male and female nature and roles, but they determined the meaning of the reality they symbolized. A perception of the function of bodily organs molded the consciousness of men and women for centuries. And there was no question that he who was an active principle was somehow greater in being than she who could be only a principle of passivity.[20]

Now in the history of Christian conceptualizations of agape, two trends are apparent. On the one hand, there has been a tendency to describe agape as wholly passively received in the human person from God and wholly actively given by the human person to his or her neighbor.[21] The primacy of the active principle is maintained in such a way that in the

[19] Letty M. Russell, "Women and Ministry," in Hageman, pp. 54–55.

[20] Were there space here, it would be interesting to speculate on the reasons for some variations on this theme. Thus, why did the seventeenth century sustain the myth of female passivity, yet give rise to a belief that women's sexuality was insatiable?

[21] See, e.g., Anders Nygren, *Agape and Eros*, tr. P. Watson (New York, 1969) pp. 75–80, 92–95, 127; Outka, pp. 49–52; Norman Snaith, *The Distinctive Ideas of the Old Testament* (New York, 1969) pp. 174–75.

relation between God and the human person, only God can be active, and in the relation between the Christian and his or her neighbor, Christian agape must be wholly active.[22]

On the other hand, where there has been a theology of grace which allows for secondary causality and freedom, both activity and receptivity are allowed in the response of Christian agape to God and to neighbor. That is to say, love of God is receptive not only in the sense that the power and the act of love are received from God as grace, but in the sense that love for God is awakened by the received revelation of God's lovableness and responds in active affirmation; and love of neighbor is likewise awakened by the lovableness of the neighbor, and only when it is so awakened (when it has so received the beauty of the neighbor) is it an actively affirming response.[23] It is an important irony, however, that those theological traditions which have tended to allow both receptivity and activity in the integral reality of Christian love have also tended to identify woman with love and man with active mind.[24]

Now the fact that receptivity has been a stumbling block both in the self-understanding of women and some theologies of Christian love is readily apparent. We can see it first in the effort of women to transcend "old order" understandings of themselves. A major part of this effort has been the struggle of women to reject identification in terms of bodily structures. Voices raised in the women's movement five or six years ago were more often than not stressing the unacceptability of the "anatomy is destiny" dictum. They had come to see the inadequacies of traditional interpretations of the structure of the human self which tied sexual identity and social roles too closely to biological givens. A certain kind of identification with the body had to be transcended if women were to achieve the personal identity which had so long eluded them. A body objectified by the other had become objectified for the self; and too simple interpretations of bodily structures led to conclusions about women's identity which were in contradiction to women's own experience. The old understandings of body and woman and receptivity had to be left behind.

Similarly, flight from receptivity in modern theologies of Christian love parallels a general fear of receptivity in a modern age when for

---

[22] The major difficulties which this position sees with allowing agape to be active vis-à-vis God and receptive vis-à-vis one's neighbor are the difficulties of preserving total divine causality in grace and the difficulties of the emergence of egocentricity in "preferential" love.

[23] This view of agape is found most representatively in the Roman Catholic tradition of a theology of Christian love.

[24] See n. 14 above.

Sartrean man "to receive is incompatible with being free,"[25] and for "protean man" everywhere there is a "suspicion of counterfeit nurturance."[26] But such fears are the result of an experience and an interpretation of receptivity which is oppressive, deceiving in its illusory offer of meaning and happiness, destructive in its enforced passivity. It is not only women but all persons who can sense that certain forms of receptivity, of passivity and submission, are not appropriate for the human person and never truly constitutive of Christian love.

New light can be shed, however, on the meaning of receptivity for all persons. Women have found important access to that light, paradoxically, by returning to considerations of bodily structures. Their move to transcend reference to bodily structures and processes was never complete; for at the same time that women were rejecting anatomical determinism, they were also taking more seriously their relation to their own bodies, seeking a way to integrate embodiment with personal selfhood and womanhood. The very forcefulness of the negation of the body as sole determinant of identity and social function allowed an undercurrent of interest in a feminist rediscovery of the body to emerge dialectically as a major theme for today's voices in the women's movement.

In their efforts to reclaim their bodies, women finally took seriously the scientific discoveries of the nineteenth and twentieth centuries which showed, e.g., that even at the physiological level the female body is never only a receptacle for male sperm. Knowledge about the ovum, and the necessity of two entities (sperm and ovum) meeting in order to form a new reality, forever ruled out the analogy of the earth receiving a seed which was whole in itself and only in need of nourishment to grow.[27] Suddenly enwombing took on a different meaning, and inseeding had to be conceptualized in a different way. Even the passivity of the waiting womb had to be reinterpreted in the face of discoveries of its active role in aiding the passage of the sperm. Receptivity and activity began to coincide.

There are dangers, of course, in women's new efforts to understand and

[25] Marcel puts these words in the mouth of the early Sartre; see Gabriel Marcel, *The Philosophy of Existentialism*, tr. M. Harari (New York, 1964) p. 82.

[26] Robert Jay Lifton, "Protean Man," in *The Religious Situation: 1969*, ed. D. Cutler (Boston, 1969) p. 824.

[27] While the ovum was discovered only in the nineteenth century, Hippocrates had taught that woman's participation in reproduction includes a positive contribution. This was taken up into philosophy and theology by the Franciscan school in the Middle Ages, but there was as yet no acknowledgment of equal contributions from male and female principles. The male contribution was considered "efficient cause," and the female contribution still "material cause." See Bonaventure, *In Sent.* 2, d. 20, q. 2.

to live their embodiment. First, if it is only women who take seriously human existence as embodied, they may simply reinforce past stereotypes which identify woman with body and man with mind. Secondly, if women fall into the trap which Freud did—i.e., by taking account of the body in only some of its manifestations and not the body as a whole—distortions will once again be introduced into the self-understanding of both men and women. Thus, e.g., to fail to see all the ways in which, even at a physical level, men's bodies receive, encircle, embrace, and all the ways women's bodies are active, giving, penetrating, is to undermine from the start any possibility of growing insight into patterns of mutuality in relationships between persons.[28] Finally, there is the danger of forgetting that bodily structures and processes, whether in themselves or as symbolic of something beyond themselves, cannot provide the key to the whole of personal identity. They do, after all, demand to be transcended, so that we come to recognize all the possibilities of activity and receptivity which belong to both men and women, not as masculine and feminine poles of their beings, but as full possibilities precisely as feminine or precisely as masculine.

But if insight can be gained into active receptivity and receptive activity at the level of human embodiment, there is also a way to further insight in the experience of Christian agape. Receptivity is indeed at the heart of Christian love, and it does indeed lead finally to receptive surrender and to a life of active and receptive self-sacrifice. But it may be that we can grasp the meaning of receptivity in Christian agape only by seeing it in the broader context of Christian faith. Theological interpretations of Christian beliefs have pointed to a mystery of receptivity in the life of God Himself, in the incarnation of the Son, his life, death, resurrection, and return to the Father, in the dwelling of the Spirit in the Church, in the life of grace which is the sharing of human persons in the life of the triune God. "The Father, who is the source of life, has made the Son the source of life" (Jn 5:26). "I can do nothing by myself . . . my aim is to do not my own will but the will of Him who sent me" (Jn 5:30). "God gives the Spirit without reserve. The Father loves the Son and has entrusted everything to him" (Jn 3:34–35). The Son's incarnate existence as God-man is an existence of receiving, of utter openness to the Father, of finally receptive surrendering unto death, and in death beyond death

[28] This, I take it, constitutes a morally significant factor in understanding homosexuality as well as heterosexual relations. There is not the opportunity here to pursue this topic, but it is of utmost importance to juxtapose these insights with the testimony of the contemporary gay community that the "new generation" of homosexuals does not reject their given sexual identity even though their sexual preference is for persons of the same sex.

into life, and into new assumption into the life of the Father.[29] The Church is alive with that same life only because and in so far as it receives the Spirit of Christ, the Spirit of the Father (Jn 4:14, 6:37, 14:15-19, 15:5-5). Human persons, subsistent receptors of their very being, awaken into life and consciousness, into love and communion, even into the love of God and communion with Him and all persons in Him, only through the mystery of their capacity to receive, their possibility of utter openness to the creative and created word of God.

Christian love, no less and indeed radically more so than any other form of human love,[30] is essentially receptive in relation to both God and neighbor. It is God's self-communication which enables Christian love, and that self-communication includes the manifestation of His lovableness for the conscious reception in and response of Christian love. And Christian love of neighbor is radical love not in that it involves no reception of the one loved, but because the one loved is received according to his or her deepest reality (her existence in God in Christ Jesus) and responded to with an active affirmation that reaches to that reality.

But all this receptivity at the heart of Christian existence is not in any way only passivity. "To receive," as Marcel has noted, can mean anything from passive undergoing to a receiving which is an active giving, as when a host "receives" a guest.[31] The receiving which is the Son's in relation to the Father is an infinitely active receiving. The receiving which is each human person's from God, and from one another within a life shared in God, is an active participation in the active receptivity of Christ, awakening, growing, reaching to the coincidence of peak receptivity with peak activity. Theologians who worry that if agape is active in relation to God, God's power will not be preserved, or theologians who worry that if agape is receptive of neighbor it will inevitably be a self-centered love, fail to understand that receiving can be self-emptying, and giving can be self-fulfilling. They fail to see the meeting between lover and beloved (whether God or a human person) which is utterly receptive but utterly active, a communion in which the beloved is received and affirmed, in which receiving and giving are but two sides of one reality which is other-centered love. Theologians or any persons who persist in identifying woman with love and man with knowledge, or who neglect to find in self-sacrificial love the coincidence of opposites (giving

---

[29] For a brief but excellent summary of the element of receptivity in the life of Jesus, see Hans Urs von Balthasar, *A Theology of History* (New York, 1963) pp. 25–30.

[30] See Jules J. Toner, *The Experience of Love* (Washington, D.C., 1968) p. 95.

[31] See Marcel, *Creative Fidelity*, tr. R. Rosenthal (New York, 1964) pp. 89–91.

and receiving), fail to understand the reality of either man or woman and fail to see the absurdity of withholding the possibilities of great Christian love from the heart of all persons.

Mutuality on a Trinitarian Model

There is a further step that we can take in trying to understand the reality of women and men, the nature of the love which can be between them, and the model of interpersonal relationship which is offered to them in Christian revelation. That step is to the doctrine of God. It is suggested by the fact that Christian theology has failed to grant equality to women precisely in so far as it has failed to attribute to women the fulness of the image of God. All persons are created in the image and likeness of God, but men participate in the *imago dei* primarily and fully, while women have long been thought to participate in it secondarily and partially. It is not surprising, then, that the only way to move beyond a long-standing inability to conceptualize and actualize patterns of relationship which do not depend upon a hierarchical model is to see whether sexual identity does indeed give graded shares in the *imago dei*. At the same time we may see whether God's own self-revelation includes a revelation of a model of interpersonal love which is based upon equality and infinite mutuality.

If we are to pursue the question of whether women as women can be understood to be in the image of God, we must ask whether God can be imaged in feminine as well as masculine terms.[32] The Christian community has traditionally tried to articulate its understanding of the inner life of God in the doctrine of the Trinity, and it is here that we might expect to find also the fullest meaning for the *imago dei*. Certain cautions, however, are in order. First, the Christian doctrine of God has never ceased to affirm that God is a transcendent God whose reality is beyond all of our images and who cannot be understood to be either masculine or feminine. Nonetheless, we do use images to help our understanding of God; and since God holds all the fulness of being, it is as legitimate to say that the perfections of masculinity and femininity are in God as to say that they are not in God. There will, of course, be radical limitations to any use of masculine or feminine images of God; but there are radical limitations to the use of any images—including those of fatherhood and sonship, or those of word and wisdom, or those of memory, understanding, and will.

[32] This does not eliminate the need to consider woman as person participating in the *imago dei*. To go to this without considering also woman as woman participating in the *imago dei* does not, however, meet the historical problem of identifying man as the primary sharer in the image of God.

It is important for us to bear in mind, however, two special limitations of masculine and feminine imagery. (1) Given no history of careful delimitation of the imagery (such as we do have for the images of fatherhood and sonship), constant care must be taken to place it within a clear affirmation of the unity of God.[33] (2) Any use of masculine or feminine imagery, whether in relation to God or not, runs the risk of being caught once again in reifying notions of the masculine and the feminine. I shall say more about this second concern later.

There are, I suggest, in traditional Roman Catholic Trinitarian theology,[34] grounds for naming each of the persons in the Trinity feminine as well as masculine. "Fatherhood" is the image traditionally used for the First Person of the Trinity. In the first two centuries of Christian thought it connoted primarily the Godhead as the creator and author of all things,[35] but it soon began to signify the unoriginated "begetting" by the First Person of the Second Person. The exclusive appropriateness of the image of fatherhood is beyond question in an age when the sole active principle in human generativity was thought to be male. No absolute necessity remains for limiting the image to that of masculine generativity, however, when it becomes clear (as it has in our own day) that the feminine principle of generativity is also active and self-contributing. There is, in other words, no reason why the First Person of the Trinity cannot be named "Mother" as well as "Father," no reason why creation cannot be imaged as coming forth from the ultimate womb, from the ultimate maternal principle. Neither image is sufficient (since in the human analogue neither male nor female principle can be the whole source of life), but either is appropriate; and perhaps only with both do we begin to return the power to images which they had in a simpler day.

"Sonship" is the image traditionally used for the Second Person of the Trinity. Once again, the appropriateness of this image is unquestionable in an age when human sons were the always desired human offspring, and when relationships between fathers and sons could often be marked with greater equality and mutuality than could those between husband and wife.[36] But there is, again, no absolute reason why the Second Person cannot be named "Daughter" as well as "Son." There is, on the contrary,

[33] In other words, not only must modalism be eschewed but "social" theories of the godhead as well; see Claude Welch, *In This Name: The Doctrine of the Trinity in Contemporary Theology* (New York, 1952) pp. 29-34, 133-51, 252-72.

[34] These same reflections could be applied to the Trinitarian theology of, e.g., Karl Barth.

[35] See J. N. D. Kelly, *Early Christian Doctrines* (New York, 1958) pp. 83-95.

[36] I am passing over here the question of the influence of reflection on the Incarnation on these views; see Kelly, chaps. 4-5.

good reason to suggest that the Second Person is better imaged when both the images of sonship and daughterhood are used.[37]

There is, however, another way in which feminine imagery may be ascribed to the Second Person of the Trinity. A large part of the history of the doctrine of the Trinity is a history of attempts to express the relationship between the First and Second Persons in a way that avoids subordinationism. From the Apologists to the Council of Nicaea the attempts were unsuccessful. Nicaea affirmed the equality and the unity of the two Persons, but the images still faltered.[38] "Fatherhood" and "sonship" (even when elaborated upon in terms of Father and Logos or light, etc.) were simply not capable of bearing the whole burden of the reality to be imaged.

With Augustine new images were introduced (being, knowing, willing; mind, self-knowledge, self-love; memory, understanding, will) which described a triune life in which all that the Father is is communicated to the Son, and all that the Son receives is returned to the Father, and the life of utter mutuality, communion, which they share, is the Spirit.[39] This life—imaged by analogues from the human mind—is still attributed, however, to Persons whose primary names are "Father" and "Son" (and "Spirit"). It is the further elaboration of this same basic description which is to be found in the rest of the history of the theology of the Trinity in the Western Church and in the official teachings of the Church.[40]

Given this articulation of the life of the Trinity, however, is it not possible to introduce images of masculinity and femininity which are no longer those of parent and child? Does not a feminine principle of creative union, a spousal principle, express as well as sonship the relation of the Second Person to the First? Is not the Second Person revealed as infinite receptor, in whom peak receptivity is identical with peak activity? Is it not possible on this account to describe the First Person as masculine and the Second Person as feminine and the bond which is the infinite communion between them (the Spirit of both) as necessarily both masculine and feminine? Do we not have here revealed a relationship in which both the First Person and the Second Person are infinitely active and infinitely receptive, infinitely giving and infinitely

[37] Tavard suggests the view that the Holy Spirit be considered as imaging daughterhood in the Trinity. This does not, it seems to me, adequately account for the theology of spiration. See Tavard, p. 198.

[38] Athanasius, e.g., still needed to draw upon such images as "stream" and "source" to try to express the relation of Father and Son. The Cappadocians still referred to the Father as cause and the Son as caused.

[39] De trin. 5, 12; 5, 15–17; 8, 1; 15, 5 and 10; In Ioan tract. 99, 6.

[40] For a concise summary of the official doctrine of the Church regarding the Trinity, see Karl Rahner, The Trinity, tr. J. Donceel (New York, 1970) pp. 58–79.

receiving, holding in infinite mutuality and reciprocity a totally shared life? Do we not have here, in any case, a model of relationship which is not hierarchical, which is marked by total equality, and which is offered to us in Christian revelation as the model for relationship with Christ and for our relationships in the Church with one another?

But let me return here to the caution I noted earlier, namely, that to use the images of masculinity and femininity to represent the Godhead runs the risk of sealing yet more irrevocably the archetypes of the eternal masculine and the eternal feminine. The God of Christianity is a transcendent God, one who breaks all archetypes and who can continually call us beyond their limitations in our own lives. It is surely the case that we do not want to find yet one more way to imprison women or men in what are finally falsifying notions of gender identity. We began these considerations, however, as part of a process—a process which may in fact lead necessarily beyond all sexual imagery to notions only of transcendence. What is important is that there be room in the process for women to know themselves as images of God, as able to be representatives of God as well as lovers of God. In addition, we cannot dismiss out of hand the possibility of finding in God's self-revelation grounds for understanding femininity in a way that begins to shatter its previous conceptual limitations, and that begins even to revolutionize archetypes. Finally, both the struggle of Trinitarian theology through the centuries to deny any subordination of the Second Person to the First, and the struggle of women and men to achieve equality and mutuality in more and more patterns of relationship, may well be served by adding the image of masculine-feminine polarity to past images of fatherhood and sonship.

New Patterns of Relationship: Relevance of Christian Justice

The Good of the Individual

There is a sense in which, once we have considered the norms of Christian love vis-à-vis patterns of relationship between women and men, we have already also considered the norms of Christian justice. At least in the theory of Christian justice to which I would subscribe, justice is itself the norm of love. What is required of Christians is a just love, a love which does indeed correspond to the reality of those loved. Thus, in a strict sense, justice requires that we affirm for persons, both women and men, what they reasonably need in order to live out their lives as full human persons and, within the Christian community, what they need in order to grow in their life of faith. It is therefore clear that to refuse to persons, on the basis of their sex, their rightful claim to life, bodily security, health, freedom of self-determination, religious worship, education, etc., is to violate the norms of a just love. Any pattern of relationship, in home, church, or civil society, which does not respect persons in these needs and claims is thereby an unjust pattern of relationship.

We have already seen the demand which a just love then makes for rejecting institutionalized gender differentiations and for affirming equality of opportunity for all persons regardless of their sex. Feminists have sometimes gone beyond an egalitarian ethic, however, to a "liberation" ethic in their delineation of the norms of justice for society and the churches.[41] The liberation ethic, in this sense, asserts that equal access to institutional roles is not sufficient to secure justice, since institutions and roles are themselves at present oppressive to persons. The reality of both men and women is such that "the social institutions which oppress women as women also oppress people as people"[42] and must be altered to make a more humane existence for all. While the goal of a liberation ethic is ultimately the common good, it nonetheless asserts important claims for a just love in terms of the reality of individuals who are loved.

The Common Good

If traditional principles of justice are to be brought to bear in forming new patterns of relationship, then it is not only the good of individuals which must be taken into account but the common good of all. It is just here that moral discourse often breaks down when arguments are advanced for basic egalitarian patterns of relationship between men and women. At least three important areas of consideration suggest themselves if we are to discern seriously the moral imperatives in this regard.

1) From the standpoint of the Roman Catholic ethical tradition, it is a mistake to pit individual good against the good of the community, or the social good, when what is at stake is the fundamental dignity of the individual. If it is the case, then, that the reality of woman is such that a just love of her demands that she be accorded fundamental personal rights, including equality of opportunity in the public world, then to deny her those rights is inevitably to harm the common good. "The origin and primary scope of social life is the conservation, development and perfection of the human person. A social teaching or reconstruction program . . . when it disregards the respect due the human person and to the life which is proper to that person, and gives no thought to it in its organization, in legislation and executive activity, then instead of serving

---

[41] See analysis in Jo Freeman, "The Women's Liberation Movement: Its Origins, Structures, and Ideas," in Dreitzel, pp. 213-16.

[42] Ibid., p. 214. This is the argument given by some women against ordination of women in the Roman Catholic Church.

society, it harms it. . . . "[43] On the basis of such a view of the common good, all arguments for refusing women equality of opportunity for the sake of safeguarding the "order" of society, church, or family must fall.

2) In the "old order," as we have seen, it was argued that the common good (which consisted primarily in some form of unity) could best be achieved by placing one person at the head of any community. Strong utilitarian rebuttals can now be offered against this view of the nature of authority.[44] The tradition from which it comes has itself shifted, through the adoption of the principle of subsidiarity, from a hierarchical to an egalitarian model of social organization in contexts of civil society.[45] To extend the shift to include relationships between men and women, it is necessary to argue that in fact the good of the family, church, etc. is better served by a model of leadership which includes collaboration between equals.

Thus, e.g., it can be argued that present familial structures which give major responsibility for the rearing of children to the mother do not, after all, provide the greatest good for children.[46] Or familial structures which entail a sharp split between the public and private worlds entail also strains on marital commitment[47] and a dichotomy between public and private morality.[48] Similarly, ecclesiastical structures which reserve leadership roles to men do not provide the needed context for all persons to grow in the life of faith. Within the confines of such structures God is not represented in the fulness of triune life, and the vacuum which ensues is filled by false forms of chauvinism in the clergy and religiosity in the congregations. On the basis of this form of argument, hierarchical patterns of relationship are judged unjust not only because they violate the reality of individual persons but because they inhibit or undermine the common good.

3) If the ultimate normative model for relationships between persons is the very life of the Trinitarian God, then a strong eschatological ethic suggests itself as a context for Christian justice. That is to say,

[43] Pius XII, Christmas Address, 1942, in Vincent A. Yzermans, ed., *The Major Addresses of Pope Pius XII* 2 (St. Paul, 1969) 54.

[44] Other forms of rebuttal, on deontological grounds, can be offered as well. These may be inferred, however, from our discussion thus far.

[45] See the historical analysis of this shift in David Hollenbach, *The Right to Procreate and its Social Limitations: A Systematic Study of Value Conflict in Roman Catholic Ethics* (unpubl. diss., Yale University, 1975) chap. 3.

[46] See Alice S. Rossi, "Equality between the Sexes; An Immodest Proposal," in Robert J. Lifton, ed., *The Woman in America* (Boston, 1964) pp. 105–15.

[47] See Martha Baum, "Love, Marriage, and the Division of Labor," in Dreitzel, pp. 83–106.

[48] See Beverly Wildung Harrison, "Ethical Issues in the Women's Movement," address given to the American Society of Christian Ethics, 1974.

interpersonal communion characterized by equality, mutuality, and reciprocity may serve not only as a norm against which every pattern of relationship may be measured but as a goal to which every pattern of relationship is ordered. Minimal justice, then, may have equality as its norm and full mutuality as its goal. Justice will be maximal as it approaches the ultimate goal of communion of each person with all persons and with God. Such a goal does not merely beckon from the future; it continually impinges upon the present, demanding and promising that every relationship between women and men, and between women and women and men and men, be at least turned in the direction of equality and opened to the possibility of communion.

The kinds of changes that are needed in the patterns of relationship between women and men are changes which are finally constituted in and by a moral revolution. It is difficult to imagine how such changes can be effected without a continuing process of conversion of thought and of love in the individual and in the community. I began this essay by suggesting that theology and ethics have an important role to play in such a process. Theological and moral insight do not come easily, however, in areas where centuries of thought and behavior have skilled us in selective vision. Surely some structures will have to change before minds and hearts can change. Surely laws and structures can begin to change without filling the hiatus between old and new understandings. We are talking, however, about a revolution that must occur in the most intimate relations as well as the most public. Without continuing changes in understanding and love, I doubt that we shall be able to effect sufficiently radical structural changes in the public sphere or structural changes at all in the world of our private lives. "We may sometimes decide to act abstractly by rule . . . and we may find that as a result both energy and vision are unexpectedly given . . . but if we do leap ahead of what we know we still have to try to catch up. Will cannot run very far ahead of knowledge, and attention is our daily bread."[49]

[49] Iris Murdoch, *The Sovereignty of Good* (New York, 1971) p. 44.

IV

HOME AND WORK: WOMEN'S ROLES AND THE TRANSFORMATION OF VALUES

ROSEMARY RADFORD RUETHER

Howard University

WOMEN IN Western societies are apt to identify the question of women's liberation with the "right to work." The discussion of the rights of women often involves heated controversy over how it is possible for women to "go out to work" and still "take care of the home" and "be mothers." The home-work dichotomy splits male and female on opposite sides of the economic system, locating men on the side of production, women as managers of the consumer support system. When women gain the right to enter a profession, it is still very hard for them to compete with men on an equal footing, since they are also presumed to be in charge of this domestic support system. Even the childless or unmarried woman is handicapped in relation to a married male on the job who has a wife who cleans his house, cooks, shops, and plans the household, thus freeing the man for full-time attention to the "job." In this system woman's work remains invisible and unpaid. It is this double bind that is the primary reason why so few women have been able to take advantage of work opportunities even when, theoretically, they are open to them in industrial societies.

People in modern society tend to assume that this role of women is static and primordial, that women were always "unproductive" members of society. The liberation of women focuses on the integration of women into paid work roles. However, in actuality, this split of home and work, with its consequent segregation of women from "productive" or exchange-value labor, is characteristic of industrialization. The real history of women and the changing structure of the family, the relationship of the home to the economic system, is concealed when we suppose that the way these appear today is the primordial role of the family and of women. If one were to ask an African woman in a traditional village if she would like to "leave the home" and "go out to work," she might have difficulty understanding what is meant. In such societies the home, embedded in the tribal community, is the unit of economic production. Here women do much of the productive labor. They are the chief agriculturalists and produce most of the handicrafts. They sow and harvest the fields, which often belong to the women. They command the transformatory processes that turn the raw into the cooked, herbs into medicines, raw materials into clothes, baskets, and pots. Often marketing is in their hands. Men protect the village from aggression, conduct war, clear and fence the

71

fields, and make weapons. The grown men are freed by the work of women and youth in order to "palaver," to engage in the political and social discourse of village government. Women are the productive laborers of society.[1] Here there is no split between home and work, because the economy still has its original locus in the home.

WOMEN AND WORK IN PREINDUSTRIAL SOCIETIES

The picture of women in many preindustrial societies is found in Proverbs 31:10–31:

She seeks wool and flax and works with willing hands. . . .
She rises while it is yet night and provides food for her household and tasks for her maidens.
She considers a field and buys it, with the fruit of her hands she plants a vineyard. . . .
She perceives that her merchandise is profitable;
Her lamp does not go out at night;
She puts her hands to the distaff and her hands hold the spindle. . . .
Her husband is known in the gates when he sits among the elders of the land.
She makes linen garments and sells them;
She delivers girdles to the merchant. . . .

In this picture we see women as the primary workers and managers of the economic realm, freeing men for the roles of political discourse "at the gates." This role did not disappear with the urban revolution, although women and men's roles became less equalitarian than they had been in village life and sharp class divisions appeared. Not only did women continue to be workers in peasant life, but the latifunda of the great landed families were often largely managed by the wife as an extension of a family-centered economy, while the men occupied themselves with war and politics. This was to a large extent true even of the plantations of the American South. Lacking an industrial base, plantations managed by the wives supported the economy that was squandered by their husbands in the Civil War.[2] As long as the economy was centered on the family, women had an important economic role and even an economic bargaining power in society, despite the patriarchal character of the political system that might define women as dependent and rightless.

The transition from rural to urban life was an important turning point in the history of women. The urban revolution originally affected only a small segment of society, however, while the rest of society remained

[1] David Hapgood, *Africa: From Independence to Tomorrow* (New York, 1970) pp. 35, 48.
[2] Anne Firor Scott, *The Southern Lady: From Pedestal to Politics, 1830-1930* (Chicago, 1970) chap. 1.

agrarian and in a family-centered handicraft economy. But the urban revolution created a new elite group of males whose power was no longer based on the personal prowess of the hunter or warrior, but on an inherited monopoly of political power, land, and knowledge. The political sphere, which had already fallen into the hands of males in village society by and large, could now be monopolized by this elite to define women and lower classes in a dependent and inferior relation to themselves. Generally we find women excluded not only from political leadership (although they may be place holders for male heirs) but from those professional roles in culture and religion that buttress political power. Scribes and priests exclude women programmatically, although no biological differences would have prevented women from entering these fields on equal terms. It is from these classes that we also get those religious laws and ideologies that codify the doctrines of female inferiority in classical societies.

Yet various professions often remained in women's hands in classical societies which they were subsequently to lose. In general, we may say that roles remain open to women as long as they are based more on experience and folk knowledge. Once the training necessary to enter them becomes professionalized, women are excluded. The exclusion of women from education in classical societies becomes the chief means of excluding women from the entire process of the reflection upon and transmission of culture, as well as access to the training necessary for all the valued professional roles.

Medicine was often monopolized by women in earlier societies. Pharmacy was an extension of their role as cooks and gatherers of herbs. As mothers, they were also midwives and healers of injuries and diseases. Certain "wise women" often specialized in these healing arts in villages. As medicine became professionalized, sometimes a few women were allowed to participate in the early stages. There were women in the schools of medicine in Spain in the eleventh and twelfth centuries in medieval Europe, for example. But generally professionalization meant both the exclusion of women from the necessary training for the profession and a gradual proscription of their earlier exercise of it based on folk knowledge.[3] This is particularly true when scribal and priestly exclusions of women join together. Such an exclusion of women from the study of medicine is represented by the decree issued by the faculty of the University of Bologna in 1377 A.D.:

And whereas woman is the fountain of sin, the weapon of the Devil, the cause of man's banishment from Paradise and the ruin of the old laws, and whereas for

---

[3] Barbara Ehrenreich and Deirdre English, *Witches, Midwives and Nurses: A History of Women Healers* (Old Westbury, N.Y., 1972).

these reasons all intercourse with her is to be diligently avoided; therefore we do interdict and expressly forbid that any one presume to introduce into the, said college any woman, whatsoever, however honorable she be. If this nonwithstanding anyone should perpetrate such an act, he shall be severely punished by the Rector.[4]

The effect of such exclusion of women is sometimes a dual system. There is the trained doctor for the upper classes and the folk "wise woman" for the poor. The result in the Middle Ages was not always an improvement of medicine, because university medical training was highly theoretical, based on classical authorities without experimental verification, while the medicine of the "wise woman" was based on experience and practice. But there was also magic mixed up with it. The great persecution of old women as witches in the Late Middle Ages down to the eighteenth century had, as one aspect, the crushing of the wise woman as folk doctor and pharmacist. Soon after, the professionally trained doctor also displaces the woman as midwife as well.[5] This new male hegemony in obstetrics had the side effect of an outsider's approach to the woman in delivery as a "patient" who is ill, whose body is treated as an object, rather than as an active participant in a natural process.

In Europe in the seventeenth century women's traditional role in crafts meant that some guilds, especially those associated with weaving and clothmaking, were female. Women also were trained in many crafts as assistants to their husbands. The proximity of shops and homes and the family aspect of guild membership meant that a widow often continued her husband's craft. In the seventeenth century there was a concerted elimination of women in crafts through professionalization and new forms of organization and through licensing that specifically forbade woman's participation. For example, women traditionally had been brewers, but new laws forbade the granting of licensing for brewing to women. The tradition of women in skilled crafts, as entrepreneurs and owners of taverns and businesses, continued longer in colonial America, where the frontier situation made the working woman still valuable. The elimination of women in business and crafts that affected Europe in the seventeenth and early eighteenth centuries only became general in America at the end of the eighteenth century.[6]

[4] Quoted in August Bebel, *Women under Socialism* (New York, 1971; reprint of 1904) p. 205.

[5] T. R. Forbes, *The Midwife and the Witch* (New Haven, 1969).

[6] Alice Clark, *Working Life of Women in the 17th Century* (London, 1919; New York, 1968) *passim*.

INDUSTRIALIZATION AND THE "CULT OF TRUE WOMANHOOD"

Industrialization is a second critical turning point in the socioeconomic history of women. On the one hand, it added a new economic dependence of men to the legal dependence that had been imposed on women in classical patriarchy. This had already been the case of upper-class women, but working-class women could still be self-supporting as long as the economy was family-centered. Industrialization progressively removed all self-supporting functions from the home, refashioning the family as a sphere totally dependent on an economic system outside of it. Women's role was also refashioned from that of an active laborer in vital economic processes to that of a manager of consumption and an ornament to her husband's economic prowess.[7]

But industrialization also created new frustrations and contradictions for a larger mass of women, increasingly deprived of active participation in the life of society. This frustration made feminism a mass movement, rather than treatises written by a few educated women of the upper classes. Industrialization also forced many poor women out of the home into doubly oppressive conditions of the factories. The liberal doctrines of equal rights began to be taken up by women and by workers who had not been included in those declarations of the "rights of man" declared by the victorious bourgeois of the French and the American Revolutions. The efforts to press woman into her newly limited and intensified role in the home created new ideologies of women's "natural" difference from men. But the revolt against this stifling sphere also began the systematic challenging of the classical patriarchal status of women as property and political dependents on men.

Industrialization completed the reshaping of the role of the home and the ideologies of womanhood and childhood that had begun under bourgeois commercial society. The home is privatized as an intensive center of personal life and nurture. The retainers, servants, and other dependents that have lived with their masters, even in relatively modest households, are gradually thrust out and the nuclear family withdraws into itself. Many family functions, such as childbirth, that have been public occasions, withdraw into secrecy. The home loses its more open, public character. Bedrooms cease to be areas of public socializing, although the great halls of the aristocracy keep these traditions longer. As the family withdraws into intensified private life, the concept of childhood is reshaped into an increasingly extended period of nurture and shaping of a malleable being. Women's role, in turn, is defined by

[7] Ann Gordon, Mari Jo Buhle, and Nancy Schrom, "Women in American Society: A Historical Contribution," *Radical America* 5, 4 (July–August 1971) 25–30.

this intensified domesticity and increasingly prolonged concept of childhood dependency.[8]

The ideology of "true womanhood" or the "lady" shaped and reflected this intensified domestication of the middle-class woman. The cult of the lady and the idealized Home also played a crucial compensatory role in the new industrial society that was being formed. Although built on the earlier aristocratic traditions of courtly love, it was popularized in the nineteenth century as part of the middle-class reaction against seculari-zation, social revolution, and industrial society, with their threats to traditional values. The Home and Womanhood were to be everything that the modern industrial society was not. Here in the home patriarchy and the natural aristocracy of "birth" still held sway in male-female relations, although democratic concepts were everywhere else challeng-ing this concept. Here the religious world view of fixed certainties could be maintained in an age of growing unbelief. Here emotionality and intimacy held sway in a world dominated outside by unfeeling technolog-ical rationality. Here sublimated spirituality compensated for the outward capitulation to the fierce materialism of industrial competition. Here an Eden of beauty and peace walled the bourgeois at home off from the ugly work world of the factories. The home was, above all, the realm of nostalgic religiosity, to be cultivated by women, to which men could repair to escape the threatening outside world of doubt, insecurity, and social restiveness. Women were to remain precritical and insulated against this threatening world, in order to preside over a home where men could preserve their faith in those values in which they no longer believed but wanted to believe that they still believed. The almost religious veneration of the home and womanhood in Victorian society must be seen in this context of escape and compensation for the threats to all these traditional values posed by the industrial revolution.[9]

This idealization of woman in the home as effectively removed her from the "real world" of men and public affairs as had her earlier denigration as that "devil's gateway, font of sin, and unsealer of the forbidden fruit." It is said that women are "too pure," too noble, to descend into the base world of work and politics. To step out of her moral shrine to work or to vote, to attend universities with men, and mingle with them in the forums of power is to sully her virtue and destroy instantly that respect which accrues to her in the "sanctuary" of the

[8] Philip Aries, *Centuries of Childhood: A Social History of Family Life* (New York, 1962) esp. pp. 353-404.

[9] Barbara Welter, "The Cult of True Womanhood, 1820-1860," *American Quarterly* 18 (1966) 152-74; also Dorothy Bass Fraser, "The Feminine Mystique, 1890-1910," *Union Seminary Quarterly Review* 27, 4 (Summer 1972), and *Suffer and Be Still: Women in the Victorian Age*, ed. Martha Vicinus (Bloomington, Ind., 1973).

home. This "down from the pedestal" argument became the chief tool by which social conservatives in the Church and society rebutted every effort of the rising women's movement to enlarge the public sphere of women. Much the same arguments are used today against the Equal Rights Amendment.

These arguments reveal the fundamental ambiguity of the male ideology of "femininity." These characteristics are seen simultaneously as unchangeably rooted in woman's biological "nature," and yet as something that can be lost instantly as soon as she steps out of her assigned social role. In the early twentieth century the Catholic bishops of the United States put themselves solidly on record against women's suffrage. An interview with Cardinal Gibbons reveals the line of the argument:

"Women's suffrage," questioned the Cardinal. . . . "I am surprised that one should ask the question. I have but one answer to such a question, and that is that I am unalterably opposed to woman's suffrage, always have been and always will be. . . . Why should a woman lower herself to sordid politics? Why should a woman leave her home and go into the streets to play the game of politics? Why should she long to come into contact with men at the polling places? Why should she long to rub elbows with men who are her inferiors intellectually and morally? Why should a woman long to go into the streets and leave behind her happy home, her children, a husband and everything that goes to make up an ideal domestic life? . . . When a woman enters the political arena, she goes outside the sphere for which she was intended. She gains nothing by that journey. On the other hand, she loses the exclusiveness, respect and dignity to which she is entitled in her home.

"Who wants to see a woman standing around the polling places; speaking to a crowd on the street corner; pleading with those in attendance at a political meeting? Certainly such a sight would not be relished by her husband or by her children. Must the child, returning from school, go to the polls to find his mother? Must the husband, returning from work, go to the polls to find his wife, soliciting votes from this man and that. . . ? Woman is queen," said the Cardinal, in bringing the interview to a close, "but her kingdom is the domestic kingdom."[10]

This split between woman's sphere in the home and the male world of work created a new ideological dualism which divided the feminine from the masculine, the private self from the public world, morality from facts. Religion, driven into the private realm by secularization, also participated in and was shaped by this split. This split partially reversed the older typologies of female "nature." Whereas classical Christianity unhesitatingly saw women as less religious, spiritual, and moral than

---

[10] *N.Y. Globe*, June 22, 1911 (Documents of the Catholic Bishops against Women's Suffrage, 1910–1920; Sophia Smith Collection, Smith College).

men, nineteenth-century culture typically saw women as inherently more moral, spiritual, and religious than men. Whereas earlier culture had regarded women as more sexual than men, almost insatiably so, Victorian womanhood was regarded as almost asexual. The "true woman" is almost incapable of feeling sexuality, and sexual desire is banished from her mind. Carnality is ceded to the male nature, as part of his rough dealings with the "real world" of materialism and power. Religion likewise recedes into the "feminine" world of spirituality divorced from truth or power. The material world is now seen as the "real world," the world of hard, practical aggressivity, devoid of sentiment or morality.

Rationality is still located in the man and "his world," but it loses the quality of wisdom and becomes that functional rationality that is the tool for manipulating matter through science. Reason is split from morality, making reason "value-free" and morality sentimentalized. Religion especially falls victim to this sentimentalization of spirituality and morality. Morality and religion fall into the realm of "private man," in the home, *de facto* the realm of women. The ethical split between "moral man" (private man) and "immoral society" (public man) unconsciously is split along the lines of work and home, masculine and feminine. Christian virtue, agape, comes to be seen as peculiarly "feminine." Christ too in nineteenth-century religion comes to be seen typically as a "feminine" figure, no longer the Christ Pantocrator of Christendom. The Church and the clergy function, like women, to create a nostalgic place of escape and compensation for an evil public world. But this realm of Church, home, and women also is the tacit support of the secular realm of male power, by pacifying the private self in relation to it. Christian virtue is both politically conservative and yet apolitical. It is "feminine" in a way that makes it also "unrealistic" and "out of place" in the world of "manly men."

The Victorian cult of true womanhood was a class myth. Industry, together with a still existing servant class, made possible a new group of leisured middle-class women who displayed through their delicacy, elegance, and idleness the wealth of the new economic leaders.[11] But the myth of the lady also ignored the large numbers of working women driven into the factories to work long hours at pitiable wages. Its sublimated leisure culture of affluence was built on sexual and social oppression.[12] The asexual "purity" of the "good woman" had its underside in the proliferation of houses of prostitution.[13] Its affluence was built on the

---

[11] See Thorsten Veblen, *The Theory of the Leisure Class* (1899; New York, 1912) pp. 171–79, 338–57.

[12] Bebel, *op. cit.*, pp. 146–66.

[13] See K. Chesney, *The Victorian Underworld* (London, 1970) pp. 306–64; also E. M. Sigsworth and T. J. Wyke, "A Study of Victorian Prostitution and Venereal Disease," in

exploitation of factory labor. These two forms of oppression mingled in the poor woman, who, often unable to survive on her low factory wages, turned to prostitution. Work itself was seen as a kind of "fall" from purity, destroying that "femininity" and "purity" of the lady. Thus the class division between the lady and the working woman also fissured into the dual ideologies of the pure asexual feminine and evil carnal femaleness. Since the cult of true womanhood made the leisured woman normative, woman going to work could only be viewed as a downfall from the sanctity of home.

Nineteenth-century working women also developed their own political struggle and articulated their own needs, which differed radically from middle-class feminism. The vote, education, and professions were the class privileges of the sisters of those in power that did not speak to the condition of working women. Middle-class feminism often spurned working women or reached out to them only in the patronizing form of moral uplift for the fallen. Working women organized around their economic needs, better wages, and working conditions. But they generally found little help from their working brothers in the union movement. Women's work was either not taken seriously as real economic need or else the low wages of women were regarded as a threat to male wages. It was assumed that women work for "luxuries," not real support, despite the numbers of households headed by women. They are regarded as unreliable workers whose biology makes them irregular and who can be expected to stay on the job only until they get married. Doubtless the bad conditions often made these assumptions self-fulfilling prophecies.

Male unionists have seldom fought for equal pay for equal work for women, but instead have either ignored them or sought to segregate them in special types of low-paid work which did not threaten their own wages.[14] Fundamentally, women's work comes to be structured into job-support systems, such as stenography, which aid male work, or are used as a surplus labor force to be hired in times of added need, such as wartime, and fired when this need recedes. Despite the numbers of women in the work force today (about 40%), neither the ideology of womanhood nor the planned relations of home and work have been willing to adjust to this reality. Women at work still have to find *ad hoc* solutions for childcare, housekeeping help, performance of domestic work for themselves and their husband and children. "Women's work" in the home is still presumed to be theirs in a work world that makes no effort to adjust to the special reality of women. The world of work still organizes

Suffer and Be Still, pp. 77–99, and S. Marcus, *The Other Victorians: A Study of Sexuality and Pornography in Nineteenth Century England* (New York, 1974).

[14] Eleanor Flexner, *Century of Struggle: The Women's Rights Movement in the United States* (New York, 1972) chaps. 9, 14, and 18.

itself as though workers were male and have nonworking wives providing for their domestic needs.

THE SOCIALIST CRITIQUE OF WOMEN'S ROLE

The utopian socialists of the early nineteenth century recognized that their critique of the family and private property involved a criticism of the role of women. Both sexual liberation and equal work roles for women were part of the program of the St. Simonians, Owenites, and Fourier-ites. Marx and Engels extended and deepened this connection between socialism and the liberation of women. Their experience with working women in English factories alerted them to the class character of the standard myth of the delicate lady, incapable of hard labor. There they saw women working ten and twelve hours a day under brutal conditions, only to return home to care for their domestic chores as well. But they also concluded that industralization, despite its doubly brutal conditions for women, was creating the economic basis for the emancipation of women. Marx and Engels and subsequent Marxists have hinged their concept of women's emancipation upon the restoration of women to the world of production. Only when women have autonomous incomes from their own labor will they have the economic basis for personal equality with men. As long as women are economic dependents on men, marriage is a degrading exchange of sexual rights and domestic labor for economic support. However softened by custom, its reality remains that of a kind of slavery and economic bondage. Autonomous work and independent income are the bases for all other rights and dignities of women. Without it, all rights and dignities are extended to her on the sufferance of males, who still retain the title to them in their own hands. In the *Origin and History of the Family, Private Property and the State*,[15] Engels worked out their view of the relation between the subjugation of women to the rise of private property and women's deprivation of an autonomous role in production. This they saw beginning to be restored by industrialism, as far as the working-class woman was concerned.

Engels believed that communism would establish complete equality between men and women by integrating women into all spheres of work equally with men. Women would receive the same education and could enter any occupation. The economic independence gained from work would be the foundation of their personal independence. They would no longer have to sell their sexuality for economic security or have their income and property owned and managed by their husbands, be coerced into marriage, or kept in marriages grown cold, by economic need. Marriage could return to being what Engels believed it had been

[15] Originally published in Zurich, 1884.

originally, before the rise of the patriarchal system: a free personal relationship between two persons based on mutual compatibility, entered into and dissolved without economic coercion. Engels believed this would lead to stable monogamous relationships, which corresponded to the "natural love instincts" of humanity, which had been distorted by the economic power of one partner and the subordination of the other into hypocrisy and infidelity.

Contrary to Marx's expectations, communist revolutions did not take place in advanced industrial countries but in countries engaged in overthrowing feudal and colonial regimes and just beginning to enter the industrial revolution. Women in prerevolutionary Russia or China had not yet experienced the expanded work roles or the enlarged education and civil rights of Western industrialism and liberalism. Their status was still that of chattel of fathers and husbands, who could be married, sold, and even killed at will.[16]

Communist revolutions have made good on the Marxist belief in the union between female emancipation and proletarian revolution by sweeping transformations of the status of women. Marriage codes established the complete civil equality of women, and comprehensive childcare and even communal kitchens, maternity leave and guaranteed re-employment, and campaigns to transform cultural consciousness strove to open the world of work to women on an equal basis. In China this policy of female emancipation demanded a literal uprooting and re-creating of the Chinese family.[17] Article 6 of the Constitution, adopted in September 1946, declared: "The People's Republic of China abolishes the feudal system which holds women in bondage. Women shall enjoy equal rights with men in political, economic, cultural, educational, and social life. Freedom of marriage for men and women shall be enforced."[18] All forms of concubinage and forced marriage were abolished, and divorce was to be granted by mutual consent. But the communalization of work conditions and the home, carried out much more radically in China than in Russia, has been the social basis for equality of women on the job and in their personal relations. The private work of women in the home has become communal work, freeing women on the job from the handicap of the double shift of home and work.

Women in the West can recognize the more systematic integration of women into work in Marxist countries. Communist regimes have been willing to recognize what liberal industrialism has always avoided,

---

[16] Sheila Rowbotham, *Women, Resistance and Revolution: A History of Women and Revolution in the Modern World* (New York, 1972) pp. 134–40, 170–83.

[17] *Ibid.*, pp. 141–59, 184–99.

[18] *Ibid.*, pp. 184–85.

namely, that women cannot be equal on the job until there is a social reorganization of the economic relations of home and work and the unpaid roles of the home are no longer placed solely on the backs of women. As long as working women must solve this problem on an individual basis, paying out of their meager salaries for substitute homeworkers, only a small elite, often unmarried or childless, can hope for significant careers, while those who must work as heads of households are forced into desperate contradictions which often leave the vital roles of the home neglected. Women are made to feel guilty for this failure, instead of society taking responsibility for adjusting the relationship of work and home in just and rational ways.

However, women may well ask whether the social values created by the Marxist solution are a sufficient answer to the historic dependency of women. This is not only because women, especially in Eastern Europe and the Soviet Union, are often left with considerable residue of the unpaid second shift of the home, handicapped thereby on the job and still subject to sexual stereotyping of work. Even more, one might ask whether the Marxist solution does not make a male concept of alienated work the exclusive pattern for life and values. The Marxist solution envisions the integration of women into this type of alienated labor by drastically reducing the work of the home, collectivizing it in the public sector.

But what is called the "home" is nothing less than the original base of personal autonomy in the self-governing familial community, which has greatly shrunk in its economic, political, and cultural functions due to the alienation of these functions into public patterns of socialization. Marxism proposes to emancipate women by totalizing this process of alienation and collectivization, leaving the home little more than a bedroom and a nucleus of fleeting personal relations. As one function after another is collectivized outside the family, the family progressively loses its self-determination and becomes totally determined by social forces over which it has no power. The shrinking of the home, then, becomes the means of creating the totalitarian society where the self has lost its autonomous base. Socialists, as well as feminists, must rethink the social role of the home, if they are committed to a society of freedom as well as a society of equal work roles.

Socialism is based on a concept of women's rights that unquestionably assumes that this process is one of obliteration of the female sphere into the masculine sphere, that is to say, the alienation of local self-determination into macro-collectivization. The values cultivated in the home, the values identified with women, are thereby also obliterated for an exclusive definition of society through the values of conflict, work, and repression. Communism totalizes the society of alienated work and warfare, instead of, as Marx himself envisioned, abolishing this society. One must ask whether a society which seeks both freedom and equal work roles, both justice and humanization, must not envision the process of socialization the other way around, not by completing the historic process of alienating the functions of the home, but by resocializing the home by bringing access to work and political decision-making back into a more integral relationship to it. Communalization of home and work that puts the ownership and decision-making over these spheres in the hands of the local community represents a kind of socialization which restores rather than destroys the sphere of self-determination. The communal patterns of China, as the base for constructing the larger networks of society, or the kibbutz patterns embedded within the larger social system in Israel, are possible models for this development. Women are reintegrated into the larger world of work and decision-making, and society takes responsibility of communal childraising, not so much by abolishing the family and the home as by re-embedding it in a "tribe," or a network of relationships whose concrete functionings can be governed by the local group itself. Working and living complexes must still be integrated into larger structures of planning and exchange, but this does not mitigate against the possibility of a system where local communities make the concrete decisions that shape their own lives.

The bringing of work back to relationship to the base of autonomous community life also suggests the shaping of society by different values than those of alienated work and conflict, which have been, historically, shaped by the male roles. A humanized society must be one reintegrated into those values cultivated in the female sphere: co-operation, mutual support, leisure, celebration, free creativity, and exploration of feelings and personal relations. The priorities of human life must be re-examined. Work itself must be seen as a means to the end of self-expression, mutual help, and fulfillment of being, rather than all existence shaped by a program of alienated labor. We do not exist in order to work, but we work in order to be—not merely in the sense of minimal survival, but in the sense of that fulfillment of being when work is reunified with creative self-expression and takes place in the framework of a community of mutual affirmation. It is this vision of the recovery of the world of work for women, which is at the same time the dealienation of work and the rediscovery of community, that must be the distinctive value which women should bring to the question of work.

V

WOMEN AND MINISTRY

ELIZABETH CARROLL, R.S.M.

Center of Concern, Washington, D.C.

THE WOMEN'S MOVEMENT constitutes a call of the Church to profound renewal in its ministry, a renewal which broadly affects the structures of the Church and asks for a deep conversion in persons.

Before Vatican II, Catholics who thought "Church" thought hierarchy. This emphasis had placed laymen and all women, so far as social expression of Church was concerned, in a passive stance, dependent upon the initiatives and continuing directives of the clerical order. Movements resulting from lay persons' dynamic relationship with God in prayer and reflection on daily experience were deflected into roles and limited by rules which expressed the perceptions of a totally male hierarchy and sense of ministry. Vatican II stirred hearts by its insights, steeped in biblical tradition, into the nature of the Church. The Church is mystery, is a sacrament of union with God and of unity of persons, is people related to God through Christ,[1] is ever anew responding in the Spirit to the signs of the times.[2]

Women in particular resonated with this teaching, experiencing a sense of being Church in a dimension which was new to them. The earlier emphasis on roles which had separated women from the Church as hierarchy gave way before the Council's teaching on "the exalted dignity proper to the human person." "The rights and duties" of the person "are universal and inviolable." These include "the right to choose a state of life freely . . . the right to education . . . to a good reputation . . . to activity in accord with the upright norm of one's own conscience . . . ."[3] The call to end discrimination by reason of sex[4] indicated that woman was to be included in the full dignity to be accorded the person.

These teachings, together with the whole cultural movement towards a fairer valuation of woman,[5] awakened in women a new consciousness of their potential. As they grew in self-respect, they experienced a new sense

---

[1] Constitution on the Church, no. 1 (tr. *The Documents of Vatican II*, ed. W. M. Abbott [New York, 1966] pp. 14–15); no. 10 (p. 27).

[2] Constitution on the Church in the Modern World, no. 4 (*Documents*, p. 201).

[3] *Ibid.*, no. 26 (*Documents*, p. 225).

[4] *Ibid.*, no. 29 (*Documents*, pp. 227–28). It is noteworthy that Vatican II, while giving a direction toward the value of personhood, did not develop the application of this teaching to woman or deal with women in the Church.

[5] The contemporary women's liberation movement traces its origins to Simone de Beauvoir, *The Second Sex* (New York, 1953), and Betty Friedan, *The Feminine Mystique* (New York, 1963). A superb historical treatment of women in the Church is George Tavard's *Woman in Christian Tradition* (Notre Dame, 1973).

of responsibility as Church. Many women felt called to the Scriptures, where "the Father who is in heaven meets His children with great love and speaks with them."[6] With new eyes they found in the Gospels evidence which challenged their previous mind-sets. They noted that Jesus had broken through all the categories and taboos of His times to reveal what respect He had for women, what expectations He placed upon them. With awe, yet with courage drawn from His promptings, many women experienced an urgency to render the institutional Church more revelatory of its redeeming Lord, more responsive to peoples' needs.

Though the Council spoke of "a variety of ministries"[7] and stated that all believers share in the mission of Christ,[8] the ministers recognized in the documents were primarily bishops, then priests and deacons. These ministers, organized hierarchically, were set apart from the rest of the Church by a graded participation in holy orders.[9] Some women felt a call to this life of orders. But for most women, the pressure was that of the vision which had been clearly set forth: the Church of witness, of community, of ministry.[10] They were conscious of needs, of the aspirations of people for a better life, a more human self-understanding, a deeper relationship with God and with one another. People were there to be served. When the whole Church did not move decisively in these directions, those women whose consciousness had been raised tended to make decisive choices: either they departed the Church, surrendered to apathy, or, confident in the Spirit, they deepened their experience of the Word, particularly as found in the Gospels. Here these latter found the essential insights on ministry.

This paper will attempt to chronicle this odyssey, to explicate (1) Jesus' revelation about ministry, his assimilation of women into that ministry: *gospel*; (2) the forces within the early Church and subsequent history which seem to have been at work in diminishing the participation of women in ministry: *tradition;* (3) the dynamic of the contemporary women's movement as it may affect ministry: *hope*.

GOSPEL

The gospel of Jesus is word and deed. Luke portrays for us Jesus, filled with the Spirit, announcing his program of ministry in the passage from Is 61:1-2 which is fulfilled in him:

---

[6] Constitution on Divine Revelation, no. 21 (*Documents*, p. 125).

[7] Constitution on the Church, no. 18 (*Documents*, p. 37).

[8] *Ibid.*, no. 10 (*Documents*, p. 27); Decree on the Apostolate of the Laity, no. 2: "the laity share in the priestly, prophetic, and royal office of Christ" (*Documents*, p. 49).

[9] Constitution on the Church, no. 20 (*Documents*, p. 40). Cf. Raymond E. Brown, *Priest and Bishop: Biblical Reflections* (New York, 1970) pp. 53–55.

[10] Constitution on the Church, no. 10 (*Documents*, p. 27); no. 9 (p. 25); Constitution on the Church in the Modern World, no. 32 (*Documents*, p. 230).

The Spirit of the Lord is upon me,
because he has anointed me
to preach good news to the poor,
to proclaim release to the captives
and recovery of sight to the blind.
He has sent me to set at liberty those who are oppressed,
to proclaim the acceptable year of the Lord.[11]

The Evangelists, Luke in quite a literal way, present Jesus fulfilling that program among the poor, the sick, outcasts, and women. Wherever there is need or prejudice, Jesus breaks through categories, rejects taboos, declares himself "Lord of the Sabbath," and offers freedom of spirit as the weapon against oppressive rules and limiting roles.[12] Repeatedly Jesus empowers the weak and patiently points out to his disciples that his (and their) mission is not to be greater than others but to serve them.[13]

The key to the ministry of Jesus appears succinctly toward the end of Mark's "Way Passage,"[14] where Jesus says: "For the Son of man also came not to be served but to serve, and to give his life as a ransom for many."[15] On the Way, women as well as the Twelve accompanied Jesus, going with him that eventful journey from Galilee to Jerusalem.[16] The verb *diakonein*, "to serve," appears infrequently in the Gospels.[17] Nevertheless, it is a very important term, for Jesus uses it to characterize and identify his mission and what he expects of his followers.[18] The contexts in which this verb appears and its restricted use are especially significant. It describes the criterion to be used at the Last Judgment and expresses Jesus' reason for coming;[19] in the course of Jesus' life he serves or ministers to many people. But besides Jesus, only angels and women are listed as the subject of this verb, and only angels and women are "ministers" to Jesus himself.[20] Jesus asked for and accepted ser-

[11] Lk 4:18 RSV.

[12] See Margaret Brennan, "Disturbing the Perceptual Patterns: A Reflection on the Liberation of Men," *Origins*, July 17, 1975, pp. 97–100.

[13] Mk 9:35; 10:43–44; Mt 20:26–27; Lk 22:24–27.

[14] Mk 8:22—10:52.

[15] Mk 10:45.

[16] Lk 8:1–3; 24:10; Mk 15:40–41; 16:9; Mt 27:55–56; Jn 19:25.

[17] The verb only appears 18 times among the four Gospels. It is "not found in the Septuagint or other Greek versions of the Old Testament including the Apocrypha" (*A Concordance to the Greek Testament*, ed. W. F. Moulton and A. S. Geden [4th ed. rev.; Edinburgh, 1963] pp. 202, xii*).

[18] Lk 12:37; cf. 17:8; 22:26–27.

[19] Mt 20:28; Mk 10:45; Lk 22:27.

[20] Cf. Mk 1:13; cf. Lk 22:43; 8:3; Mt 8:15.

vices in public from women; this was unorthodox for a Jewish man in his day.[21]

Ministry as discipleship. To be a disciple was to learn from Jesus, to absorb his teachings into a life pattern, and to teach them to others. Women were surely among the disciples of Jesus. Mary the mother of Jesus is described by Luke as one who "heard the word of God and kept it."[22] Witness also Mary of Bethany, who "sat at the Lord's feet and listened to his teaching."[23] Mary won approval from Jesus in the act of repudiating a "woman's role" and appearing to Martha to violate a rule of hospitality. Martha too must be counted a disciple of the Lord; for she shared with him his precious dialogue on the resurrection of the dead and made her declaration of faith: "Yes, Lord; I believe that you are the Christ, the Son of God. . . . "[24] To Mary she communicated the message "The Teacher is here. . . . "[25]

Just as Mary of Bethany broke womanly tradition to join herself as a disciple to Jesus, even more did the woman from Samaria violate conventions (and Jesus with her), speaking to and learning, in a public place, from a Jewish man.[26] This Samaritan woman, autonomous and rational, drew Jesus and was drawn by him into an ever deeper conversation. He taught her of the gift of inner life which he brought, led her to a state of conversion, and declared himself the Messiah. And the woman proclaimed him: "Many Samaritans from that city believed in him because of the woman's testimony."[27] Some of the most important elements of Jesus' self-revelation were spoken in these discourses with women: the resurrection (to Martha), the life of grace (to the Samaritan).

Women are represented not only as hearing but as remembering the Lord's words. Lk 2:52 tells us this of Mary who "kept all these things in her heart." Of the message at the tomb it is recorded of the women

---

[21] Donald Senior, *Jesus: A Gospel Portrait* (Dayton, 1975) pp. 74-75.

[22] Lk 11:27-28; 8:19.

[23] Lk 10:39. The lesson of Lk 10:38-42 (Mary and Martha) is enveloped by Lk 10:25-37 (the good Samaritan) and Lk 11:1-4 (the Lord's Prayer). Like Acts 6:1-4, these passages emphasize that human services must be complemented by prayer and service of the word. On discipleship see Brown, *op. cit.*, pp. 21-26; D. Senior, "The Mother of Jesus and the Meaning of Discipleship," *Sign*, May, 1975, pp. 5-8; Jean Delorme, "Diversité et unité des ministères d'après le Nouveau Testament," in *Le ministère et les ministères selon le Nouveau Testament*, ed. Delorme (Paris, 1973).

[24] Jn 11:20-27.

[25] Jn 11:28.

[26] Jn 4:7-42. See Bruce Vawter, "The Gospel according to John," in *Jerome Biblical Commentary* (Englewood Cliffs, N.J., 1968) 63:76, p. 431.

[27] Jn 4:39.

that "they remembered his words."[28] Jesus gives no hint of a repudiation of women as unable to hear or understand or remember his word. He testified to the discipleship of his own mother when he complemented her role of physical motherhood, elevating and universalizing her relationship as among those who "hear the word of God and do it."[29]

The great lesson of discipleship was the Cross: "If any man would come after me, let him deny himself and take up his cross and follow me."[30] How graphic must have been this Gospel challenge to the women after they had succored Jesus along the Way of the Cross! Even in these terrible straits he had responded to their sympathy and anguish by teaching them, preparing them for the days when their discipleship would be tested.[31] In fact, the response of the women who accepted the invitation to follow Jesus, to be with him on the Way and in his sufferings, is the one point of relief from the otherwise consistent emphasis in the Gospels on failure in discipleship.

Ministry as witness. The early Church verbalized a criterion for witness of Jesus: those "who have accompanied him during all the time that the Lord Jesus went in and out among us...."[32] Women fulfilled this requirement, for they accompanied Jesus and his disciples on that decisive last journey from Galilee to Jerusalem.[33] "He journeyed through towns and villages preaching and proclaiming the good news of the kingdom of God. The Twelve accompanied him, and also some women," Mary Magdalene, Joanna, Susanna, and many others.[34] There is no evidence in the Gospels that any one of these women faltered when the apostles failed Jesus. It is among the Twelve, chosen personally by Jesus (men, to symbolize the New Israel as representative of the Twelve Tribes[35]), that we find those who deserted, denied, betrayed him. According to the fourth Gospel, the women with the Beloved Disciple stood firm, witnessing the crucifixion.[36] Women watched Jesus' burial.[37]

---

[28] Lk 24:8. Memory is regarded by contemporary theologians as an integral part of the act of faith. See Edward J. Kilmartin, "Apostolic Office: Sacrament of Christ," THEOLOGICAL STUDIES 36 (1975) 255.

[29] Lk 8:21.

[30] Mt 16:24-25; Mk 8:34; Lk 9:23-24.

[31] Lk 23:27.

[32] Acts 1:21. The text 1:21-22 makes explicit the choice of a male because the place of Judas among the Twelve is to be filled. The expression "from the baptism of John" probably does not literally imply the presence of the Twelve but is a reference to the beginning of the gospel; see Mk 1:1-4.

[33] Mk 15:40-41.

[34] Lk 8:1-3.

[35] David M. Stanley and Raymond.E. Brown, "Aspects of New Testament Thought," *Jerome Biblical Commentary* 78:173, p. 797.

[36] Jn 18:15-18, 25-27; 19:25-27.

[37] Mt 27:61; Mk 15:47; Lk 23:55.

Women were singled out as the first witnesses to the Resurrection,[38] the first to whom the risen Lord appeared. It is amazing that the Gospels (written when the attitude toward women in the early Christian community was already tightening) recorded these facts. The story of Jesus' choice of women, told by all four Evangelists, accentuates the apostles' disbelief, even as it reinforces Jesus' habit of disregarding a limiting tradition (the Jewish nonacceptance of women as witnesses).[39]

Ministry as apostleship. During the lifetime of Jesus the term "apostle" seems not to have been used. It came into use only after the resurrection of Jesus, particularly through the influence of Paul. The Twelve were then called apostles, "those sent." But others besides the Twelve were also called apostles.[40] Paul applied the term not only to himself and many other men, but perhaps even to a woman.[41] The Samaritan woman, one of the earliest persons recorded by John as receiving an important revelation from Jesus, became a self-appointed apostle, with her work blessed by the Lord.[42] Certainly women were sent on the most important mission of all: they were commissioned by Jesus to "Go and tell my brothers to go to Galilee, and there they will see me."[43]

Ministry as service. Jesus accepted from women the kind of service which the Church has continually recognized as fitting for women to give: the ministry of providing for bodily needs in the form of food and those ameliorations of environment which make living more human. Certain women, we are told, "used to follow him and look after him...," assisting him and his followers out of their own resources.[44] Jesus not only accepted this service from women but performed miraculous cures which enabled women to serve him. He healed the mother-in-law of Peter, who then "got up at once and began to wait on him."[45] Of

---

[38] The message to the women is rendered in Mt 28:1-10 by an angel, then Jesus; in Mk 16:9 by Jesus; in Lk 24:1-11 by two men; in Jn 20:1-18 by two angels, then Jesus. Though Luke does not record Jesus' appearing to the women, he does acknowledge women as witnesses of Jesus' resurrection, presents them as remembering Jesus' message (given to them in Galilee) and reminding the disciples.

[39] See Roland de Vaux, *Ancient Israel: Its Life and Institutions* (New York, 1961) p. 156.

[40] Stanley and Brown, *JBC*, p. 798.

[41] 1 Cor 1:1; 15:5-7; James: Gal 1:19; Barnabas: Acts 14:14; 1 Cor 9:6; 4:9; Gal 2:9; Andronicus and Junias: Rom 16:7. Junias (Iounian) can be translated Junia (or some mss. Iulia) and was thought by Chrysostom and others to be a woman. See Stanley and Brown, *JBC* 78:179, p. 798; Joseph A. Fitzmyer, "The Letter to the Romans," *JBC* 53:138, p. 330.

[42] Jn 4:7-42.

[43] Mt 28:10. See Brown, *op. cit.*, p. 28: "in the Jewish notion of apostolate the one sent . . . represents the one who sends, carrying not only the sender's authority but even his presence to others."

[44] Lk 8:3.

[45] Mt 8:14-15; Lk 4:38-39; Mk 1:29-31.

the women who provided for Jesus Luke remarks: they "had been healed of evil spirits and infirmities."[46]

Ministry as receiving Jesus' power and becoming instruments of the Spirit. Women attracted the power of Jesus in cures,[47] in being raised from the dead,[48] and in forgiveness of sins.[49] The woman with a hemorrhage drew power from Jesus apparently without his consciously willing it.[50] At Cana, Mary the mother of Jesus was an instrument of Jesus' clarification for us of his power, even to the point of anticipating his "hour" of glorification.[51] In periods relating to crucial events in Jesus' life, women were the recipients of heavenly messages empowering them: Mary at the Annunciation, to bring forth Jesus; Magdalene and the women at the empty tomb, to proclaim the risen Lord.[52] Women also are represented as receiving the Spirit of Jesus directly, most notably Mary his mother,[53] but also Elizabeth.[54] Women were present at the Pentecostal effusion of the Spirit.[55]

Ministry as offering intercessory prayer and worship. In Matthew's Gospel many people "came to Jesus," some to test him, some to ask a favor for themselves or others, some to offer Jesus the respect and honor he deserves. Women are never numbered among those who test Jesus, but, perceiving his real identity, they come to Jesus to make intercession or to offer him praise and adoration. The prayerful message of Martha and Mary evoked a favorable response from Jesus when he raised Lazarus from the dead.[56] Jesus yielded to the persevering, humble prayer of even a non-Jewish woman, a Canaanite,[57] who desired to feed from the crumbs. In the parable of the unjust judge, Jesus chose a woman as a model for perseverance in prayer.[58]

The proclivity of women to worship is graphically presented in the confessions of Martha and Mary[59] and in the public praise of him by the

[46] Lk 8:2.

[47] Lk 8:43–48; 13:10–13.

[48] Lk 8:49–56; Mt 9:18–26; Mk 5:21–43.

[49] Lk 7:48.

[50] Mt 9:20–22.

[51] Jn 2:1–11. John usés his typical literary method of dialogue and represents Mary as evoking Jesus' power and inviting him to anticipate his "hour" of glory.

[52] Lk 1:26–38; Mt 28:1–8; Mk 16:5–8; Lk 24:5–7.

[53] Lk 1:26–38.

[54] Lk 1:39–45.

[55] Acts 1:14; 2:1–4.

[56] Jn 11:3–5; 43–44. In the dialogic form common to John, the prayerful message of Lazarus' sisters arouses Jesus' concern. The spoken faith of Martha in his ability to heal Lazarus is built upon by Jesus to evoke her deeper expression of faith in the resurrection of the dead and his own manifestation of power over death.

[57] Mt 15:22–28.

[58] Lk 18:2–8.

[59] Jn 11:21–27; 20:16–18.

woman crippled for eighteen years.[60] Presence with him at his sacrifice on the cross, reverence for his body,[61] were so important that they took precedence over all the fears which the women must have had. The watchful presence of the women and Beloved Disciple at the cross is symbolized in the celebration of the sacraments by the accepting Church.[62] Women who greeted and worshiped the risen Lord responded in faith to this new form of Presence among them. They gave immediate "obedience of faith"[63] by bearing their Good News to the incredulous disciples.

Ministry as predictions of the future sacraments. In explaining why Jesus is happy to associate with sinners, Luke presents him teaching three parables. Between the parable of the lost sheep[64] and that of the prodigal[65] he inserts one on the woman searching for and rejoicing in the recovery of a small coin.[66] The mercy of God is allegorized through the activity of women as well as of men. Women as well as men are encouraged to seek out and promote the conversion of sinners. These figures of God's mercy prepare the way for the sacraments of baptism and penance. The Gospels also present women as ministers of unction.[67] Mary won Jesus' acclaim for having at great expense anointed his body before he died.[68] After Jesus' death, it was the women who were preoccupied to purchase spices and go to the tomb to anoint him.[69] This association of anointing with preparing the body for death and for burial may well have influenced the rite of the Anointing of the Sick.

The peak of sacramental ministry inheres in the offering of the Eucharistic Sacrifice. Theological manuals used to teach that the priest "confects the body and blood of Jesus." The question was seriously asked, and answered negatively, whether woman can perform such a function.[70] If the Spirit utilized the female powers of Mary's body to incarnate the Son of God, the Church may well recognize His will to use other female powers, for example in orders, to symbolize that incarna-

---

[60] Lk 13:11-13.

[61] Mt 27:55-56; Lk 23:55-56; Mk 16:1-3.

[62] Mk 15:40-41; Lk 23:49; Jn 19:25-30. See John H. McKenna, "Eucharistic Epiclesis: Myopia or Microcosm?" THEOLOGICAL STUDIES 36 (1975) 267: "Christ's sacramental offer of himself finds its complete realization only in the sacramental acceptance of this offer by the faithful."

[63] Rom 1:5; 16:26.

[64] Lk 15:3-7.

[65] Lk 15:11-24.

[66] Lk 15:8-10.

[67] Lk 7:46; Jn 11:2; 12:1-3; Mk 14:8; 16:1.

[68] Mt 26:13.

[69] Mk 16:1; Lk 23:56.

[70] See Haye van der Meer, *Women Priests in the Catholic Church?* (Philadelphia, 1973) pp. 143-53.

tion.

The Eucharist celebrates the entire paschal mystery and re-presents the mission of Jesus. Related to his mission at each step was the participation of a believing community. Jesus' ministry as a call to discipleship presented models for the sacramental life of the Church. Those partaking with Jesus at the Last Supper, the women and the Beloved Disciple at the cross, and the women after the Resurrection offered that presence, memory, loving faith, and service which are integral to the Eucharist.[71]

The various forms of ministry performed by women may seem dimly related to the ordered functions of preaching, teaching, administering the sacraments, and organizing the community of followers of Jesus until we remember that these forms were inchoate also in terms of male disciples and even the Twelve.[72]

In the post-Resurrection period women equally with men received the charisms of the Holy Spirit.[73] Paul's insistence that Gentiles need not be circumcised before embracing Christianity opened to women the possibility of baptism and full membership in the Church. Doctrinally and in his personal relations with women[74] Paul appeared to appreciate the equal status of women with men in Christ. But the pressures brought to bear against this equality must have been overwhelming, especially as

---

[71] When Jesus describes his ministry along the Way to Jerusalem as "I have come not to be served but to serve and to give my life as a ransom for many" (Mt 20:28), he invites the disciples to be like him. In Mark's account of the Last Supper these latter words are echoed as a concrete example of Jesus' sacrificial ministry (Mk 14:24). The fulness of discipleship implies that every level of human life is touched by Jesus' own saving ministry. No comparison of Gospel texts makes this more obvious than the accounts of the Last Supper events in the Synoptics (Mt 26:26-28; Mk 14:22-25; Lk 22:14-20) and Paul (1 Cor 11:24) taken together with that of John (Jn 13:1-14). Paul and the Synoptics preserve the tradition of the Passover meal, Paul and Luke especially underlining the commemorative aspect of this meal in the words of Jesus "Do this in memory of me." John omits the account of the offering of Jesus' body and blood, but retains the formula "As I have done, so you must do," applied in this instance to Jesus' humble service of washing his disciples' feet. John apparently desires to widen the scope of the commemorative action of the Church, reminding Christians that a Eucharistic celebration without service to others is meaningless and empty, that the Eucharist and service cannot be separated. John does not neglect the Eucharist, as the discourse of Jesus on the Bread of Life in chap. 6 shows. This context emphasizes how closely Jesus linked human service (in multiplication of loaves that prompted the discourse) with the fulfilment of spiritual needs. Paul, too, inserts his account of the Eucharist into the context of the mutual concern the members of a community should have for one another. Luke makes the same point with his banquet theme, where the poor, the outcasts, and women are opposed to the rich, the revered, the Pharisees.

[72] See Brown, op. cit., pp. 13, 17-20, 34-43.

[73] Acts 1:14; 2:1-4.

[74] Gal. 3:27-28; Rom 16.

regards the difficult Corinthians. Clearly, women were early represented among the prophesiers.[75] Their homes may well have served as churches.[76]

Widows constituted a special group, as in Judaism, as the recipients of food and social services. The fact that these widows later became an established order in the Church indicates that they may well have performed individual ministry in gathering the community together, communicating the message of the risen Lord, praying, and prophesying.[77] Chronologically, the first reference to any term later applied to order in the Church is that of "deacon," used for Phoebe, a woman deeply respected by Paul. He urges the Christian community to receive her and help her in every way possible because of the role of leadership she has exercised in the Church. Whatever the "deacon" meant in Paul's lifetime, the same Greek term is used for men and women.[78] The Pastorals witness to an organization of widows and the continuance of women as deacons.[79] By the third century the *Didascalia* indicated that bishops, presbyters, deacons, and deaconesses had clerical office, while widows and virgins were recognized as of nonclerical status.[80] When minor orders were enumerated in the *Apostolic Constitutions*, that of deaconess was included. It seems apparent that women played an "immense and irreplaceable role . . . in the growth of the early Church."[81]

The evidence of women in roles of discipleship, witness, apostleship,

---

[75] Acts 21:8-9; cf Eph 2:20. See *The Jerusalem Bible*, ed. Alexander Jones (London, 1966) p. 221, note m: "particular individuals are so specially endowed with the charisma that they are always referred to as 'prophets', Ac 11:27; 13:1; 15:32; 21:9, 10. These normally occupy the second place after the apostles in the order of charisma, 1 Co 12:28-29; Ep 4:11; but cf. 1 Co 12:10; Rm 12:6; Lk 11:49; this is because they are the appointed witnesses of the Spirit, Rv 2:7, etc., 1 Th 5:19-20, whose 'revelations' they communicate, 1 Co 14:6,26,30; Ep 3:5; Rv 1:1, just as the apostles are witnesses to the risen Christ, Rm 1:1+; Ac 1:8+, and proclaim the kerygma, Acts 2:22+." The prohibition against women prophesying, "women should keep silent in all such gatherings" (1 Cor 14:33b-35) is considered by a growing body of commentators to be an interpolation influenced by a post-Pauline reaction to certain heretical groups; see A. Feuillet, "La dignité et le rôle de la femme," *New Testament Studies* 21 (1975) 163, n. 2.

[76] Acts 12:12; Rom 16:5. Six of the persons greeted in Rom 16 are women. The word used for Phoebe in Rom 16:2 is *prostasis*, a noun derived from the verb *prostasso*, meaning "to order validly," "pertaining to those who have the right to command" (p. 37). It asserts, as it is used, e.g., in Acts 10:33, authority and also dependence on God (p. 38); cf. G. Friedrich, ed., *Theological Dictionary of the New Testament* 8 (Grand Rapids, 1972) 37-39.

[77] Mary Lawrence McKenna, *Women of the Church* (New York, 1967) pp. 35-62.

[78] Rom 16:1. The same Greek noun is used for a man. Cf. Phil 1:1; 1 Tim 3:11.

[79] 1 Tim 5:3-16; 3:11. See Peter Hünermann, "Conclusions regarding the Female Diaconate," THEOLOGICAL STUDIES 36 (1975) 325-33; McKenna, *art. cit.*, pp. 35-63.

[80] McKenna, *art. cit.*, p. 66.

[81] Hünermann, *art. cit.*, p. 325.

serving, being empowered, worship, and symbolic actions cuts across the tradition presented by all four Gospels. Jesus' ministry to and acceptance of women must have been a very important part of the gospel, preserved even "against the grain" of the Jewish and later the Gnostic influences that tended to reduce Jesus' startling freedom with women. The presentation of this material suggests that it was such an integral part of the Gospel tradition that it could not be rejected or weakened. As is said of the woman who anointed Jesus, "whenever this gospel is preached in the whole world, what she has done will be told in memory of her."[82] The Gospels talk about the words and works not only of Jesus but of women as well.

TRADITION

"Venerable tradition"[83] has been proffered as the reason for excluding women from official ministry, even of a lay character.[84] Such tradition is not static. Its validity may be measured by such characteristics as the following: whether it (1) derives from the example of Jesus, (2) is constant, (3) is revelatory of sound doctrine, (4) cannot be changed. When the women's issue is studied in the light of these questions, a firmer basis for the influence of tradition on women's ministries may be achieved.

Example of Jesus

The exclusion of women from ministry does not derive from the example of Jesus. There is one saying of Jesus which is most consistently quoted in the Gospels and the writings of Paul: the "great commandment" or the "love command." Both Paul and the Evangelists attempt to show the growth and development of the early Church as evidence of the Christian community's effort to interpret the love command. Fidelity to this command provided the criterion for resolving new disputes as the Church confronted new issues.[85]

---

[82] Mt 26:13.

[83] See Constitution on Divine Revelation, no. 10 (*Documents*, pp. 117-18): "Sacred tradition and sacred Scripture form one sacred deposit of the word of God.... [The] teaching office is not above the word of God but serves it." No. 8 (p. 116): "This tradition which comes from the apostles develops in the Church with the help of the Holy Spirit. For there is a growth in the understanding of the realities and the words which have been handed down."

[84] Paul VI, "Motu Proprio on Minor Orders," *Origins*, Sept 21, 1972, p. 203.

[85] E.g., Mt 5:44; 19:19; 22:37-39 and par.; Jn 13:34-35; Gal 5:6; 1 Cor 13; 1 Jn 4. See Victor Furnish, *The Love Command in the New Testament* (Nashville, 1972); Ceslaus Spicq, *Charity and Liberty in the New Testament* (Staten Island, N.Y., 1965); *id.*, *Agape in the New Testament* (St. Louis, 1963); Gerard Gilleman, *The Primacy of Charity in Moral Theology* (Westminster, Md., 1959).

Paul demonstrated a prophetic understanding of the role of this mandate when he challenged Peter and the other Jewish Christian authorities for their refusal to allow the Gentiles free entrance into the Church.[86] Paul chastises Peter for submitting to convention and thus failing to apply the lesson of Jesus' central teaching.[87] This confrontation and its settlement emphasized the love command as the absolute criterion for settling disputes in the Christian Church. As such, it presents a meaningful model for resolving the question of the role of women in the Church, both as to ways of proceeding and as to content.

No mention is made in the New Testament of any dispute over the baptism of women. But if the narrower view had prevailed and circumcision of the foreskin of males had been made a prerequisite for baptism, women would have been denied Christian baptism. It is interesting that the great Pauline doctrinal proclamation of equality is thought to be part of a baptismal formula:[88] "There is neither Jew nor Greek, there is neither slave nor free, there is neither male nor female; for you are all one in Christ Jesus."[89]

The exclusion of women had its origin, however, early in Christian history when the young Church was unable to continue the radicalism of Jesus' position against the ingrained customs of society.[90] The Gospels hint that the male followers of Jesus had difficulty in understanding and assimilating Jesus' concept of women.[91] Consideration of the depth and extent of antifeminism in the Jewish world of the first century A.D.[92]

[86] Acts 15:1-31; Rom 2:25-29; 3:30; 1 Cor 7:17-19; 8:1-13; Gal 2:1-10; 6:15.

[87] Gal 2:11-21.

[88] See Joseph A. Fitzmyer, "The Letter to the Galatians," *JBC* 49:24, p. 243.

[89] Gal 3:17-28.

[90] Jewish society honored women only within the home in subjection to husband or father; cf. de Vaux, *op. cit.*, pp. 39-40. Philo wrote: "The women are best suited to the indoor life, which never strays from the house, within which the middle door is taken by the maidens as their boundary, and the outer door by those who have realized full womanhood" (*De spec. leg.* 3, 169). Josephus insisted: "The woman, says the Lord, is in all things inferior to the man. Let her accordingly be submissive, not for her humiliation but that she may be directed; for the authority has been given by God to the man" (*In Flaccum* 89). The common physiological knowledge of the time emphasized the inferiority of woman, her passivity in procreation, and the need of the female for longer embryonic development; see Tavard, *op. cit.*, p. 62. The dualistic philosophy of Plato exaggerated the differences between men and women, leading later to St. Augustine's conclusion that spirit was symbolized by man, flesh by woman (*Expositio in Joannem* 1, 13 [*PL* 35, 1395]).

[91] Jn 4:27; Mt 26:7-10; Lk 24:9-11. Note the apocryphal *Gospel of Thomas:* "Simon Peter said to them, 'Let Mary go out from among us, because women are not worthy of the Life.' Jesus said, 'See, I shall lead her, so that I will make her a male, that she too may become a living spirit, resembling you males. For every woman who makes herself a male will enter the kingdom of heaven'" (E. Hennecke, *New Testament Apocrypha*, Logion 14, pl. 99, 18-26, ed. W. Schneemelcher [London, 1963] p. 299).

[92] See de Vaux, *op. cit.*, pp. 39-40.

causes the "remembering" (inclusion in the writings which became the New Testament) of the respectful, nonpatronizing attitude of Jesus toward women to be a miracle in itself—a testimony to biblical inspiration. Jesus' approach to woman as person is to be distinguished from both streams of thought about women apparent in the Old Testament, that of the accursed temptress and that of the embodiment of heavenly wisdom.[93] To some extent in St. Paul and certainly in the Pastorals, Jesus' attitude toward women was being submerged.[94] A critical turning point in the history of the Church was in process.

Although Paul taught clearly that Christ's redemptive acts broke into history and destroyed the effects of the sin of Adam, his writings reflect an awareness that these effects still dominated society.[95] Accordingly, comments ascribed to him on the text of Genesis 1, where male and female are declared, as humankind, to be the image and likeness of God, are ambiguous. Is the passage which claims that man "is the image and glory of God; but woman is the glory of man. . . . Neither was man created for woman, but woman for man"[96] an ironic repetition of the argumentation of Paul's times? In the next verses Paul stresses the interdependence of man and woman.[97] Christian tradition, however, did not see this dictum as irony (if it was) but allowed it to deflect from or deter efforts to realize the ideal of Gal 3:27-28. So also, the injunction that "the women should keep silence in the churches"[98] is in contradiction to his testimony to women as prophesiers and coworkers with him.[99] The Pauline community later registered doubts about Paul's Christological vision for all humankind and the freedom of women in ministry which he had promoted. The first letter to Timothy[100] contradicts Paul's first letter to the Corinthians 11:7-10 in attributing sin solely to Eve and thus missing the point of Paul's theology: "Sin entered the world through one

[93] See Tavard, op. cit., pp. 17-26.

[94] Paul: 1 Cor 11:3-10; 14:33b-36; Col 3:18; Eph 5:22-24; Pastorals: Tit 2:3-5; 1 Tim 2:11-15. Robin Scroggs, "Paul: Chauvinist or Liberationist?" Christian Century 89 (1972) 307, considers 1 Cor 14:33b-36 as a post-Pauline gloss. He also considers Col and Eph deutero-Pauline.

[95] Gn 3:1-16. See Tavard, op. cit., p. 31. Note ibid., p. 45: "the advent of the New Creation has, in principle, restored mankind to a paradisiac, prelapsarian state. The Christian woman is no longer under the curse by which she was made servant to her husband and bound to a chain of painful pregnancies triggered by her desire for him." Cf. Robin Scroggs, "Paul and the Eschatological Woman," Journal of the American Academy of Religion 40 (1972) 291.

[96] 1 Cor 11:7,9. See the commentary of Scroggs, "Paul and the Eschatological Woman," pp. 294-95, 297-303.

[97] 1 Cor 11:11-12.

[98] 1 Cor 14:34; see note 75 above.

[99] Rom 16; 1 Cor 11:5; Phil 4:2-3; see also Acts 21:9.

[100] 1 Tim 2:14.

man" (Adam-humankind) whose countertype is Christ, the savior of all humankind.[101] This letter also indicates that woman is to be saved by childbearing (by the fulfilment of her curse), not by baptism.[102] The letters to Titus and to Timothy make no mention of prophecy (testified to as an office of women in Acts and Corinthians),[103] but rather forbid women to teach[104] and restrict widows and deaconesses to the totally private functions common in Jewish society in the first century A.D.[105]

Unfortunately, such positions were put forward at the period when the Church was organizing, beginning to institutionalize its ministry.[106] The exclusion of women which had been so marked in Hellenistic Jewish religion therefore affected Christian patterns decisively.[107]

The ministry of women through the ages developed under the shadow of sexual bias in society reinforced by the institutionalization in the first and second centuries of an all-male hierarchical priesthood. This shadow blighted the development of a tradition of equality of sexes as achieved through baptism.

Inconstancy of the Tradition

The tradition of the exclusion of women from official ministry in the Church is not constant. It is not constant because at root there are two traditions: that of Jesus and the earliest Church, which had some partial echoes in history, and that of the institutionalizing period of the Church (about 60 to 100 A.D.), which limited women in ministry and excluded them from priesthood. In the first tradition is Phoebe, revered by Paul as coworker and *prostasis* (one who has authority, who rules) in the Church. This tradition is partially continued in the diaconate of women. It is revived in the Middle Ages in the attribution of powers of episcopal jurisdiction to certain abbesses. But most ecclesiastical practice has followed the second tradition. The Church has been unable to incorporate women into its government structures.

A strong constant in ecclesiastical structures has been the need to separate the sexes, modified by the responsibility the Church assumed to

[101] See Tavard, *op. cit.*, pp. 31–35.

[102] 1 Tim 2:15.

[103] Acts 21:9; 1 Cor 11:5.

[104] 1 Tim 2:12.

[105] 1 Tim 5:3–16; 3:11.

[106] The pastoral letters reflect the complex situation of the Church between 60 and 100 A.D. Of this period Tavard comments: "The liberty recognized by Paul must now be channelled through regular institutions: that of widowhood stands out, that of matrimony offers the only proper way of life, since it is through motherhood that they will obtain salvation" (*op. cit.*, p. 35). See Brown, *op. cit.*, pp. 35–38.

[107] For worship, Jewish women entered only the outer court, the women's court of Herod's temple; see de Vaux, *op cit.*, p. 317.

provide "care of souls." Strongly affecting that constant and affected by it is the presumed inferiority of women. It was segregation of sexes and the need to care for women in ways which would not threaten the purity of priests which led to the development of orders of widows and deaconesses, widows dominantly in the Western Church, deaconesses in the Eastern. The widows,[108] gathered at first as recipients of the Church's bounty, grew in importance from apostolic times through the third century as the Church's chief representatives into the world of women: teaching, nursing, praying, providing works of charity.[109] Though within the limits specified the widows exercised a ministry broad and useful, honored by the Church, they had no part in the sacramental system, no influence upon the total structure or policies of the Church, and depended for their livelihood upon the charitable contributions of the faithful as dispensed by the clerics.

In the Eastern Church segregation of women extended even to the sacramental system. Therefore deaconesses,[110] besides undertaking a ministry to women like that of the widows in the west, were also deliberately incorporated into the clerical rank alongside the deacon to assist with ministry to women. The deaconesses were chosen and ordained by the bishop with imposition of hands, and prayer invoking the Holy Spirit for grace to discharge the office properly. Their main liturgical function was assisting at the baptism of women, though they also distributed Communion to women and children, administered extreme unction to women, and performed auxiliary tasks at the Eucharist. Their service was directed always to women, instructing them for baptism, providing spiritual guidance, visiting the sick, nursing, acting as their advocate and companion in approaching the bishop or deacon.[111] Like the widows, the deaconesses were obviously a response to the social segregation of the sexes.

That the deaconesses were not to be given any assignment which gave them authority outranking man[112] is a manifestation of male superiority not quite in the spirit of Christ; that they were not to function at the altar

---

[108] M. L. McKenna, op. cit. (n. 77 above) pp. 35–63; H. Leclercq, "Veuvage, Veuve," DACL 15/2, 3015.

[109] In some circumstances, as in the entourage of St. Jerome, these women became really learned in the Scriptures and courageous in the scope of work undertaken; see M. L. McKenna, op. cit., pp. 126–29.

[110] "Deaconess" (diakonissa) is an ecclesiastical term deliberately coined in the third century; cf. M. L. McKenna, op. cit., pp. 64–94; also Hünermann, op. cit., pp. 325–33. The deaconesses never became popular in the West, though some canons deal with them. See M. L. McKenna, op. cit., pp. 129–40.

[111] M. L. McKenna, op cit., pp. 69–73, 76–79. See Constitutiones apostolorum 3, 2, 3 (ed. F. X. Funk [Paderborn, 1905] p. 185).

[112] Hünerman, art. cit., p. 328.

during the consecration of the Eucharist[113] may well have been a continuation of the Old Testament menstrual taboo.[114] Nonetheless, from the third to the sixth centuries women played a vital role in the extensive and intensive missionary and charitable activity of the Church; some (deaconesses) served within the ordained clergy.

The ascetical ethos which elevated chastity as the Christian priority began to assume structural forms in the third century. The "companies of virgins,"[115] begun as a positive response to the gospel call to virginal discipleship of Christ, interacted with and finally absorbed the orders of widows and deaconesses, giving promise of fruitful patterns of clerical and nonclerical service.

The persistent tradition of woman as temptress was, however, given new life, accompanied by the myth that man, though powerful against the devil, was powerless before a woman.[116] As celibacy became a more pronounced ideal for the clergy,[117] the easy solution was to banish women from their companionship and even their sight. Separation from the world became not only a spiritual and psychological self-perception; it was materialized in habit, wall, and enclosure.[118] Theoretically, all channels to active ministry were closed to women. Yet the medieval ruralism provided even for cloistered nuns opportunities for social and religious influences. Some abbesses, continuing the tradition of deaconesses, exercised ecclesiastical as well as manorial jurisdiction over towns and parishes.[119] As the cloister became less common for men religious, it was formally imposed on all women wishing officially to serve the Church.

[113] Epiphanius, *Adversus haereses* 79 (*PG* 42, 743 f.).

[114] Lv 15:19-29. Origen forbids women to enter a church building at the time of their menstrual period; see Tavard, *op. cit.*, p. 95; Roger Gryson, *Les origines du célibat ecclésiastique* (Paris, 1970).

[115] M. L. McKenna, *op. cit.*, pp. 95-110.

[116] Tertullian's "you are she who enticed the man whom the devil dare not approach" (*De cultu feminarum* 1, 1) continues on even into the twentieth century; see van der Meer, *op. cit.*, p. 50.

[117] Legislation forbidding priests to have intercourse began as early as the fourth century in regional councils. In 1050 Pope Leo IX began the effort to abolish the marriage of priests throughout the Church. In 1123 ordination became an impediment nullifying marriage. Clerical celibacy was reaffirmed by the Council of Trent. See Tavard, *op. cit.*, p. 119.

[118] See Valentine Schaff, *The Cloister* (Cincinnati, 1921) pp. 26-56. The sixth-century rule for women of Caesarius of Arles prescribes strict cloister. Before the twelfth century, regulations of cloister were issued by various regional councils. Boniface VIII imposed perpetual cloister on all women who had made profession. The Council of Trent confirmed the legislation of Boniface VIII and extended it to all women religious. Efforts to enforce and tighten this legislation were made by Pius V. In 1900 bishops were directed to enforce cloister even on sisters in simple vows.

[119] Joan Morris, *The Lady Was a Bishop* (New York, 1973); see van der Meer, *op. cit.*, pp. 106-128, for discussion on the nature of this jurisdiction.

With the rise of cities, the functions which monasteries had performed for people on their own estates became irrelevant. Yet new structures to allow women to make a contribution as Church of social and spiritual assistance were frustrated.[120] During the Renaissance, women tried to respond in forms like the Oratory of Divine Love, where men and women devoted themselves to the appallingly bad social conditions of Italy.[121] Despite the needs of society and the good work accomplished by women, the Council of Trent reiterated the imposition of cloister upon all women who wished to serve the Church.[122]

The long struggle of women in the Church from the seventeenth to the nineteenth century for greater opportunities for service eventuated in the recognition within canon law of "active" congregations of women religious—still, however, dominated by a cloistral mentality.[123] Their position in the Church never rose above that of "widows," did not even attain the ecclesiastical importance of deaconesses. The opportunity for higher ecclesiastical studies was closed to women.[124] All theology and canon law have been solely male in source and outlook. Official documents since Vatican II have reiterated the exclusion of women from ministry or assigned them an inferior place within it.[125] It is this second tradition that is becoming untenable. Events, including concern for human rights and for the fullest implementation of justice as part of the

[120] Women associated with both St. Francis and St. Dominic were strictly cloistered and did not participate in the peripatetic preaching of men. Yet, in the thirteenth century large numbers of women participated in new forms of "apostolic life," in chastity and poverty. These groups perplexed the Church, because they did not fit into established categories. A struggle ensued. Pressure was brought on the Curia to recognize and incorporate these women into the Church. The Curia sought to place them under the jurisdiction of the male orders. When these latter opposed such an arrangement, the Curia eventually turned to the bishops to provide pastoral care and impose discipline. See Brenda M. Bolton, "Mulieres sanctae," in Sanctity and Secularity: The Church and the World, ed. Derek Baker (Oxford, 1973) pp. 77-95. Bolton concludes: "The general ecclesiastical attitude to women was, at best, negative if not actively hostile. Nor, indeed, was a women's vocation necessarily regarded in a serious light." See also R. W. Southern, Western Society and the Church in the Middle Ages (Baltimore, 1970) pp. 240-272.

[121] Richard L. De Molen, "The Age of Renaissance and Reformation," in The Meaning of the Renaissance and Reformation, ed. De Molen (Boston, 1974) pp. 22-23.

[122] Session 25, De regularibus, c. 5. Yet see Georges Goyau, La femme dans missions (Paris, 1933) for a survey of the beneficent missionary work of women religious.

[123] See Leon Joseph Suenens, The Nun in the World (Westminster, Md., 1963). The struggle of women religious against this cloistral mentality since Vatican II has influenced the proposed New Code for Religious, where equality is posited between men and women save for contemplative women, who still have obligations not imposed on contemplative men. See Review for Religious 34 (1975) 63-65.

[124] Pontifical faculties of theology have been opened to women only in the last decade.

[125] Paul VI, "Motu Proprio on Minor Orders," Origins, Sept. 21, 1972, p. 203.

love command, call for a re-examination of the first tradition.

Sound Doctrine

The tradition of the exclusion of women from official ministry in the Church does not rest upon sound doctrine. This structure of the subordination of women and their exclusion from the active ministry of the Church flourished upon a substructure of scriptural commentaries and canonical legislation[126] which helped the men of the Church to justify their exclusivism and the women of the Church to interiorize their inferiority. Though certainly no one today would teach as sound, unchanging doctrine views such as these of Thomas Aquinas (admittedly taken out of context), they do represent a chain of commentary which has persisted through the ages and is therefore bound to influence attitudes, even unconsciously.

[Woman is] something deficient or accidental. For the active power of the male intends to produce a perfect likeness of itself with male sex. If a female is conceived, this is due to lack of strength in the active power, to a defect in the mother, or to some external influence like that of a humid wind from the south. . . . [127]

Nature has given men more intelligence.[128]

The reason why women are in a subordinate and not a commanding position is because they lack sufficient reason, which a leader above all needs.[129]

It was necessary for woman to be made, as the Scripture says, not as a helpmate in other works than generation, as some say, since man can be more efficiently helped by another man in other works, but as a helper in the work of generation.[130]

. . . since it is not possible in the female sex to signify eminence of degree, for a woman is in the state of subjection, it follows that she cannot receive the sacrament of orders.[131]

Contemporary women are reminded of the thought of Duns Scotus: "The Church would not presume to deprive the entire female sex, without any guilt on its part, of an act which might licitly pertain to it [Scotus is speaking of ordination], being directed toward the salvation of women

---

[126] Canon 968, 1: "A baptized male alone can validly receive sacred ordination."

[127] *Sum. theol.* 1, q. 92, a. 1, ad 1m.

[128] *Ibid.*, ad 2m.

[129] *In 1 ad Cor. lectio 7, Super ep. s. Pauli lectura* (ed. R. Cai [Rome, 1953] 1, 402).

[130] *Sum. theol.* 1, q. 92, a. 1.

[131] *Ibid., Supplementum,* q. 39, a. 1.

and of others in the Church through her. For this would be an extreme injustice, not only toward the whole Church but also toward specific persons."[132] So huge is the injustice that Duns Scotus cannot conceive of the Church being responsible for it. He traces its source to the inscrutable will of Christ. The solution of an unjust God is unacceptable as a doctrinal basis for the continued exclusion of women from official ministry.

Tradition Not Unchangeable

The tradition of the exclusion of woman from ministry is not unchangeable. It is response to the world and its antifeminine culture that caused the Church to delimit the role of woman from what it had been with Jesus and in the earliest Church. It is response to the world and the cultural aspirations of personhood, equality, and feminism which should lead the Church to reconnect its tradition with its earliest sources.

The Church cannot be taken seriously as being "in the modern world" unless it takes the aspirations of women seriously. Vatican II (unintentionally indeed) forced on the Catholic mind the issue of transformational reform, discontinuity.[133] The Church must examine sinfulness and grace in its own structures as well as in persons and worldly society.[134]

HOPE

The women's movement affords a providential opportunity for the Church to move into a better confrontation with the gospel concerning both women and ministry. The fundamental dynamic of the movement in its Christian aspects stresses personhood as a value for women and men, and envisages structures respectful of persons.[135] It thus seems consonant with God's design in creating humankind, male and female, "in the image and likeness of God." It affords our Church the opportunity to become "a clearer revelation of Christ" by imitating Jesus in cutting through societal role fixations and dealing with persons, male and female, as real and gifted human beings. Pope Paul has said: "In the contemporary effort to promote 'the advancement of women' the Church

---

[132] John Duns Scotus, *In librum 4 sententiarum*, d. 25, q. 2, scol. 2 (*Opera omnia*, ed. L. Vives [Paris, 1894] 19, 140).

[133] Cf. Walter J. Burghardt, "A Theologian's Challenge to Liturgy," THEOLOGICAL STUDIES 35 (1974) 235; Michael A. Fahey, "Continuity in the Church amid Structural Changes," *ibid.*, pp. 427–28.

[134] Fahey, *art. cit.*, p. 421. Note *General Catechetical Directory*, nos. 65–67.

[135] Dorothy L. Sayers, *Are Women Human?* (Grand Rapids, 1971); Sally Cunneen, *Sex: Female; Religion: Catholic* (New York, 1968) esp. pp. 22–46.

has already recognized a 'sign of the times' and has seen in it a call of the Spirit."[136]

Call of Women to Personhood

The women's movement calls woman to define herself as a human person, equal in capacity, in aspiration, and in sinfulness with men. Modern women reject definition of themselves by role and are unwilling to have their physiological differences from men serve to express their total reality or to limit it arbitrarily. Aware of the potential for diverse human development which they share with men, they see their sexuality as a gift but do not accept the role limitations of "the feminine" imposed upon them by Church and society. Created, equally with men, as image of God, to exercise creative intellect, freedom of choice, and affectivity in a wide variety of roles, they think of themselves as autonomous,[137] not merely relational. As autonomous, they strive to build honest relationships and to fulfil vocational roles as free persons.

Contemporary Catholic women have felt impelled by the Spirit to respond to human needs, not only in the personal expression of prayer or in other interpersonal spheres of immediate care and concern, but in the public domain. They seek to be sharers of interpersonal grace and channels of societal grace, whether this grace is shown forth in ecclesiastical or in secular forms.

Women are actually serving as associate pastors, members of pastoral teams, and even as administrators of parishes. In many parishes they act as directors of religious education, conducting much of the preparation of adults as well as children for the sacraments. Many undertake programs for the elderly which include community organizing, personal counseling, prayer, and liturgical participation. As extraordinary ministers of the Eucharist, many women bring the Sacrament to the aging and bedridden. Hospital chaplaincies and campus ministries include and are often headed by women. The preaching of retreats, work with the Christian Family Movement, Cursillos, Marriage Encounter groups,

[136] Paul VI, "Address on International Women's Year," *Origins*, May 1, 1975, p. 718.

[137] For this approach to herself, modern woman finds confirmation in the attitude depicted in the Scriptures of Jesus toward women. In the preparation for his incarnation, Mary is approached not relationally, as a minor, through her father or her fiancé, but as an autonomous woman, fully capable of an intelligent, free, loving response. Jesus expresses the desire that she be revered not because she is physically his mother but because she is a woman of faith. So also with other women. We know nothing of the marital status of Mary and Martha. What was important to the Evangelists was that Jesus loved them, trusted them, taught them, found them worthy to share his ministry. Reverence for the Samaritan woman even in her sinfulness caused Jesus to ignore roles and to encourage her initiative and sense of responsibility.

teen-age organizations, and charismatic prayer groups engage the skills of many women. Hispanic women and black women offer general and specialized ministry to their people. Some women, particularly in campus ministry, preach homilies, distribute Holy Communion, arrange and participate in communal penance services, prepare students for marriage, teach inquiry classes, plan liturgies, do private and group counseling.

With the same motivation of ministry, other women are studying and seeking to change the political, economic, and social structures which anonymously and pervasively cause great poverty and alienation. They undertake advocacy roles for the poor, for prisoners, for the dependent and helpless. Whether through Catholic Charities or in a federal or state office or staff position or in a public interest capacity, women undertake to put into practice the goals of the *Call to Action* of Pope Paul and the Synod of 1971.[138]

Through the demands of such ministries women become aware of their personal needs and weaknesses, out of which, if they are able to be faithful, they must grow. In a less artificial setting than formerly characterized women, they find in openness to pain and struggle an access to the grace of the Spirit which alone makes ministry effective.

Call of Men to Personhood

The women's movement looks upon men as victims of role distortion equally destructive to them as to women.[139] The masculine image sets priority upon being in control, dominating, winning. The economic system asks men that they be single-mindedly competitive and profit-oriented. They are expected to be the all-successful providers for wife and family, with work as their justification for living. Such roles must be questioned. Men in ministry will ask whether the roles established for them in the Church are derived from social custom or from the gospel.

The women's movement calls men to accept their sexuality,[140] to deal with it in ways which do not entail the exclusion or belittlement of women. It asks them to deal honestly with women as human beings with the same human range of hopes and fears, capabilities and defects, sensitivities and goals as they have. Whereas in women the imaging of God in freedom and intellectual development has often been hindered, in men it is the affective which society tends to crush. Sensitivity to the

---

138 M. Thomas Aquinas Carroll, *Experience of Women Religious in the Ministry of the Church* (Chicago, 1974).

139 Walter Farrell, *The Liberated Man* (New York, 1974); Jack Nichols, *Men's Liberation* (New York, 1975); Gene Marine, *A Male Guide to Women's Liberation* (New York, 1972).

140 See esp. Don Goergen, *The Sexual Celibate* (New York, 1975).

feelings and needs of others must be seen as neither male nor female, but as human. Intuitional as well as rational forms of intellectual process must be respected.

Call of Women and Men to New Relationships

The appeal of the women's movement to Christians is the hope it holds forth of translating into concrete experience Jesus' command to human beings to love one another.

When relationships between men and women are not truly mutual, relationships among women as well as those among men are distorted. If men are cast in a role which expects of them that they "put down" women face to face or among their male friends, their respect for themselves and for each other is bound to be diminished. If they feel they can only praise women for performing in ways that are essentially subservient or anonymous, then women's attitudes toward one another will be negatively affected and men may base their self-respect on a false superiority.

The consequences of this lack of genuine mutuality in male-female relations are not insignificant. Distortions in relationships bring about distorted personalities. Women become deviously submissive or hostile in a desperate effort to survive psychically. Men become insensitive, even violent in their modes of self-expression.

Because women suffer from an all-pervasive domination by men, they have learned to retrieve some sense of mastery by manipulating men. Manipulation is nondevelopmental for the one who practices it and the one on whom it is practiced. If Christian values (and the ideals of the women's movement) are to inform male-female relations, both the need to manipulate and the act of manipulation must be overcome. Otherwise man and woman are treating each other as things.

The alternative for both man and woman is the cultivation of a basic reverence, an approach to each other in mutual honesty and trust. There seems no reason why men and women who are mature in their sexuality, faithful to the commitments they have made, should not enter into relationships of deep friendship and build support groups for one another. This would seem to be a natural step to the ideal of community which Jesus preached and lived. Mutuality of spiritual direction could be immensely helpful in promoting the wholeness of both men and women.

Such mature, honest, developmental relationships are indispensable if real co-operation in the ministry is to be attained. Women must be accepted as working *with* others for the promotion of the kingdom, not working *for* men. The call of the women's movement, then, which at least in this regard coincides with Jesus' call to love and to community, urges women and men so to assimilate their sexuality that they can look upon one another as persons, partners in the divine enterprise of promoting charity.

Call of Church to Structural Reform in Ministry

Human beings create structures.[141] Structures are ways of being together (or not being together) and of working together (or not working together) which in their origins are subject to all the manifold motivations of humankind. Structures readily become objectified, take on a life of their own, and to a great extent control the human beings within them. Structures become interiorized to such a degree that alternative ways of relating seem unthinkable. Yet, as persons break through societal myths which have formed them, they find themselves in tension with the structures. The women's movement is provoking such a tension.

The Church is a social structure, formed and reformed by human decisions through the ages.[142] Christ founded the Church on men and women who responded to his call, determined in particular ways how they would pray and celebrate the Eucharist, how they would be ministered to and governed.[143] Vatican II profited from a new historical consciousness to make radical changes in the Church's self-understanding[144] and thereby performed the most human (and divine) task a community can undertake: to create structures wherein persons are freed for responsible action in service, justice, and love. The Council modeled or eulogized such qualities as freedom of spirit, respect for persons, community, and such processes as subsidiarity, collegiality, and an accountability which is growth-productive.

Despite striking initiatives toward change, the image still projected by ministry in the Church is that its structures promote fear and apathy rather than freedom of spirit. In law, the Church is identified with the clergy. "Office" means hierarchical office. Elements which do not have an "official" character are neglected. Societal demands of position, advancement, power, the responsibilities of hierarchical control appear to weigh heavily upon and to limit personal fulfilment of ministry. The attribution of jurisdiction only to the clerical order successfully elimi-

[141] Andrew Greeley, "Sociology and Church Structure," *Concilium* 58 (1970) 26.

[142] *Ibid.*, p. 27: "the greatest problem the Church as an organization faces is the pervasive human temptation to canonize as essential relationship patterns that evolved to meet the needs of one era. . . . " See William F. Ryan, "Mindsets and New Horizons for Discernment," in *Soundings* (Washington, D.C., 1974) pp. 4–6; William R. Callahan, "The Impact of Culture on Religious Values and Decision Making," *ibid.*, pp. 8–12.

[143] Brown, *op. cit.;* cf. the biblical evidence in Acts on Peter, who "went here and there among them all," obviously exercised authority (9:32), but in conjunction with "the apostles and the elders" (14:2).

[144] Cf. Burghardt, *art. cit.*, p. 235.

nates laymen and all women from decision-making roles in the Church. The relationships are those of a power structure, wherein conformity is rewarded and obedience becomes the primary virtue.

Women who wish to minister hesitate to move into this structure. They consider it depersonalizing, destructive of the Christian spirit of ministry. They find that Jesus directed his most frequent warnings against the manifestations of this structural model. In alternative personnel models proposed, obedience is not discarded but emphasis is placed upon each person's obedience to God through searching out "the needy and the poor," through internal submission to the Spirit in identifying talents and weaknesses, and through confirming the personal and communal discernment with appropriate person or board. Personal responsibility for choices is thus established. The will of God becomes the object of a dynamic search into self and into the needs of Church and society. Initiative and zeal are set free. The "mission spirit" is not restricted to foreign lands. In such a process, authority performs the absolutely necessary function of setting free and developing the talents of others, of establishing a climate in which freedom before the Spirit and co-operative endeavors can grow.

As those who minister experience the effects of such a climate, the fostering of community will become a more realizable goal. Expectations upon ministry will change as churchgoers discover what it means to "be church." Those individual ministries will thrive which have their basis in concern for humanizing persons as well as perpetuating sacramental channels of grace.

In a setting of respect for persons and personal decisions, subsidiarity will allow many needs to surface and be met by co-operative effort in a small localized area. Collegiality in goal-setting and decision-making flourishes in an atmosphere of trust. This total freeing up of persons through confidence in them and trust in God's working with them is not a neat, orderly process, but it can be unified, as the level of self-responsibility rises, to a system of accountability which is not fear-filled but looked upon as a means to further growth.

If the Church would reorganize its structure in a model such as this, the integration of women would be facilitated, and women would greatly strengthen ministry. If discernment and full development of talents as related to needs is the goal, each member of a team, man or woman, does what he or she is most skilled in. Leadership is not fixed, but shifts as special expertise is needed. As the Church takes seriously its functions of service, proclamation of the word, and community building as a necessary base for the administration of the sacraments, it will have to legitimize the ministry of women. Such a legitimation, involving change of one of the oldest mind-sets in the Church, can be accomplished only if there is profound trust in the Holy Spirit and awareness of the discontinuity which has been as much a providential mark of the Church as has continuity.[145]

The hierarchical order is itself a structure devised by men over the ages. Jesus did not establish orders of priesthood.[146] He taught, encouraged, ordered persons—men and women—to serve. He established a community of "priestly people" symbolized as the New Israel by the Twelve. In various local churches the Christians developed methods of organizing themselves, in some places through collegial bodies of "overseers," the *presbyteroi-episkopoi*, in others through leaders appointed by Paul and his disciples. The development of this ordering was especially marked in the second century. During the third century a redistribution of ecclesial functions was undertaken, entailing the creation of the entire lower clergy, priests, deacons, deaconesses, and the minor orders (only recently discontinued).

A first step required if women are to be fully integrated into the Church is to legitimate their present ministries. The kind of legitimation that is needed is not a paraliturgical or even a liturgical service. What is primarily needed is a forthright and total acceptance of women in the positions they occupy as human persons with human and professional rights and responsibilities, including the right to education. Furthermore, women need that legitimation which enables them to complete, vis-à-vis those they serve, the ministry they exercise toward those in need. Women serving in ministry to the dying teach, counsel, comfort, inspire, then step aside for the often mechanical rendering of the sacrament of the sick by a priest. Women in counseling of youth or the alienated enter into a truly sacramental relationship of sharing and are prevented from the sacramental sign of absolution. Women whose ministry is to the sick and the aging need to be legitimized as extraordinary ministers of the Eucharist, so that the reception of the body of the Lord might, in the context of an already established relationship of shared faith and prayer, be a real communion.[147] The sacraments would thus fit naturally into the whole movement of conversion and humanization which is the object of ministry, and would be rescued from the magical interpretation that commonly results from the often too hurried and formal intervention imposed on the ordained

[145] Cf. Fahey, *art. cit.*, pp. 426–28.

[146] Brown, *op. cit.*, pp. 13–20.

[147] At one time in the Church, women were not permitted to baptize even in emergencies when a layman might. This discipline has been altered. Women are acknowledged as ministers of the sacrament of matrimony.

priest.

The ordained minister functions in an especially symbolic way in the Eucharist. The bishop and later the priest were seen to act in the person of Christ, especially in pronouncing the words of institution.[148] Women were said to be excluded from these offices because only males were thought to be able to represent the male Jesus.[149] This line of thought would lead logically to the conclusion that women do not share in the redemptive acts of Jesus, a view which the Church never embraced. The reality of the presence of Christ in the Eucharist, however, derives from his resurrection as the culmination of his self-offering and sacrifice on the cross. It is the risen Christ who is rendered present by the Spirit evoking faith from the "faithful" at the Eucharist.[150]

The president draws together the faith expression of the assembly in helping them to be present to the word of God proclaimed, to remember the saving acts of Jesus, and to deepen confidence that the Spirit will bring the risen Christ to reality within and among them.[151] The president then represents Christ because and to the extent that he represents the faith of the Church.[152]

From this insight into the Eucharistic mystery it follows that the faith of the whole Church would be better represented if women as well as men were called forth to preside.[153] Such a representation would fulfil the many initiatives of Jesus in associating women as well as men with his ministry. It would be for women a validation of their personhood, a legitimizing of whatever partial ministrations of sacraments might be accorded to their particular form of service.

This vision of the Eucharist and of the place of women in its ministry provides a wholeness to theological anthropology which is otherwise lacking. Avery Dulles, for instance, writes: "Man shares in the divine life, not in a divine, but in a human way, consonantly with his nature as man."[154] But man is male and female. Since "sacraments have a dialogic structure,"[155] they must not perpetuate the dominant-submissive struc-

---

[148] Kilmartin, *art. cit.*, p. 244.

[149] Van der Meer, *op. cit.*, pp. 128–43.

[150] Kilmartin, *art. cit.*, p. 254.

[151] The ordained minister may be seen "as a sort of symbolic point of convergence where Christ's offer of himself and the assembly's believing response to this offer find expression. Nevertheless, it is the whole assembly which, through the ordained minister, calls upon God to make His presence felt here and now. It is through the whole assembly that God realizes the Eucharist" (J. H. McKenna, *art. cit.*, p. 272).

[152] *Ibid.*, pp. 255–58.

[153] *Ibid.*, p. 263.

[154] Avery Dulles, *Models of the Church* (New York, 1974), p. 60.

[155] *Ibid.*, p. 62.

ture of man-woman relations. If "man" shares in the divine life in a human way, through "the body with all its movements and gestures,"[156] it must be through the female as well as the male body.

Women are disaffected from the institutional Church because it represents a power relationship and because this power is often insensitively administered. Many women have discovered talents in themselves for building community. In visitation to the aging, in youth retreats and counseling, they experience the fulfilling quality of the ministry of service. The ministry of justice involves them in confrontation with the powers of Church and state and business establishment. Women are gaining confidence in paraliturgical prayer and reflection on the gospel message. All these factors combine to forecast a gradual separation from the Church as sacrament and proclamation of the word if these remain the forbidden land for women as ministers. As sacrament and word are now administered within the law of the institutional Church, they are almost entirely prerogatives of the Church of imposing structures and minimal community, where the faithful congregate, not the Church as service and community model. If men remain the sole representatives of the Church of sacrament and word, and women predominantly the ministers in the Church of service and community, and if man/woman relations in the Church continue to deteriorate, a serious break within the ministry will occur.

Women were created by God as sharers in the same human nature as men. Both men and women were intended to show forth the image of God. The dominance of men over women, however first arrived at, is expressed in Genesis as one of the effects of sin. That Jesus overcame sin is a promise that the effects of such sin will be eliminated through the grace-filled efforts of human beings. Christ's transforming power has been at work through the ages: Jewish male circumcision ceased to be a necessary prerequisite for reception of baptism, which therefore was available also to women; Christians now admit the structural and human evils of slavery; the full empowerment of woman becomes a similar possibility. The Gospels are very much concerned to present women as authentic persons, as dependable witnesses to truth and faith. Jesus promised the action of the Holy Spirit in his Church. The Spirit inspired Peter and Paul to demand the non-Judaizing of Christian Gentiles; the Spirit inspired numerous Christians to end slavery as a creditable Christian institution; the Spirit today is believed by many women to be calling them to the priesthood. Justice would seem to require that these women who feel called by the Spirit to priestly office should have their charisms personally tested, not categorically dismissed. Rejection of

[156] *Ibid.*, p. 60.

women from the ordained ministry by men seems to women an obvious contradiction of the gospel.

The renewal of the Church would profit from the renewal of ministry brought about by the full acceptance of women into ministry. The fostering of more honest relationships between men and women, wherein women would be freed from the need to manipulate and men would be freed from the need to dominate, would reveal new sources of energy and fresh ways of looking at structures. The Church in its humility, its sense of serving persons, the love it would thereby witness, would give, as is its profound destiny, a clearer revelation of Christ.

VI

ROLES OF WOMEN IN THE FOURTH GOSPEL

RAYMOND E. BROWN, S.S.

Union Theological Seminary, N.Y.C.

THERE ARE several ways of approaching the biblical evidence pertinent to the contemporary debate about the role of women in the Church and about the possibility of ordaining women to the priesthood. One approach is a general discussion of first-century ecclesiology both in itself and in its hermeneutical implications for the present. How does one read the NT evidence about the foundation of the Church and the institution of the sacraments, and to what extent is that evidence culturally conditioned? Following the teachings of the Council of Trent, Catholics have spoken of the institution of the priesthood at the Last Supper. Does that mean that at the Supper Jesus consciously thought of priests?[1] If he did not and if the clear conceptualization of the priesthood came only toward the second century, does the fact that men exclusively were ordained reflect a divine dispensation? Or are we dealing with a cultural phenomenon which can be changed? In other words, do we work with a "blueprint ecclesiology" wherein Jesus or the Holy Spirit has given us a blueprint of church structure in which virtually no changes can be made? While I regard the discussion of these questions as most important, I have written on them elsewhere and shall not repeat my observations here.[2]

A second approach to the biblical evidence is to discuss the explicit texts that refer respectively to the equality and the subordination of women in society and cult. I am not convinced of the usefulness of such a

---

[1] In this question care is required in interpreting Trent: "If anyone shall say that by the words 'Do this for a commemoration of me,' Christ did not institute the apostles priests. . .let him be anathema" (Denzinger-Schönmetzer 1752). The fathers of Trent did not distinguish between the Jesus of the historical ministry and the developed Christological picture of Jesus presented in the Gospel accounts of the ministry written thirty to sixty years later; thus they did not speak simply of Jesus but of Christ. Today, in loyalty to the 1964 statement of the Pontifical Biblical Commission on Gospel historicity (see *Jerome Biblical Commentary* [Englewoods Cliffs, N.J., 1968] art. 72, sect. 35), Catholics would have to acknowledge that the divinity of Jesus was recognized *after* the Resurrection and that eventually it was this fuller appreciation of Jesus as the Christ, the Son of God, that was made part of the Gospel accounts of his ministry. Therefore, institution of priests by *Christ*, as taught by Trent, which cites words reported by Luke and Paul (but not by Mark and Matthew), may imply more than was apparent at the historical Last Supper.

[2] One of my Hoover Lectures delivered at the University of Chicago in January 1975 treated this subject; it is now published in *Biblical Reflections on Crises Facing the Church* (New York, 1975). To what I have said there I would add only a plea for accuracy. The statement is sometimes made that there were no women priests in NT times. Since in the NT itself the term "priest" is applied to Christians *only* in the broad sense of the priesthood

discussion, since for every text pointing in one direction there is usually a countertext. If Eph 5:24 states that wives must be subject in everything to their husbands, Eph 5:21 introduces that section by commanding "Be subject to one another." If 1 Cor 11:7 says that the man (*anēr*) is the image and glory of God, while woman is the glory of man, Gn 1:27 states that both man and woman are in the image of God. If 1 Cor 14:34 rules that women should keep silence in the churches,[3] 1 Cor 11:5 recognizes the custom that women pray and prophesy—and prophecy is the charism ranking second after apostleship (1 Cor 12:28), to the extent that Eph 2:20 has the Church, the household of God, built upon the foundation of apostles *and prophets*. I might continue listing contrary voices, but then we would still have the question of how to evaluate the voices that stress subordination. Once more we would have to ask: Is that purely a cultural pattern or divine revelation?

I prefer here to follow a third approach and to consider the general picture of women in one NT work, the fourth Gospel, and in one NT community, the Johannine community.[4] I have chosen the fourth Gospel because of the perceptive corrective that the Evangelist offers to some ecclesiastical attitudes of his time—his should be a voice heard and reflected upon when we are discussing new roles for women in the Church today. I presuppose[5] that the Evangelist was an unknown Christian

---

of the people (1 Pt 2:5; Ap 5:10—i.e., a priesthood of spiritually offering one's life as a sacrifice according to the demands of the gospel), it would seem warranted to affirm that the term "priest" was just as applicable to women as it was to men in NT times. If the more precise claim is made that women did not celebrate the Eucharist in NT times, there is simply no way of proving that, even if *one may well doubt that they did*. We know very little about who presided at the Eucharist in NT times. Yet, there is some evidence that prophets did, for prophets are said to be involved in liturgy (*leitourgein* in Acts 13:2) and to give thanks (*eucharistein* in *Didache* 10, 7); and certainly there were women who prophesied (1 Cor 11:5; Acts 21:9).

[3] It is frequently argued that 1 Cor 14:34b-36 is not genuinely Pauline. H. Conzelmann, *1 Corinthians* (Philadelphia, 1975) p. 246, states: "The section is accordingly to be regarded as an interpolation."

[4] This paper is a development of remarks prepared for the session of the Pontifical Biblical Commission in April 1975. In treating the Gospel, while maintaining that the Evangelist has tradition about the ministry of Jesus, I take for granted that he reports that tradition through the optic of his own times, so that he tells us something about the role of women in his own community. I shall use the name "John" for the Evangelist even though I do not think he was John son of Zebedee; it is more open to discussion whether the Beloved Disciple was John. All the narratives in the Gospel dealing with women will be discussed except the story of the adulteress in 7:53—8:11, which is a later and non-Johannine insertion into the Gospel.

[5] The evidence for these presuppositions may be found in my commentary on John in the Anchor Bible (2 vols.; Garden City, N.Y., 1966, 1970). In particular, see the section on Johannine ecclesiology, pp. CV-CXI.

living at the end of the first century in a community for which the Beloved Disciple, now deceased, had been the great authority. I do not think that the Evangelist was either antisacramental (in a Bultmannian sense) or antiecclesiastical. He took for granted the church situation of his time, which included both structure and sacraments; yet he counteracted some of the tendencies inherent in that situation by writing a Gospel in which he attempted to root the Christians of his time solidly in Jesus. They may be members of the Church, but the Church does not give God's life: Jesus does. And so, in order to have life, they must inhere in Jesus (Jn 15:1–8). The sacraments are not simply church actions commanded or instituted by Jesus; they are the continuation of the power that Jesus exhibited in signs when he opened the eyes of the blind (baptism as enlightenment) and fed the hungry (Eucharist as food). At the end of the first century, when the memory of the apostles (now increasingly identified with the Twelve) was being increasingly revered, the fourth Gospel glorifies the disciple and never uses the term "apostle" in the technical sense,[6] almost as if the Evangelist wishes to remind the Christian that what is primary is not to have had a special ecclesiastical charism from God but to have followed Jesus, obedient to his word. In short, it is a Gospel that seeks to make certain that in the inevitable structuring of the Church the radical Christian values are not lost. What information does such a perceptive Evangelist give us about the role of women?

I

There is not much information about church offices in the fourth Gospel[7] and, a fortiori, about women in church offices. Perhaps the only text that may reflect directly on this is 12:2, where we are told that Martha served at table (*diakonein*). On the story-level of Jesus' ministry this might not seem significant; but the Evangelist is writing in the 90's, when the office of *diakonos* already existed in the post-Pauline churches (see the Pastorals) and when the task of waiting on tables was a specific function to which the community or its leaders appointed individuals by laying on hands (Acts 6:1–6).[8] In the Johannine community a woman

---

[6] Cf. 13:16 for *apostolos* in the nontechnical sense of "messenger." *Apostellein*, "to send" (seemingly interchangeable with *pempein*), occurs for sending on a mission, but women can be involved in a mission too. See n. 9 below.

[7] Although John knows of the existence of the Twelve as a group during Jesus' ministry (6:70), their names are not listed, nor is there a description of their call as a group.

[8] Originally this scene referred to the selection of leaders for the Hellenist Christian community. Although we do not know if titles were used at this early period, the closest parallel in the titulary used in later church structure would be "bishop." Luke looks back on the scene from the 80's, and he may have thought that their work was comparable to that done by the deacons in his time, especially if he had begun to think of the apostles as bishops.

could be described as exercising a function which in other churches was the function of an "ordained" person. But, except for that one passage, our discussion must center rather on the *general* position of women in the Johannine community.

Let us begin with the story of the Samaritan woman. In the sequence of reactions to Jesus found in the dialogues of chaps. 2, 3, and 4, there seems to be a movement from disbelief through inadequate belief to more adequate belief. The "Jews" in the Temple scene are openly skeptical about his signs (2:18-20); Nicodemus is one of those in Jerusalem who believe because of Jesus' signs but do not have an adequate conception of Jesus (2:23 ff.); the Samaritan woman is led to the brink of perceiving that Jesus is the Christ (Messiah; 4:25-26, 29) and shares this with others. Indeed, the Samaritan villagers believe because of the woman's word (4:39, 42: *dia ton logon [lalian] pisteuein*). This expression is significant because it occurs again in Jesus' "priestly" prayer for his disciples: "It is not for these alone that I pray, but also for those who believe in me through their word" (17:20: *dia ton logon pisteuein*). In other words, the Evangelist can describe both a woman and the (presumably male) disciples at the Last Supper as bearing witness to Jesus through preaching and thus bringing people to believe in him on the strength of their word. One may object that in chap. 4 the Samaritan villagers ultimately come to a faith based on Jesus' own word and thus are not dependent on the woman's word (4:42). Yet this is scarcely because of an inferiority she might have as a woman—it is the inferiority of any human witness compared to encountering Jesus himself. A similar attitude may be found in chap. 17, where Jesus prays that those who believe in him through the word of his disciples may ultimately be with him in order that they may see glory (17:24).

That the Samaritan woman has a real missionary function is made clear by the dialogue between Jesus and his male disciples which precedes the passage we have been discussing. In 4:38 we have one of the most important uses of the verb *apostellein* in John.[9] Jesus has just spoken of the fields being ripe for the harvest—a reference to the Samaritans coming out from the village to meet him because of what the woman has told them (4:35 following 4:30). This is missionary language, as we see from the parallel in Mt 9:37-38: "The harvest is plentiful, but

---

[9] See n. 6 above. Another usage of *apostellein* is in 17:18: "As you [Father] sent me into the world, so I sent them into the world," which precedes the prayer "for those who believe in me through their word" (17:20)—even as *apostellein* in 4:38 precedes the references in 4:39, 42 to those who believe in Jesus through the woman's word. A third significant usage of "send" (*apostellein* and *pempein*) is in the postresurrectional appearance of Jesus to the disciples: "As the Father has sent me, so do I send you" (20:21). In the next paragraph of my paper I shall discuss the priority John gives to the appearance of the risen Jesus to a woman disciple.

the laborers are few; therefore pray to the Lord of the harvest that He send out laborers into the harvest." But curiously the harvest of the Samaritans verifies the saying "One sows, while another reaps" (Jn 4:37). Jesus explains this to his male disciples: "What I sent [apostellein] you to reap was not something you worked for. Others have done the hard work, and you have come in for the fruit of their work." Whatever this may have meant in reference to the history of the Samaritan church,[10] in the story itself it means that the woman has sown the seed and thus prepared for the apostolic harvest. One may argue that only the male disciples are sent to harvest, but the woman's role is an essential component in the total mission. To some extent she serves to modify the thesis that male disciples were the only important figures in church founding.

The phenomenon of giving a quasi-apostolic role to a woman is even more apparent in chap. 20. Essential to the apostolate in the mind of Paul were the two components of having seen the risen Jesus and having been sent to proclaim him; this is the implicit logic of 1 Cor 9:1-2; 15:8-11; Gal 1:11-16. A key to Peter's importance in the apostolate was the tradition that he was the first to see the risen Jesus (1 Cor 15:5; Lk 24:34). More than any other Gospel, John revises this tradition about Peter. Mt 28:9-10 recalls that the women who were leaving the empty tomb were the first to encounter the risen Jesus, but in Matthew they are not contrasted with Peter. In Jn 20:2-10 Simon Peter and the Beloved Disciple go to the empty tomb and do *not* see Jesus (also Lk 24:12, 24); in fact, only the Beloved Disciple perceives the significance of the grave clothes and comes to believe. It is to a woman, Mary Magdalene, that Jesus first appears, instructing her to go and tell his "brothers" (the disciples: 20:17 and 18) of his ascension to the Father.[11] In the stories of the angel(s) at the empty tomb, the women are given a message for the disciples; but in John (and in Matthew) Mary Magdalene is sent by the risen Lord himself, and what she proclaims is the standard apostolic announcement of the Resurrection: "I have seen the Lord." True, this is not a mission to the whole world; but Mary Magdalene comes close to meeting the basic Pauline requirements of an apostle; and it is she, not Peter, who is the first to see the risen Jesus.[12] Small wonder that in some

[10] See the discussion in my commentary (n. 5 above) pp. 183–84.

[11] A similar instruction to go and tell Jesus' "brothers" is found in the parallel appearance to the women in Mt 28:10.

[12] The tradition that Jesus appeared first to Mary Magdalene has a good chance of being historical—he remembered first this representative of the women who had not deserted him during the Passion. The priority given to Peter in Paul and in Luke is a priority among those who became official witnesses to the Resurrection. The secondary place given to the tradition of an appearance to a woman or women probably reflects the fact that women did not serve at first as official preachers of the Church—a fact that would make the creation of an appearance to a woman unlikely.

Gnostic quarters Mary Magdalene rather than Peter became the most prominent witness to the teaching of the risen Lord.[13] And in Western Church tradition she received the honor of being the only woman (besides the Mother of God) on whose feast the Creed was recited precisely because she was considered to be an apostle—"the apostle to the apostles" (*apostola apostolorum*).[14]

Giving to a woman a role traditionally associated with Peter may well be a deliberate emphasis on John's part, for substitution is also exemplified in the story of Lazarus, Mary, and Martha. The most famous incident in which Peter figures during the ministry of Jesus (and his other claim to primacy besides that of witnessing the first appearance of the risen Jesus) is the confession he made at Caesarea Philippi, especially in its Matthean form (16:16): "You are the Christ, the Son of the living God." Already the disciples had generally confessed Jesus as a "Son of God" (no definite article in Mt 14:33), but it is Peter's more solemn confession that wins Jesus' praise as a statement reflecting divine revelation. The closest parallel to that confession in the four Gospels is found in Jn 11:27: "You are the Christ, the Son of God";[15] and it appears on the lips of a woman, Martha, sister of Mary and Lazarus. (And it comes in the context of a major revelation of Jesus to Martha; it is to a woman that the mystery of Jesus as the resurrection and the life is revealed!) Thus, if other Christian communities thought of Peter as the one who made a supreme confession of Jesus as the Son of God and the one to whom the risen Jesus first appeared, the Johannine community associated such memories with heroines like Martha and Mary Magdalene. This substitution, if it was deliberate, was not meant to denigrate Peter or deny him a role of ecclesiastical authority, any more than the introduction of the Beloved Disciple alongside Peter in crucial scenes had that purpose. If I interpret John correctly, at a time when the twelve apostles (almost personified in Peter, as in Acts) were becoming

[13] *The Gospel according to Mary*, in E. Hennecke and W. Schneemelcher, *New Testament Apocrypha* 1 (Philadelphia, 1963) 342–44.

[14] J. A. Jungmann, *The Mass of the Roman Rite* (New York, 1950) p. 470, n. 55. The use of "apostle" of Magdalene is frequent in the famous ninth-century life of her authored by Rabanus Maurus: Jesus instituted her apostle to the apostles (*PL* 112, 1474B), she did not delay in exercising the office of the apostolate by which she had been honored (1475A), she evangelized her coapostles with the news of the Resurrection of the Messiah (1475B), she was elevated to the honor of the apostolate and instituted evangelist (*evangelista*) of the Resurrection (1479C).

[15] In my commentary on John (n. 5 above) p. 302, I show how the elements of Matthew's account of Peter's confession at Caesarea Philippi are found scattered in John: e.g., Andrew, Simon Peter's brother, confesses Jesus to be the Messiah when Andrew is calling Simon to follow Jesus, and on that occasion Jesus changes Simon's name to Cephas (1:40–42); Simon Peter as spokesman of the Twelve confesses Jesus to be the "holy one of God" (6:69); ecclesiastical authority is given to Simon Peter in 21:15-17.

dominant in the memory of the ministry of Jesus and of church origins, John portrays Simon Peter as only one of a number of heroes and heroines and thus hints that ecclesiastical authority is not the sole criterion for judging importance in the following of Jesus.[16]

The importance of women in the Johannine community is seen not only by comparing them with male figures from the Synoptic tradition but also by studying their place within peculiarly Johannine patterns. Discipleship is the primary Christian category for John, and the disciple par excellence is the Disciple whom Jesus loved. But John tells us in 11:5: "Now Jesus loved Martha and her sister [Mary] and Lazarus." The fact that Lazarus is the only male in the Gospel who is named as the object of Jesus' love[17]—nothing similar is said of the Twelve—has led some scholars to identify him as the Beloved Disciple.[18] And so it is noteworthy that John would report that Jesus loved Martha and Mary, who seem to have been better known than Lazarus.[19] Another proof that women could be intimate disciples of Jesus is found in chap. 20. In the allegorical parable of the Good Shepherd John compares the disciples of Jesus to sheep who know their shepherd's voice when he calls them by name (10:3-5). This description is fulfilled in the appearance of the risen Jesus to Mary Magdalene as she recognizes him when he calls her by her name "Mary" (20:16). The point that Mary Magdalene can belong to Jesus' sheep is all the more important since in 10:3-5 the sheep are twice identified as "his own," the almost technical expression used at the beginning of the Last Supper: "Having loved his own who were in the

[16] Such an attitude can be detected in the Synoptic tradition as well. Matthew is the Evangelist who gives Peter the most exalted role as the recipient of the keys of the kingdom of heaven (16:19), but Matthew would never make Peter first in the kingdom. That is a primacy specifically denied even to members of the Twelve (Mt 20:20-26). The criterion for primacy in the kingdom, as distinct from the Church, is not ecclesiastical authority or power but total dependence on God, whence the model of the little child (18:1-4). At a time when we are engaged in a necessary debate as to who among the baptized can be ordained to priesthood or bishopric, it may be useful to remind ourselves that it remains more important to be baptized than to be ordained, more important to be a Christian than to be a priest, bishop, or pope.

[17] See also Jn 11:3, 11, 36, where *philein* and *philos* are used of Lazarus. The significance is not different from the use of *agapan* in 11:5; both verbs are used of the Beloved Disciple (*philein* in 20:2; elsewhere *agapan*).

[18] See the discussion in my commentary (n. 5 above) p. xcv.

[19] Notice the order of names in 11:5. Moreover, in 11:1-2 Lazarus is identified through his relationship to Mary and Martha. The reason for this may be that the two women were known in the wider Gospel tradition (Lk 10:38-42), whereas Lazarus is a peculiarly Johannine character (at least as a historical figure; cf. Lk 16:19-31) who is introduced into the Gospel by being placed in a family relationship to Mary and Martha. This is not unlike the introduction of the Beloved Disciple into well-known scenes by placing him in a relationship to Peter.

world, he loved them to the end" (13:1). On the analogy of the Synoptic Gospels, conservative scholars have argued that the participants in the Johannine Last Supper scene were the Twelve. Be that as it may,[20] it is clear that John has no hesitation in placing a woman in the same category of relationship to Jesus as the Twelve would be placed if they are meant by "his own" in 13:1.

II

It is as a continuation of this idea that I now turn to John's treatment of the mother of Jesus, who appears in the fourth Gospel at the first Cana miracle and at the foot of the Cross. There are many symbolisms that John may have intended his reader to associate with the mother of Jesus; in my commentary on the two scenes I have explained some of them at length. But here I am concerned only with discipleship and with the relative importance of men and women in the Johannine community. I shall be concise, since I do not want this paper to be more than a note and since elsewhere I have given detailed arguments.[21]

Let us begin with the wedding at Cana. Many theorize that there was a pre-Johannine form of the story. One form of this theory suggests that John drew the basic Cana miracle story from a tradition of the *preministry* career of Jesus—a tradition wherein the Christology of the ministry was anticipated by describing Jesus as endowed with divine power and knowledge during his youth, when he was still living with his family.[22] In this tradition Jesus spoke freely of his divine mission and worked miracles in order to help family and friends. It is borne witness to in the apocryphal Gospels of the second century (e.g., *The Infancy Gospel of Thomas*) and in one other place in the canonical Gospels, namely, the scene in Lk 2:41-50 where as a youth Jesus shows extraordinary knowledge and refers to the Temple as his Father's house. This background would explain many peculiar features in the story of the water changed to wine at Cana: Jesus is still up in the highlands of Galilee (where he does not work miracles in the Synoptic tradition); he has not yet left his home and moved to Capernaum, which will be the center of his public ministry (2:12); he is in the family circle of his mother and brothers (2:12) and he is attending the wedding of a friend of the family (2:1-2); his

---

[20] The "his own" at the beginning of chap. 13 are the replacement of an older "his own" who refused to receive him (1:11); and so, whether or not the Twelve are placed in the scenario of the Last Supper as "his own," in many passages of chaps. 13-17 they are the representatives of all who believe in Jesus.

[21] In the last of the Hoover Lectures (the one on an ecumenical understanding of Mary) mentioned in n. 2 above and published in the same collection; there I approach the Johannine evidence concerning Mary from another angle—a quest for the historical Mary.

[22] This is a development of the thesis proposed by B. Lindars, *The Gospel of John*

mother expects him to use his miraculous power to solve the shortage of wine at the wedding (2:3); the miracle he performs is particularly exuberant (about 100 gallons of wine from the six stone jars mentioned in 2:6).

I have described one form of the theory that a pre-Johannine story underlies the present Cana narrative. There are other forms of this theory, but almost all propose that there was no response of Jesus such as now appears in 2:4—a response which makes the story very hard to understand. It is a seeming refusal; and yet Jesus' mother goes ahead as if he had not refused, and Jesus does what she requested. The substance of the pre-Johannine story may have gone thus:[23]

Now there was a wedding at Cana of Galilee and the mother of Jesus was there. Jesus himself and his disciples had been invited to the wedding celebration. But they had no wine, for the wine provided for the wedding banquet had been used up. The mother of Jesus told the waiters: "Do whatever he tells you." There were at hand six stone water jars, each holding fifteen to twenty-five gallons. "Fill those jars with water," Jesus ordered. . . .

Such a popular picture of Mary's ability as a mother to intervene in Jesus' activities, to ask for a miracle for her friends and to have it

---

(London, 1972) pp. 126–27. It supposes the legitimacy of several attitudes in modern Gospel research. *First*, in the course of early Christian preaching the Christology developed "backwards": the role of Jesus as the Messiah, the Son of God, was first understood in relation to the future (the Parousia), then in relation to the present (the Resurrection), and finally in relation to the past (the ministry). As part of a reflection on what Jesus was before the Resurrection, Christology was pushed back to his youth and to his conception/birth. Thus, Mark, the first Gospel, has no infancy story but concentrates on Jesus as Son of God during the ministry; the later Gospels, Matthew and Luke, have infancy stories which took their final shape after the story of Jesus' ministry had been preached. In Lk 2:41–50 a once-independent story of Jesus as a youth has been appended to the story of Jesus' conception/birth, leaving us the awkward sequence wherein Mary who has been told that Jesus is the Son of God does not understand when he speaks about his Father (2:50). *Second*, the modern Roman Catholic exegete, following the directives of Pius XII, recognizes the existence of different types of literature in the Bible, including fiction and popular stories which can be inspired by God just as well as history. And so there is nothing contrary to Catholic teaching in supposing that an Evangelist on rare occasions took over stories (of undefinable historicity) from popular traditions about Jesus—certainly that happened in both infancy narratives. Inerrancy comes into play, not in reference to either the origin or historicity of a story like that of Cana, but in reference to its teaching "that truth which God wanted put into the sacred writings for the sake of our salvation" (Vatican II, *Dei Verbum*, no. 11). As we shall see, John did adapt the story to make it conform to the genuine Gospel picture of Jesus' relationship to his family. All of this is treated in detail in the lecture referred to in the preceding note.

[23] The best reconstruction of the pre-Johannine miracle material is found in R. T. Fortna, *The Gospel of Signs* (Cambridge Univ., 1970), and I offer here a translation of the first part of his Greek reconstruction of the pre-Johannine Cana miracle story. I (and others) do not agree with Fortna that a whole pre-Johannine gospel can be reconstructed, but all admit that the best evidence for a pre-Johannine miracle collection is in the two Cana miracles which John himself numbers in sequence (2:11, 4:54).

granted, did not correspond with the oldest Gospel tradition about Jesus' attitude toward family. In Mk 3:31–35 we find Jesus strongly rejecting intervention by his mother and brothers in favor of obedience to God's will. And so, when John brought this miracle story into the Gospel, he modified it by inserting 2:4,[24] where Jesus carefully dissociates himself from his mother's interests ("Woman, what has this concern of yours to do with me?") and gives priority to the hour dictated by his heavenly Father ("My hour has not yet come").[25] Thus the fourth Gospel agrees with the other three that Mary had no role in the ministry as Jesus' physical mother. The Jesus who asked his disciples not to give any priority to family (Mk 10:29–30; Mt 10:37; Lk 14:26) was not himself going to give priority to family. This interpretation of Jn 2:4 is valid whatever theory one accepts about the origins of the Cana story.

If one had just Mk 3:31–35, the only scene common to the Synoptics in which the mother and brothers of Jesus play a role, one might conclude that Jesus completely rejected them from his following. According to Mark, when Jesus was told that his mother and brothers were outside asking for him, he replied: "'Who are my mother and my brothers?' And looking about at those who sat around him, he said: 'Here are my mother and my brothers!'" He then stated that whoever did the will of God was his brother and sister and mother—in other words, his disciples take the place of his family. But this was not Luke's understanding of Jesus' intent. His version of the scene (Lk 8:19–21) omits the Marcan words I have italicized above and reads thus:

Then Jesus' mother and his brothers approached him, but they could not reach him because of the crowd. He was given the message: "Your mother and your brothers are standing outside waiting to see you." But he replied: "My mother and my brothers are those who hear the word of God and do it."

For Luke, the hearers of the word of God do not *replace* Jesus' mother and brothers as his true family; for his mother and brothers hear the word of God and do it and so are part of the true family of disciples. Luke preserves Jesus' insistence that hearing the word of God and doing it is constitutive of his family, but Luke thinks that Jesus' mother and brothers meet that criterion. That this is a correct interpretation is confirmed by Acts 1:14,[26] where, among the 120 "brethren" who

[24] Fortna points out that this verse, besides creating logical difficulties, is written in the characteristic prose of the Evangelist, something that is not true of the pre-Johannine story Fortna has reconstructed. It is worth noting that in Lk 2:49 a similar modification of the parents' claims appears: "How is it that you sought me? Did you not know that I must be in my Father's house [about my Father's business]?"

[25] The "hour" pertains to the heavenly Father's domain: "The hour had come for Jesus to pass from this world to the Father" (13:1).

[26] Another confirmation is found in Lk 1:38, where Luke dramatizes Mary's reaction to

constitute the believing community after the Resurrection-Ascension, Luke lists "Mary the mother of Jesus and his brothers."

This is also John's understanding of the role of Jesus' mother in relation to discipleship, as we see from the other scene in which she appears (19:25–27). At the foot of the Cross there are brought together the two great symbolic figures of the fourth Gospel whose personal names are never used by the Evangelist: the mother of Jesus and the Disciple whom Jesus loved.[27] Both were historical personages, but they are not named by John, since their primary (not sole) importance is in their symbolism for discipleship rather than in their historical careers. During the ministry, as we saw in the final Johannine form of the Cana story (especially 2:4), the mother of Jesus was denied involvement as his physical mother in favor of the timetable of the "hour" dictated by Jesus' Father; but now that the hour has come for Jesus to pass from this world to the Father (13:1), Jesus will grant her a role that will involve her, not as *his* mother but as the mother of the Beloved Disciple. In other words, John agrees with Luke that Jesus' rejection of intervention by Mary did not mean that his natural family could not become his true family through discipleship. By stressing not only that his mother has become the mother of the Beloved Disciple, but also that this Disciple has become her son, the Johannine Jesus is logically claiming the Disciple as his true brother. In the fourth Gospel, then, as well as in the Synoptic scene, Jesus has reinterpreted who his mother and his brothers are and reinterpreted them in terms of discipleship.[28] If in Acts 1:14 Luke brought back the mother and brothers of Jesus as disciples after the Ascension, John chooses the "hour" when Jesus has been lifted up

---

the Christological proclamation about Jesus' divine sonship (formerly attached to the baptism of Jesus but now attached to his conception). Her response is drawn from Luke's positive understanding of the Marcan scene, namely, that she was one who heard the word of God and did it: "Let it be done to me according to your word." See R. E. Brown, "Luke's Method in the Annunciation Narratives of Chapter One," in *No Famine in the Land: Studies in Honor of John L. McKenzie*, ed. J. W. Flanagan and Anita Robinson (Missoula, 1975).

[27] John's failure to use the personal name of the mother of Jesus is striking because John is not shy of that name. "Mary" occurs some fifteen times in the fourth Gospel: for Mary the sister of Martha, for Mary Magdalene, for Mary the wife of Clopas. His insistence on the title "the mother of Jesus" or "his mother" is probably because John is interpreting a tradition about what constituted her true motherhood.

[28] I repeat what I stated at the beginning of the discussion of the mother of Jesus: this is not the only symbolism. It should be noted, too, that Mary does not become simply a disciple among many; she has an eminence as the mother of the ideal Disciple. While John and Luke move here in the same general theological direction, Luke is reinterpreting the role of Jesus' physical "brothers," i.e., relatives. John (7:5) treats the physical brothers as nonbelievers, and so he chooses to deal with the brotherhood of the Beloved Disciple, who is not a physical relative of Jesus.

(12:32) to bring onto the scene the mother of Jesus who is made the mother of the Beloved Disciple, now Jesus' brother.

I pointed out earlier that discipleship is the primary Johannine category and that John included women as "first-class" disciples by telling us that Jesus loved Martha and Mary and that Mary Magdalene was one of "his own" sheep whom he called by name. John's treatment of the mother of Jesus is a step further in that direction. If the Beloved Disciple was the ideal of discipleship, intimately involved with that Disciple on an equal plane as part of Jesus' true family was a woman. A woman and a man stood at the foot of the Cross as models for Jesus' "own," his true family of disciples.

I spoke earlier of the Samaritan woman to whom Jesus revealed himself as the source of life and the Messiah, a woman who in a missionary role brought men to him on the strength of her word. In the scene in 4:27, we are told that when Jesus' male disciples saw him speaking to her, they were surprised that he was dealing in such an open way with a woman. In researching the evidence of the fourth Gospel, one is still surprised to see to what extent in the Johannine community women and men were already on an equal level in the fold of the Good Shepherd. This seems to have been a community where in the things that really mattered in the following of Christ there was no difference between male and female—a Pauline dream (Gal 3:28) that was not completely realized in the Pauline communities.[29] But even John has left us with one curious note of incompleteness: the disciples, surprised at Jesus' openness with a woman, still did not dare to ask him, "What do you want of a woman?" (4:27). That may well be a question whose time has come in the Church of Jesus Christ.

[29] The rule that a woman should keep silence in the churches, if it was authentically Pauline (see n. 3 above), was scarcely in effect in the Johannine community, in whose gallery of heroes were the Samaritan woman who brought men to faith by her word and Mary Magdalene who proclaimed the good news of the risen Jesus.

VII

SEXIST LANGUAGE IN THEOLOGY?

GEORGE H. TAVARD

Methodist Theological School in Ohio

THE RECENT concern for nondiscriminatory language has arisen out of the newer wave of the woman-liberation movement. Black liberation was not particularly eager to change language, as no pronoun in English, or in any language I am acquainted with, connotes skin pigmentation. The term "black" came to be preferred to that of "negro" for historical, sociological, and psychological reasons, not for linguistic motives. But "she" connotes femininity and "he" connotes masculinity; "man" is used as a generic term including male and female and it also designates the male of the race. Thus the woman movement is brought to questioning, not this or that word fashion, but the very structure of language: "the problem of 'desexing language' has taken on particular importance. In North America women are seeking to find *human pronouns* which clearly interpret the fact that men and women are included in the words expressed."[1] This is not a good formulation of the question, since words themselves never interpret their own content. But it is a good indication of the range of problems that are now being faced. At a low level of sophistication, some publishers try to solve the problem by omission: authors will simply not use certain words. Thus, McGraw-Hill's guidelines to authors state: "The English language lacks a generic singular pronoun signifying he or she . . ." and give the advice: "Avoid when possible the pronoun he, him and his in reference to the hypothetical person . . . ." In a similar vein, the Journal of Ecumenical Studies has adopted an "editorial policy" as a "step toward the elimination of linguistic sexism": "Avoid the generic use of the word man. . . . Avoid referring to God with masculine pronouns. . . . Avoid other male-dominated phrases. . . . "[2]

The interest in language and the belief that the problem can be overcome through new linguistic forms did not appear in the previous literature about woman. And that was not for lack of intellectual sophistication. Simone de Beauvoir did not seem to find any problem in this area when she wrote The Second Sex.[3] Yvonne Pellé-Douël, in Etre femme, clearly indicated why this could not be a problem. Discussing woman as myth, she showed that woman had to be "demythified" in

[1] Letty M. Russell, *Human Liberation in a Feminist Perspective: A Theology* (Philadelphia, 1974) pp. 93–94.

[2] The McGraw-Hill guidelines were featured in many newspapers; for the *Journal of Ecumenical Studies*, see Vol. 11/2, Spring 1974.

[3] Simone de Beauvoir, *The Second Sex* (New York, 1953).

order to accede to the level of true symbolism; and language, because it is necessarily used at the two levels of myth and of symbol, is always ambiguous: "All language is ambiguous; it is an insufficient sign of concrete fulness."[4] In these conditions language must be interpreted and reinterpreted. But the attempt to create a nonambiguous language in which woman, man (*vir*), and generic man (*homo*) will always see themselves at their right place so that no interpretation will be needed derives from a naive conception of the symbolization process which is embodied in language.

The linguistic problem points to a deeper anthropological question. What do we mean by "man"? Under what conditions, in what circumstances, do we conceive "mankind" to include both men (*viri*) and women? To say that "man" is a generic term implies a certain attitude toward men and women. But to what reality does the generic paradigm "man" correspond? Human experience has to do with concrete men and with concrete women, never with men in general. The level of meaning at which generic man can be understood is abstract. And while there is nothing wrong with abstraction, the whole trend of modern education makes it less and less likely that abstractions are understood by the majority of people in the unreflexive moments which occupy the greatest part of their days. Thus the generic sense of terms such as "man" and "mankind" becomes what Letty Russell calls "generic nonsense": "It is generic nonsense to say that women are included linguistically when they are excluded by so many practices."[5] Superficial attempts to avoid the anthropological problem are made, as when "chairman" becomes "chairperson." A more sophisticated program looks for the root of the problem, and finds it in "patriarchy." Thus Mary Daly:

The method of liberation involves a *castrating* of language and images that reflect and perpetuate the structure of a sexist world. It castrates precisely in the sense of cutting away the phallocentric value system imposed by patriarchy, in its subtle as well as in its more manifest expressions. As aliens in a man's world who are now rising to name—that is, to create—our own world, women are beginning to recognize that the value system that has been thrust upon us by the various cultural institutions of patriarchy has amounted to a kind of gang rape of minds as well as of bodies.[6]

The notions of patriarchy and of matriarchy, which have been introduced into the discussions, are deeply ambiguous. In Jungian analysis the term "matriarchal" denotes an archetype, related to *anima*,

---

[4] Yvonne Pellé-Douël, *Etre femme* (Paris, 1967) p. 202.

[5] *Op. cit.*, p. 95.

[6] Mary Daly, *Beyond God the Father: Toward a Philosophy of Woman Liberation* (Boston, 1973) p. 9.

the Feminine archetype, which itself corresponds to the dark depths of the soul. It is counterbalanced in all human persons by the patriarchal archetype, related to *animus*, the Masculine archetype, which corresponds to the clear intellectual consciousness. This is by no means identical to a woman-man or female-male dichotomy.[7]

In ethnology matriarchy is used to designate a system of societal relationships *in time*, matrilinear filiation, in which legal ascendency is traced through the mother, the male who has responsibility for the child being usually not the father but a sibling of the mother. In patriarchy, or patrilinear filiation, legal ascendency goes through the father. But ethnological matriarchy does not imply that it is woman who holds power in the societal relationships *in space*.[8] It is therefore sheer fancy to blame patriarchy for sexist language, and still more to imagine, with Elizabeth Gould Davis, that matriarchy was, long ago, a prehistorical golden age.[9]

Thus a myth is being built around nonexistent institutions, the matriarchy and the patriarchy of the current feminist literature. Among the institutions attributed to this patriarchy there is, of course, the Church. Thus a theological problem is raised: Christian theology is accused of speaking a patriarchal, or male-chauvinist, language. This is Mary Daly's summary of the situation: "The entire conceptual systems of theology and ethics, developed under the conditions of patriarchy, have been the product of males and tend to serve the interest of sexist society."[10] The practice of designating God with masculine pronouns, the New Testament denomination of God as "Father," the Lord's Prayer, the Trinitarian designation of the Second Person as "the Son," convey the impression that masculinity is a better symbol for God than femininity. Masculine theological language is therefore attributed to a patriarchal ideology. Because theology has always (or most often) been done by males, God is given male attributes. Thus Christian theology would be *de facto* antifeminist. Although such an interpretation of the classical language about God is far from self-evident, it has been taken seriously enough for several ways of reform to be proposed. Should we, following Mary Daly, "castrate 'God'" and cut away "the Supreme Phallus"?[11] More modestly, should we, with Letty Russell, bring back into use some "forgotten names of God" which the patriarchal society of the Old Testament abandoned because of their implicit suggestion that God has "characteristics frequently thought of as being feminine"?[12] Or should

[7] See Erich Neumann, *The Great Mother* (Princeton, 1972); Ann Belford Ulanov, *The Feminine in Jungian Psychology and Christian Theology* (Evanston, 1971).

[8] See Claude Lévi-Strauss, *Les structures élémentaires de la parenté* (Paris, 1949).

[9] Elizabeth Gould Davis, *The First Sex* (Baltimore, 1971).

[10] *Op. cit.*, p. 4.

[11] *Ibid.*, p. 19.

[12] *Op. cit.*, p. 100.

we endeavor to see femininity in God, especially in connection with the Holy Spirit, in keeping with Leonard Swidler's analysis of *pneuma?*[13]

Here again the new feminism differs from the old. But if the older feminism did not denounce theological language, it may be that the "patriarchal" interpretation of it is not so obvious as one claims it to be. If Simone de Beauvoir was not a theologian, she was at least very well informed and highly articulate. Yet her interpretation of the facts, in *The Second Sex*, was quite different. She saw Christian women, especially the women mystics, as responsible for the masculinity of the divine image: "Woman seeks in divine love what the *amoureuse* seeks in that of man: the exaltation of her narcissism." This explains that mysticism comes, as it were, more naturally to woman than to the male: "It is in the shape of the spouse that God is wont to appear to woman."[14] Can the theological problem be reduced to male chauvinism? Even if it cannot be reduced to female narcissism, it would appear to be more complicated than is being suggested in much of the feminist literature. Part of the complication is that this is not a purely speculative or historical problem that could be handled with the classical tools of theological analysis. The problem touches on nontheological factors. The critics of sexist language in theology tend to focus on anthropological, sociological, and psychological components of the context of theology and religion, even though they treat anthropology, sociology, and psychology with little scientific accuracy. By and large they ignore the less-known and more abstruse discipline of linguistics, thus further weakening a case which a superficial acquaintance with other human sciences wrongly deems to be very strong.

In order to arrive at an informed judgment on the problem of sexist language in theology, I will examine first some aspects of the linguistic question. This will lead me next to some problems relating directly to the language of theology. But perhaps I ought to say here that in my view the linguistic discussion is already theological, since theology, whether it is spoken or written, is couched in human discourse, which itself depends on the fundamental structure of language.[15]

ASPECTS OF THE LINGUISTIC QUESTION

Is Language an Ideology?

The first problem concerns the assumption, made in the contemporary literature about woman and implied in the very expression "sexist

---

[13] Leonard Swidler, "God the Father: Masculine; God the Son: Masculine; God the Holy Spirit: Feminine," *National Catholic Reporter*, Jan. 31, 1975, pp. 7 and 14.

[14] *Op. cit.* (Bantam ed., 1964) pp. 634, 636.

[15] On a linguistic approach to theology, see my *La théologie parmi les sciences humaines* (Paris, 1975).

language," that language in general, or at least the English language as it
is now spoken, translates a social situation in which women are
dominated by males, the relationships of power being expressed in
particular by the prevalence of the male gender ("he," "his," "him") and
of male terms ("man," "mankind") in discourses that refer to God and to
the human race in general. Letty Russell writes: "However much a
particular person or organization may protest that the words *really mean*
human, human beings, his and hers, humankind, peoplehood, etc., the
fact remains that women are frequently left out of both the mental
structures and the social structures of our cultures."[16] In other words,
there would be a direct correlation between the structures of male-
dominated society and the structures of language: these too are male-
dominated.

Clearly, such a thesis could be accepted only as a particular case of a
broader thesis. Not only women have been dominated in society: so have
slaves, minority groups, minority races, underdeveloped tribes, the
proletariat, "natives" in colonial countries, the uneducated everywhere.
The thesis about sexist language is acceptable, from a linguistic point of
view, only if one accepts the broader thesis that there is a necessary
correlation between the structures of society and those of language. The
broader thesis, however, is in fact not accepted in linguistics.

The problem amounts to whether or not language is an ideology in the
Marxist sense of the term. That it is one was the theory of the Soviet
linguist Nicolay Jakovlevitch Marr (1864–1934). Marrism, as it is called
in textbooks of linguistics, dominated Soviet schools and research until it
was challenged by a *Pravda* article on May 9, 1950, which was signed by a
certain Arnold Tchikobava.[17] The central tenet of Marrism was that the
Marxist dialectical law applies to the formation of languages as well as to
other societal institutions: these reflect the power structure of society,
which is embodied primarily in the ownership and management of the
means of production. The evolution of languages corresponds to and
derives from the evolution of the power structure of society. All
languages, like all societies, will eventually undergo the same types of
changes in keeping with the inner dynamics of the evolution of economic
production. Each type of society initiates one type of language, so that
each moment of a language's history is a faithful copy of the historical
state of the society where it is spoken. It follows—and Marr himself drew
the conclusion—that the languages and dialects actually spoken by
proletarians throughout the world have certain common features of

[16] *Op. cit.*, p. 94.
[17] On Marrism see John Murra *et al.*, *The Soviet Linguistics Controversy* (New York,
1951); Lucien Laurat, *Staline, la linguistique et l'impérialisme russe* (Paris, 1951).

structural kinship, although they are not mutually understandable. It would also follow—though Marr did not draw this conclusion—that the languages of male-dominated women throughout the world, in whatever society they live, have certain common features which somehow make them languages of one sisterhood, in which feelings of oppression, resentment, and aspiration to freedom are reflected. It would follow that such sisterhood features could be detected by an acute observer freed from the influence of the male-imposed general structure of these languages, and also that it is possible to change one's language in keeping with the desires and images which reflect our position in society. In the words of Letty Russell, "The way people use language reflects the images in their lives and the patterns of their social behavior. As social patterns and images in church and society change, this may have an effect on our language so that it becomes more inclusive of those who find themselves 'left out.'"[18] This is a watered-down version of Marrism.

Unfortunately for the question of the sexist language, fervor does not replace competence when we deal with such a highly technical science as linguistics. Marrism was never accepted by non-Marxist linguists. And it did not last long within the Soviet Union. There is no need for me to analyze Joseph Stalin's refutation of Marrism in his *Pravda* article of June 20, 1950, "Marxism in Linguistics."[19] Suffice it to quote Bertil Malmberg's remark: "Marrism is completely abandoned today; it denied the most self-evident facts."[20] This is, of course, not to suggest that there are no relations between language and society. But these relations should be carefully studied for each language and in each society. They do not obey any general law concerning who dominates whom.

The debacle of Marrism undercuts the central idea behind the contemporary complaints about sexist language: it forbids us to believe that the use of "he," "his," "him," "man," "mankind," and similar generic terms is due to male domination in society and to a supposed male order in the formation and use of the semantic structures of English.

A countertest may be attempted. If language was an ideology, and sexist language in particular was the ideology of male power, one should expect to find a fairly stable correlation between degrees of feminine subservience in society and degrees of sexism in language. Yet the facts do not warrant such an expectation. Anyone who has consulted a Turkish

---

[18] *Op. cit.*, pp. 94–95.

[19] Joseph Stalin, *Marxism and Linguistics* (New York, 1951). Long before the *Pravda* debate, eminent linguists who were also Marxists had refuted Marr's theory, e.g., Aurélien Sauvageot, *La théorie japhétique de l'académicien Marr*, in the symposium *A la lumière du Marxisme* (Paris, 1935).

[20] Bertil Malmberg, *Les nouvelles tendances de la linguistique* (Paris, 1968) p. 37.

grammar knows that the Turkish language makes no distinction corresponding to "he," "she," "it": there is only one gender for everything and everybody. But anyone who studies the status of woman in traditional Turkish society knows that the Turkish way of life was not exactly liberal as far as women were concerned. And, far from corresponding to an evolution of the language, the revolution initiated by Kemal Ataturk was inspired by imitation of Western countries whose language is notoriously more "sexist" than Turkish.

Sex and Gender

From a more strictly linguistic point of view, one should ask: What is gender? Does gender, in the languages that have several genders, mean, imply, correspond to, suggest sex? On this point the peculiarities of the English language have beclouded the issue. For if "he" and "she" usually correspond to male and female in English and American usage (though more so in the American branch of English: in England, cats and ships are frequently "she"), this is due to a process of neutralization of everything that is not male or female ("it") and not to a primordial sexual status for "he" or "she." Gender does not mean sex, as anyone knows who speaks French, German, Italian, Spanish, or most languages of the world. It is a means of classifying nouns and of explaining the concordance between nouns and adjectives of certain categories. If it denoted or connoted sex, a French male could not be called *une personne*, the mystery of the Triune God could not be called the mystery of *la Trinité*, Madame Veil, the current Minister of Health in the French government, could not be addressed as *Madame le Ministre*, and a most peculiar transformation would take place in the organ of a French church when it passes from the singular (*il*) to the plural (*elles*). That gender is simply a taxonomic denomination that is unrelated to sex appears clearly from the fact that Swahili distinguishes among six different genders, none of which corresponds to male or female. And the Bantu languages of Southern Africa, which count as many as sixteen genders, do not suggest that Bantu culture is acquainted with sixteen sexes. Admittedly, the distinction between genders, whether these are two or sixteen, does correspond to the perception of some distinctions in nature. Thus, in Swahili, "most nouns denoting human beings fall into class I, words denoting inanimate objects into class II, names of trees, plants, etc., into class III, abstract nouns into class VI, and so on. There are many words whose classification appears arbitrary or anomalous, but this does not invalidate the statement that there is a considerable degree of correspondence between gender and a classification of nouns from a semantic point of view."[21] That in most languages male and female fall

---

[21] John Lyons, *Introduction to Theoretical Linguistics* (Cambridge, 1971) p. 286.

into different genders simply means that human beings have noticed a difference between male and female, and that most of them have found this difference important enough to call for grammatical classification.

The misunderstanding by which gender is, in much current discussion and, I suppose, in the popular mind of English-speaking people, assimilated to sex has a well-documented origin. Early Greek grammarians designated the first two genders with terms borrowed from the biological categories which Greek usage included within these genders, that is, male and female, whence masculine and feminine. The third gender, nameless in the first grammars, was called "intermediate" by Aristotle—which obviously suggests that Aristotle did not mistake gender for sex. Later grammatical practice called it "neither" masculine nor feminine, which was translated into Latin as *neuter*. The restriction of two genders to male and female in the English language, and the pooling of everything that is not male and female into the third gender, are responsible for the widespread but erroneous belief that gender means sex, that there are only two genders, and that the third is a misnomer for the nonsexual in nature and culture. The following passage from the *Journal of Ecumenical Studies* statement on "linguistic sexism" is a good example of such an error:

Upon reflection it should also be clear that the feminine-masculine imagery used in the Jewish, Christian, Muslim, and other traditions (i.e. to refer to God and to "entities such as the Church or Israel") is an attempt to express that inferior-superior, human-divine relationship in language that reflected the then, and, often, still existing inferior-superior, female-male societal relationship.[22]

The passage from feminine-masculine to female-male in this text is precisely what no linguistic correlation supports. Already in 1952 Claude Lévi-Strauss warned against hasty assimilations of linguistic patterns to observable empirical phenomena. Social attitudes, he wrote, "do not belong to the same level as linguistic structures, but to a different, more superficial, level."[23] It is precisely because they are superficial that they can be reformed. Sexist discrimination is an observable empirical phenomenon, a social attitude. But language pertains to deeper levels.

The misadventure of gender in English has a curious sequel. It is frequent to hear babies designated as "it" rather than "he" or "she." Gender being popularly assimilated to sex, it would seem natural that those whose sex is—in popular imagination if not in Freudian analysis—more potential than actual should not be "he" or "she" but "it." The inability of the Supreme Court to determine if and when a fetus becomes a person provides a dramatic illustration of the tendency to assimilate

---

[22] *Journal of Ecumenical Studies, loc. cit.*
[23] Claude Lévi-Strauss, *Anthropologie structurale* (Paris, 1958) p. 82.

personhood and developed sexual characteristics. This assimilation entails a dichotomy between the fully sexual beings and the younger developing beings whose sex, though already biologically determined and psychologically active, is not yet socially affirmed. Women are "she"; baby girls are reduced to "it"; and fetuses are no-thing. Here again Lévi-Strauss's remarks are relevant. Noting that on the one hand the Oneida language spoken among the Iroquois has different pronouns for adult women and for younger girls, and that on the other hand the Iroquois nation extended to women the widest range of rights, he suggested that there could be an inverse correlation between the social status of the adult woman and the linguistic status of the younger girl. While the adult woman is powerful, the younger girl is reduced to the status "of animals and not of human persons." He saw this correlation between "already formalized homogeneous expressions of the linguistic structure and the social structure," rather than between "language and behavior."[24] Is a similar correlation developing in the wake of the woman-liberation movement? The abortionist literature provides many an example of this phenomenon, the latest episode in the Anglo-Saxon misadventure of grammatical gender.

Generic Terms

The problem of generic terms is different from that of pronouns. "Man" in English means both human being and human male, with the result that women are not always quite sure when they are included in man-talk, and that some have come to suspect that they may never be included at all. "As women questioned the generic use of male words they were promptly put down repeatedly with ridicule," Nelle Morton complains. But she adds with some satisfaction: "Finally it became quite evident to them that male and not the generic in the male terminology was meant."[25] This is, of course, a nonscientific statement; for one should first determine if we are faced with the generic use of male terms (we use the male term "man" in the absence of a properly generic term) or with the specific use of a generic term (we use the generic term "man" because we have no other word when we want to speak of the human male as a person rather than a male). In the French language it is clearly the generic term *homme* which is used for the male. German (*Mensch, Mann*) or Swedish (*människa, man*), like Hebrew (*adam, ish*), Greek (*anthrōpos, anēr*), Latin (*homo, vir*), and many other languages use two words. In German, too, the generic *Mensch*, in the parlance of some parts

[24] *Ibid.*
[25] Quoted in Russell, *op. cit.*, p. 94.

of Southern Germany, is, in the neuter gender, used for woman.[26] Thus the linguistic problem is infinitely more complex than we may be led to believe. Why the Old English term *manncynn* (related to German *Mensch* and Swedish *människa*) disappeared from the language and left us without a generic term is anybody's guess. In any case, it is evident, from a look at Hebrew, Greek, Roman, or Germanic civilizations, that the use of two terms does not mitigate the male domination of society.

Linguistically, "man" can be treated as an ambivalent or equivocal word, a word with two meanings, the sense being determined in each case according to the rest of the discourse (the context). Or "man" (human being) and "man" (human male) can also be treated as homonyms. In either case, the problem of discriminating between two possible meanings is to be solved in the syntagmatic dimension of language. That is, one should ask: How does the word function in relation to the other parts of the discourse in which it appears? The various recent guidelines against linguistic sexism erroneously place the problem in the paradigmatic dimension: they suggest replacing the word by others, such as persons, human beings, members of the human race, they, etc. This is a shortsighted project which may lift an occasional ambiguity but leaves two basic problems untouched. First, the living meaning of terms (their denotation and connotations) emerges as they are featured in the syntagmatic order. This follows the structure of each language and cannot be tampered with without creating further ambiguities. Second, whether we select our paradigms (words) or we order them syntactically, we may always be playing a game which is not detectable at the surface of our discourse.

Language Games

In order to locate sexist language or linguistic sexism properly, we must leave the strict compound of linguistic science and enter the vaguer area of linguistic philosophy.

As I hope I have sufficiently indicated, the common mistake of the usual argumentation against sexist language is that it tries to cope with the level of what Ferdinand de Saussure, the initiator of structural linguistics, called *la langue*. Facing the constitutive structure of language, it sees evil in the inadequacy of certain paradigms, taken in their denotation as accepted in the society speaking the language in question, to express the contemporary shift of power in the male-female dialectic. By the same token, it is led to assume, gratuitously and erroneously, that

[26] According to Sachs-Villatte, *Dictionnaire encyclopédique français-allemand et allemand-français* (4th ed.; Berlin, 1917) art. *Mensch*.

the present paradigms of our language express a past power relationship in which males dominated females. This is linguistically naive and historically simplistic. But the picture changes considerably if we look at the other face of language, called by de Saussure *la parole*.[27] There is no English equivalent for the distinction between *langue* and *parole*, but we approximate the scope of the distinction if we see language as a system generally available for communication (*langue*) and as effectively used for communication by individuals (*parole*). Then the question is no longer one of language structure. It turns into the phenomenological question: What do I do when I speak? What do I do when I say, for instance, "Man is made in the image of God"? Whom do I include in this term "man"?

In the *Tractatus logico-philosophicus* Ludwig Wittgenstein wrote: "A proposition is the description of a state of things."[28] The later Wittgenstein judged rather that (in my words) a proposition is the description of a state of mind. The meaning of language, taken not as a theoretical possibility of communication but as actually communicating information from one person to others, is not to be discovered by an objective analysis of the rules of semantics and syntax at work in a discourse, but by investigation of the explicit or implicit, conscious or unconscious intention of the speaker. From this perspective language reveals, besides the generally accepted meaning of the terms used as interpreted in keeping with generally accepted grammatical rules, the state of mind of the speaker. Wittgenstein encapsulated this insight in the notion of "language games." One and the same proposition can be used according to several games. While the game comparison suggested by de Saussure when he compared the rules of grammar to those of chess[29] illustrated the objective structure of *la langue*, the game comparison of Wittgenstein intended to throw light on the subjective twist of *la parole*.

My contention is precisely that the question of sexist language must be asked and answered at the level of language games. If I wish to know what I really put under such terms as "he," "him," "his," "man," "mankind," etc., I should go way beyond, or deep within, what is revealed about words and their usage by the structure of the language I speak. I should attempt to discover what I would understand by what I say if I were not a somewhat sophisticated theologian, philosopher, linguist, engineer, author, or what not, but a child who is still unaware of the objective or generally accepted meanings and rules of this language. Thus a language game, for Wittgenstein, is not a play with words; it is a

[27] Ferdinand de Saussure, *Cours de linguistique générale* (Paris, 1971) pp. 36–39.
[28] Ludwig Wittgenstein, *Tractatus logico-philosophicus* (London, 1961) no. 4.024.
[29] *Op. cit.*, pp. 124–27.

very serious enterprise of psychological and philosophical investigation. The description of language games contained in *The Blue Book* is quite significant:

I shall in the future again and again draw your attention to what I shall call language games. These are ways of using signs simpler than those in which we use the signs of our highly complicated everyday language. Language games are the forms of language with which a child begins to make use of words. The study of language games is the study of primitive forms of language or primitive languages. If we want to study the problems of truth and falsehood, of the agreement and disagreement of propositions with reality, of the nature of assertion, assumption, and question, we shall with great advantage look at primitive forms of language in which these forms of thinking appear without the confusing background of highly complicated processes of thought. When we look at such simple forms of language the mental mist which seems to enshroud our ordinary use of language disappears. We see activities, reactions, which are clear-cut and transparent. On the other hand we recognize in these simple processes forms of language not separated by a break from our more complicated ones. We see that we can build up the complicated forms from the primitive ones by gradually adding new forms.[30]

This quotation will help us to pinpoint the true problem of sexist language. It is twofold. On the one hand, what do I, as this concrete person, really, honestly, intend to convey by such terms as are questioned in the controversy about sexist language? What does the "primitive man" in me truly mean? What image of the world, of society, of male and female, presides over my use of words? On the other hand, what do I, as this concrete person, hear when I receive a discourse in my understanding? What do I read into other people's discourses under the influence of my "primitive" or "childish" or simply favorite view of the world, of society, of male and female?

The same point may be clarified with the categories of J. L. Austin or Donald Evans.[31] When it is spoken, language not only conveys information, it also orients the speaker in the direction of a certain type of action. It is "performative." It expresses the speaker's wish to influence the world in a certain way. It reveals an attitude. It inspires a behavior. So the question of sexist language becomes: What is the underlying attitude of my use of "he," "him," "his," "man," "mankind," etc.? How do I wish to influence power struggles between male and female? Similar questions should be asked about the underlying intentions of my use of such terms as black, race, poor, proletarian, liberation, revolution, and of all that

[30] Ludwig Wittgenstein, *The Blue and Brown Books* (New York, 1965) p. 17.
[31] J. L. Austin, *How to Do Things with Words* (Cambridge, Mass., 1962); Donald Evans, *The Language of Self-Involvement* (London, 1963).

connotes relationships between individuals or groups with unequal or diverse standings in the implicit value-systems of society.

The answers to such questions may indeed reveal an astonishing amount of sexual bias in the language of most people. Many readers who have never seen themselves as male (or female) chauvinists would well be astonished if they analyzed their language games and discerned the implicit direction of their self-involvement in language referring to male and female. By the same token, the solution to the ensuing dilemmas cannot be a linguistic solution, because the dilemma itself is not linguistic. Were I a Turk, I could still play a sexist game with a language which does not express the distinction between "he" and "she": my bias could affect the tone of my voice, my smile, the twinkle in my eye, the gesture I make, the many nonlinguistic signs which accompany my speech. Were I a Swahili-speaking East African, I could likewise express my involvement in a world where males dominate females, even though the six gender categories of my language do not correspond to a feminine-masculine distinction, still less to a female-male opposition.

Similar remarks should also be made concerning myself as receiver of spoken communication; for I am likely to understand others according to my inner bias. The scholastic axiom *Quidquid recipitur ad modum recipientis recipitur* already pointed to a major aspect of human communication: Do I, in the interior game I play when I hear the speech of others, project my sexist bias into discourses that may well be perfectly innocent of linguistic sexism? This question is, of course, relevant to our present concerns. I suspect that much denunciation of sexist language in others reveals the bias of the hearer rather than that of the speakers.

Is There a Solution?

If my analysis is correct, then the problem is much more complicated than appears, and it cannot possibly be solved by superficially adjusting our choice of words to a new fashion and by pressuring authors into new vocabulary habits. At most, this will do what tokenism did to the black movement: blunt the edge of the struggle. Solutions at the level of words can only be illusory. Nietzsche's *Zarathustra* perceived this:

Oh my beasts, said Zarathustra, keep on chattering and let me listen. Your chattering refreshes me—where there is chattering, the world lies before me like a garden. How lovely it is that words and sounds exist. Are words and sounds not rainbows and illusion-bridges between what is forever divided?
Each soul has a different world. For each soul, every other soul is a hinterland.
Between two objects most similar, illusion carries the loveliest lies, for the smallest gap is the hardest to bridge. . . .

How lovely is all speaking and all lying of sounds! With sounds, our love can dance on many-colored rainbows.[32]

Which I take to mean: language reforms provide illusory solutions to human problems; for the problems pertain to a deeper metalinguistic symbolic level. They arise in the semiotic dimension of life. They belong to the meaning and reading of symbols. This insight enriched Yvonne Pellé-Douël's contribution to a philosophy of womanhood: to be a woman is to assume a certain symbolism within the fundamental human vocation.

Woman has an experimental knowledge of her feminine being, of her femininity. There are strictly feminine ways of living out the human vocation: this is an irrefutable truth. There are feminine ways of being a human being, experiences which pertain only to women as these exist in the human community, in union with a man, in society, in the divine-human relationship. There is a feminine 'existentiality.'[33]

Each woman has to discover, to endorse, to enrich, to live her own symbolic function and value among the many aspects of the feminine condition in nature and culture. In so doing, she serves both herself and humankind; for "the feminine values belong to the whole of humanity, and finally their sense is one integral sense; there are no feminine values; there are human values carried, manifested, symbolized by women."[34] To assume a symbolic vocation does not amount to being given meaning by others, by men, by the males who have hitherto presided over the organization of society and led the development of culture. Rather, one should interpret the human condition in such a way that meaning is created and becomes manifest in one's life. The challenge is to assume in intention, thought, feeling, project, and action what constitutes the purpose of language: to communicate values. Words are given values that are read as their meaning. Human persons choose their own meaning, as useful or purposeless, real or illusory, good or evil, other-centered or self-centered, Godward or self-enclosed, serving or dominating. And they express this in language.

Thus it is not, after all, surprising that when Lévi-Strauss, analyzing the elementary structures of kinship, found these structures to hinge on the prevalence of exogamic marriage due to the prohibition of incest, he compared woman to the word which speech sends from speaker to listener in order to create ties between individuals, just as the exchange

---

[32] Nietzsche, *Thus Spoke Zarathustra* (Chicago, 1957) p. 224.
[33] *Op. cit.*, p. 133.
[34] *Ibid.*, p. 160.

of women in marriage creates ties between clans and tribes.[35] To be human is to take on a semiotic dimension. It is to become language, to create values, to invent meaning, to communicate with others in speech and behavior and with the All-Other in worship, according to our insights into the depths of existence. Whatever the real one-sidedness and the verbal exaggerations of her book *Beyond God the Father*, Mary Daly comes to this conclusion as she writes: "The question itself is the beginning of an answer that keeps unfolding itself. The question-answer is a verb, and when one begins to move in the current of the verb, of the Verb, she knows that she is not a mirror."[36] A mirror reflects. A person invents. Woman is called to be a verb because this is, in imitation of God, the human vocation. She has to discover what verb she is, to create her own verb, to be what her verb means, to do what her verb says. In so doing, she will relate to "the creative drawing power of the Good Who is self-communicating Be-ing, Who is the Verb from whom, in whom, and with whom all true movements move."[37]

So the linguistic reform that is called for by the woman movement should not be satisfied with surface adjustments of our spoken tongues, as though eliminating some words and altering gender patterns could help to gauge the meaning of woman and of man (in the two senses of "man"). The demand should be for a reform in depth of our symbolisms, social, political, cultural, esthetic, and, yes, religious and theological, so that at all levels and in all dimensions women may discover their meaning, conceive their project, fulfil their service, define their expectation, refine their attention, offer their leadership, give their witness, formulate their prayer, share their worship, create their life. According to the Christian faith, there is only one key to such a spiritual renovation: dying and rising with Christ.[38] The theological tradition of St. Cyril of Alexandria preferred to say that the Logos became "man" rather than became "a man"; for the Word assumed all humankind in His dying and rising, women no less than men. To discover oneself in Christ is not a matter of language. It is a matter of what Roland Barthes calls *l'écriture:*[39] the woman who creates her life finds by the same token her own style, both her style of life and her style of communication, her style of symbolization. And, as has been shown by Jacques Derrida, there is a sense in which *l'écriture* is anterior to language.[40]

This, of course, brings us directly to the theological problems.

[35] *Op. cit.*, pp. 67–72.
[36] *Op. cit.*, p. 197; see the explanations given on pp. 33–34.
[37] *Ibid.*, p. 198.
[38] Cf. Pellé-Douël, *op. cit.*, pp. 85–161.
[39] Roland Barthes, *Le degré zéro de l'écriture* (Paris, 1953).
[40] Jacques Derrida, *De la grammatologie* (Paris, 1967).

THEOLOGICAL SEXISM?

The basic question here is simple: What are the language games of theologians? Is there, in what they have been doing since Christians began to reflect about their faith, a sex-discrimination game? Is their language, in some of its aspects, a sexist language? This is not asking if theologians have not occasionally, at times, often, or even most of the time, forgotten to examine what contributions women could bring to theology. It is not asking if they have ever thought of such a possibility. No doubt, theologians have frequently forgotten many things. They could often apply to themselves what Wittgenstein wrote of himself as a philosopher: "I do philosophy now like an old woman who is always mislaying something and having to look for it again: now her spectacles, now her keys."[41] The feminine contribution to theology may well be the mislaid spectacles, the missing keys, that are necessary to a fully human or Christian theology. The question would then be: How does it happen that theologians have never even noticed that these spectacles or these keys were missing? Have they been, unawares, both the actors and the victims of a primitive misogynist language game?

This is the contention of many today. Thus Joan Morris contends that ecclesiastics and church historians have systematically hidden the true history of woman in the Church, especially as regards the existence of women with a quasi-episcopal authority.[42] Thus Clara M. Henning affirms: "The operative law of the Church is designed to grant men—specifically priests—the absolute controlling position."[43] Thus Mary Daly states: the "denial of rationality in women by Christian theologians has been a basic tactic for confining them to the condition of moral imbecility."[44]

Many remarks could, of course, be made about each of these points. For instance, the existence of abbesses exempted from the jurisdiction of bishops and holding jurisdiction over priests has always been well known to historians. Or also: if canon law has had the effect of putting some men in controlling positions, it is both historically and logically absurd to conceive of the entire system of law as being designed to have this effect. Or yet: the tactic detected by Mary Daly must have been a notorious failure, given the great number of canonized women saints, who cannot be called moral imbeciles by any stretch of imagination.

These samples of rash escalation in the assault on theological sexism

[41] Ludwig Wittgenstein, *On Certainty* (New York, 1972) no. 532.

[42] Joan Morris, *The Lady Was a Bishop* (New York, 1973). This title is, of course, entirely misleading; the lady was never a bishop.

[43] Clara M. Henning, *Canon Law and the Battle of the Sexes*, in Rosemary Radford Ruether, ed., *Religion and Sexism* (New York, 1974) p. 286.

[44] *Op. cit.*, p. 101.

should not blind us to the genuine problem, which strikes at the heart of theology: Has Christian theology borrowed from the human male the experiential model for its description of God? Have our images of God and, by extension, our views of the mysteries of the Incarnation, the redemption, the life of grace, the sacraments, the Church, been distorted by misogynism?

Is God a Father?

It is a telling commentary on the present deliquescence of theological awareness that the process of analogical thinking as used in the God-talk of the great Christian tradition is regularly ignored or misunderstood when it comes to such questions as: Why do we refer to God as He, not as She? Why do we speak of God as our Father, of God the Father, of God the Son? Why not our Mother, God the Mother, God the Daughter? Such questions are asked at the level of images and metaphors, sometimes at that of analogy of attribution. And they assume that human discourse can be changed at will, and that anyone can invent a new metaphysics.

But can one create symbols? If our basic images are archetypal residues of millennia of human experience (as Carl Jung would see them) or translations of ontological structures inexorably enscribed in human psyche and human chemistry (as Lévi-Strauss might say) or natural precomprehensions of the divine self-revelation in Christ (as I would like to suggest), then the questions ought to be asked and answered at greater depth. Does the Christian language about "the Father, from whom every patrimony in heaven and on earth takes its name" (Eph 3:15), derive from an ontic level which should be accepted because it is first given to us, and ought to be understood because rationality seeks for understanding, but that can be tampered with only at the cost of a denial of nature and an impoverishment of culture? The superficial question remains at the level of what Yvonne Pellé-Douël calls myth;[45] the deeper question operates at the level of what she calls symbol.[46]

The answer of classical theology was given in terms of analogy. Divine Fatherhood, whether intra-Trinitarian or *ad extra*, is an analogy, a special kind of symbolization that allows us to speak of the unspeakable. But the only analogy that may be validly applied to a totally transcendental subject (and God is, of course, the only totally transcendental subject) is the analogy of proper proportionality. This does not posit anything common between the terms that are being compared, since these are strictly heterogeneous to each other. God is beyond all genus.

[45] *Op. cit.*, p. 165–95.
[46] *Ibid.*, pp. 197–226.

Nothing that is connoted by fatherhood in human experience applies to Him, which is the exact reason why the New Testament, in the Lord's Prayer, qualifies fatherhood with "heavenhood." What is true of fatherhood on earth cannot be predicated of heavenly fatherhood. God our Father in the "economic" Trinity, God the Father in the "transcendent" Trinity, are always meant of "God in heaven." As a result, to speak of fatherhood in God is to negate human fatherhood as a proper image of God. Likewise, to speak of a motherhood of God—an expression which is not unheard of in classical authors, both mystics and theologians—is to negate human motherhood as a proper image of God. All that is said by this type of language is this: in our human experience of fatherhood, of motherhood, especially when lived and understood in the light of the Christian revelation, there is trace of an element that places us on the right direction to relate to God and to understand this relationship.

Analogical nomination of God is both negative and positive. It is negative since it negates that human fathers are images of God in their fatherhood; it is positive since it affirms that the human experience of fatherhood—at its best, not in the sorry instances of too many individuals—helps us to understand our relationship to God and therefore God as the originating and dominant term of this relationship. It is negative insofar as it denies that fathering a child images the divine Fatherhood; it is positive insofar as it affirms that relating to a father helps me to understand my relation to God. The human term of the fatherhood analogy is not human fatherhood as lived by human fathers; it is the experience of human persons, women as well as men, of relating to a human father in love, gratitude, and obedience. The point of comparison for the divine Fatherhood is not human fatherhood: this would imply a point-by-point comparison, which proper proportionality denies radically. It is human filiation. This implies a proportion, that is, a correspondence of relationships, which requires four terms. God's Fatherhood *ad extra* is a short expression implying: *filiation* and *parenthood* in humankind; *human creature* and *God the Creator*. Intra-Trinitarian Fatherhood is also an epitome of the Christian revelation concerning the inner life of God: *filiation* and *parenthood* in mankind; the *Second* and the *First Person* in God. That is, my experience of human filiation helps me to understand Jesus' relationship to his divine Father, which I believe further to express the eternal relationship between the divine Word and the fontal Principle of the Divinity.

The relevance of this for our discussion is, I believe, that the sexist game has not been played by the theologians who have commented on the divine Fatherhood or by the authors of the New Testament who evoked for us Jesus' filial love for the Father, or by Jesus himself, if indeed it is correct that the appellation *Abba* in the New Testament goes back to the historical Jesus of Nazareth. The sexist game was not played by a writer like Julian of Norwich, who spoke of "God, All-Wisdom, our kindly Mother" and of "our Mother Christ": she took her point of departure in her experience of being daughter to a human mother, and she found this meaningful for her understanding of her relationship to the Word Incarnate as Jesus.[47]

If I may call this the primary level of theology, the sexist game has been played, I suspect, at the secondary level, not by metaphysicians who have carefully purified their concepts with the tools of analogical thinking, but by theological popularizers and by pastors, bishops, and priests whose preaching has shaped the popular theological language and the popular Christian mind. The advent of the scientific age has developed an empirical mentality which makes it all but impossible for most of us to think analogically in the classical sense of this term. Then analogy of proper proportionality is replaced by other types of comparison. The working concepts of God and of divine Fatherhood, far from being united in the *via negationis* which underlies classical analogy, operate along divergent lines of uncritical *affirmatio*. They waver between literalism, which takes fatherhood in man as a positive image of fatherhood in God, and liberalism, for which human appellations of God are pure metaphors. The process of popularization, which seems indispensable to the preaching of the gospel to the masses, has banalized our images of God. And, at least in regard to God as the Father, banalization is falsification. At this level the protest against the Fatherhood of God is entirely justified. One must reach "beyond god the father" in order to remain faithful to the revelation of the transcendence of God. In attempting to give life to its images and to make the gospel relevant, secondary-level theology has no doubt played language games which have aped the power games and the sexist games of society.

I tend to think, however (but I may well be wrong, and such a surmise is difficult to document), that the mind of the People of God has not been greatly misled by popular preaching and teaching and writing. At least, the Catholic concept of the *sensus fidelium* implies that the Spirit also protects and guides the faith of the people. The faith may well be right even when the theology is wrong. I doubt that most Christians think of God's Fatherhood in the terms rightly denounced by the Koran: "The Creator of the heavens and the earth—how should He have a son, seeing that He has no consort, and He created all things, and He has knowledge of everything?"[48]

[47] Julian of Norwich, *Revelations of Divine Love* (Westminster, Md., 1952) p. 119. See *Woman in Christian Tradition* (Notre Dame, 1973) pp. 144–45.

[48] *Cattle*, in A. J. Arberry, tr., *The Koran Interpreted* 1 (New York, n.d.) 161.

Should the Spirit be Feminine?

I probably would not speak to this topic but for an unfortunate essay by Leonard Swidler.[49] The suggestion is made in this article that we may call the Father and the Son "Him," but the Spirit should be called "She." The idea runs into several major difficulties. First, there are linguistic difficulties. The author argues from his belief that the Greek word for Spirit, *pneuma*, frequently used by St. Paul, is, like the Hebrew term *hochma*, feminine. However, this is a bad mistake, as anyone can see by looking up a dictionary. *Pneuma* is not feminine; it is neuter, neither masculine nor feminine. It belongs to the Greek equivalent of the English gender rendered as "it." The only traditional church languages in which the word for Spirit is feminine are the Semitic languages. Thus, to argue from Greek is a mistake. To argue from Hebrew, Aramaic, or Syriac to throw light on the proper use of gender in English would be another mistake; for gender does not have the same connotations in all languages, as shown by the fact that languages do not use the same genders for the same things. There is a third mistake in that the proposed idea assimilates gender to sex.

There is, of course, no problem about Syriac- or Arabic-speaking Christians referring to the Spirit in the feminine gender, since in their languages this entails no consequence about female symbolism. But to diversify English pronouns in order to stress a supposedly feminine —understood as female—aspect of the Spirit is another matter. The pronouns that designate the three Persons might be diversified—were this linguistically possible—if indeed the pronouns designated the relational oppositions, the relationships between the Father and the Word, the Word and the Father, the Father and the Spirit, the Word and the Spirit, the Spirit and the Word. But when Christians refer to the Father, the Son, and the Spirit—in worship, private prayer, preaching, or teaching—they think of the totality of the Divinity which relates to them and relates them to Itself. When they think of the Divinity in the shape, form, or image of one of the three Persons, it is still the divine substance as the content of the Persons which they have in mind, since the divine Persons have no other content than their common divinity or substance. Theologians occasionally reflect about the relational opposi- tions, the processions, the singularity of each Person. Mystics occasion- ally believe that they have received an ineffable experience of the relational oppositions in their wonder, their beauty, their richness; and they may attempt to describe this experience indirectly with the help of esthetic or psychological symbols. But even then, the reality which is aimed at in each Person is always the Divinity, which is identical in all three (as implied in the *homoousia* of the early councils). When we refer

[49] See n. 13 above.

to the works of God *ad extra*, which proceed from the divine power common to the three, we give glory to the three Persons in their total oneness. Accordingly, we may well say "he," "him," "his," or "she," "her," "hers," or "it," "its," about any of the three Persons, always designating the divine *ousia*, since this is the substance (*homoousia*) of each Person. Stretching somewhat the limits of language, we may say that the Divinity, the oneness, is always the noun, whereas the Persons are verbs. We could differentiate between the Persons linguistically with the help of different pronouns only if pronouns did not stand for nouns, if designations did not point to what is, if symbols had no content; for the content of the Persons is and cannot be anything else than the divine *ousia*. Pronouns cannot express the relational oppositions in the life of God. To diversify our pronouns in order to stress the singularity of each Person would be to break the simplicity of the divine Being.

Femininity in God?

Admittedly, there have been previous attempts to introduce some sort of femininity in God. In the *De trinitate* 13, 5–6, St. Augustine discarded the comparison of the three Persons to the three members of a nuclear family: father, wife-mother, child. In my *Woman in Christian Tradition* I drew attention to Julian of Norwich (Christ our Mother), to St. Gregory Palamas (Christ is our "brother ... bridegroom ... father ... mother ... "), to Vladimir Soloviev's visions of the divine Sophia, to Victor White's suggestion that the feminine dimension in God could be explored with the help of Jungian psychology.[50] But this does not constitute a tradition of divine femininity. Both Palamas and Julian spoke in reference to the Incarnation, not to the intradivine life. Soloviev's Sophia is not God; it is the soul of the world as the epiphany of God shining in Christ, in the Church, in the Virgin, and eventually in mankind transformed in the image of the Theanthropy.

Yet it is not out of place to investigate further if there is not a sense in which we may or should conceive of God as somehow feminine. This cannot be, if I am correct in my understanding of the mystery of the Trinity, at the level of the Persons. But could it not be at the level of God's manifestation of Himself *ad extra* in creation and re-creation? That humankind is created in two forms polarly related to each other is hardly an accident of the human nature. The entire animate world is created according to a similar polarity. And the mythologies and cosmogonies of most peoples have seen the whole cosmos made alive by the polarities of the Yin and the Yang—expressed, of course, in manifold cultural forms. The tradition of the Old Testament, or rather a trend within that tradition, used such images to describe the unequal polarity of the

[50]*Woman in Christian Tradition*, pp. 144–45, 158, 160–63, 146 respectively.

covenant. And it may not be purely coincidental that the first inkling of the covenant shows the Spirit of God (*rouach elohim;* LXX: *pneuma theou*) "brooding" (*merachepheth;* LXX: *epephereto*) over the waste (Gn 1:2). Brooding evokes the very feminine image of the mother bird waiting patiently for her eggs to hatch, or also (the verb can have this sense) hovering over the nest while she encourages her young ones to get up and fly. It is precisely in the process of creation that God can be seen in a "feminine" attitude, an attitude which pervades both the Old and the New Testament when writers and prophets perceive the fulness of the divine love for His people. God loves mankind with a motherly love. As "the power of the Most High" (*dynamis hypsistou*), this primordial love, in the epiphany of Lk 1:35, "overshadows" (*episkiasei*) the Virgin. Thus God, as Father, Word, and Spirit, manifests Himself to humankind in a love which human experience associates with a mother's love. The Sophia of Vladimir Soloviev was this love. The divine "energies," in Palamas' conception of the Trinity, are radiations of the divine Glory, the manifestation of the fulness of divine love.

It would seem normal that, having perceived this love in their response to it, the Christian faithful would from time to time have imagined God under the feminine traits of divine Motherhood. The Catholic and the Orthodox traditions have channeled such images toward the *ecclesia*, the soul, the Virgin Mary, rather than toward God Himself. For reasons of Trinitarian theology, they have discouraged the projection of the male-female polarity into our conception of the divine. But they have left two ways open for a theological integration of the feminine dimension of life in our concept and representation of God. There is the way of the divine Motherhood, manifested in creation and re-creation: Julian of Norwich explored it without hesitancy. And there is the way, dear to many mystics and basic to the Catholic theology of the sacrament of marriage, of an analogy between the gift of love in the transcendent Trinity and the gift of love between man and woman. As commented upon before the advent of scientific exegesis, the Song of Songs developed such an analogy. From Origen through St. Bernard to St. John of the Cross, this analogy is constantly used to describe the development and the highest degrees of the spiritual life. The mystery of the bridegroom and the bride reflects the mystery of God's inner love. We should endorse Ann Belford Ulanov's summing up of the Catholic conception of love: "The mystery of the unconditioned Divine, the Father, seeing unconditional worth in the human, the Son, and bestowing that worth in an act of self-giving love, the Spirit, is fully reflected in the mystery of unconditional love between lovers."[51] Moralists would have said "between husband and wife." But mystics have been bolder.

[51] *Op. cit.*, p. 308.

In the mystery of love between God and His creatures, God is not male and human persons female, nor is God female and human persons male. But the polarity between them is such that in the fulness of love the distinction between the two poles is abolished; for the fulness of divine love erases distinctions, integrating them into organic wholeness. Who is male, who is female, in St. John of the Cross's explanation of this verse of stanza 35 of the *Spiritual Canticle* (shorter version): *Y vamonos a ver en tu hermosura?*

Let us so act that we may be alike in beauty and that thy beauty may be such that, when one of us looks at the other, each may be like to thee in thy beauty, and may see himself in thy beauty, which will be the transforming of me in thy beauty. Thus I shall see thee in thy beauty and thou wilt see me in thy beauty; and thou wilt see thyself in me in thy beauty, and I shall see myself in thee in thy beauty; and thus I may be like to thee in thy beauty, and thou mayest be like to me in thy beauty, and my beauty may be thy beauty and thy beauty my beauty; and I shall be thou in thy beauty, and thou wilt be I in thy beauty, because thy beauty itself will be my beauty.[52]

The polarity of the Yin and the Yang is not a polarization between male and female. Feminine elements may be kept, or introduced, in the thematization of our relationship to God, where this is at all possible. But these elements belong to men as well as to women. They are at work, not only in Julian of Norwich calling Christ "Our Mother," but also in St. Angela di Foligno's spontaneous prayer to God: "My Son, my Son, do not abandon me, my Son."[53]

CONCLUSION

The danger of the woman-liberation movement in the Church is that it can distort polarity into polarization. Drawing on Jungian psychology, Ann Belford Ulanov gives timely warning:

Polarity and polarization can be understood as two ways that pairs of opposites may relate to each other. In polarity, the opposites are related to each other by mutual attraction; they are drawn to unite to each other without destroying the distinct individuality of each pole; on the contrary, the individuality of each is heightened and realized. In polarization, the opposites pull away from each other and conflict with each other. The two poles split apart and destroy the individuality of each other.[54]

Presumably, concern for neat language has not been the only motivation of the questions that are being asked about linguistic sexism in

---

[52] The translation is Allison Peers's (minus his many capital letters), *Works of St. John of the Cross* 2 (Westminster, Md., 1945) 164.

[53] *L'Esperienza di Dio amore: Il libro di Angela di Foligno* (Rome, 1972) p. 137.

[54] *Op. cit.*, p. 296.

theology. The need to provoke conflicts has played its part. One could psychoanalyze this need as the reversed *machismo* of the masculinity complex. This was already done by Marynia Farnham in relation to the early feminist movement: "Psychologically, feminism had a simple objective: the achievement of maleness by the female, or the nearest approach to it."[55] One could also "politico-analyze" it, that is, uncover the political components borrowed from the Hegelian-Marxist theory of conflicts, which one finds in most theologies of liberation. Where Frantz Fanon wrote: "La lutte elle-même, dans son déroulement, dans son processus interne, développe les différentes directions de la culture et en esquisse de nouvelles,"[56] Gustavo Gutierrez says: "el hecho histórico, político, liberadores crecimiento del Reino, es acontecer salvífico. . . ."[57] Elizabeth Gould Davis sees woman liberation as political messianism:

Only the complete and total demolition of the social body will cure the fatal sickness. Only the overthrow of the three-thousand-year-old beast of masculist materialism will save the race. . . . She who was revered and worshipped by early man because of her power to see the unseen will once again be the pivot—not as sex but as divine woman—about whom the next civilization will, as of old, revolve.[58]

Going further, Mary Daly identifies the discovery of sisterhood with the cause of causes, the final cause of the universe.[59] And Judith Plastow Goldenberg opens a mythifying perspective on the transformation, not only of humankind, but also of God, as a result of the advent of woman. She expects the superwoman to come, the Lilith, created at the beginning, of a Jewish legend. Both God and man fear her return.[60] At this point, of course, we are not in religion, in theology, or in feminine symbolism; we are in pagan mythology.

The suggestions examined in the present essay have been more sober, less mythical and less mystifying. But we should delude ourselves were we to think that questions concerning God as He or She or It, concerning the meaning of the term "man," are easy semantic plays of words that

[55] Marynia Farnham and Ferdinand Lundberg, *Modern Woman, the Lost Sex* (New York, 1947) p. 167.

[56] Frantz Fanon, *Les damnés de la terre* (Paris, 1970) p. 173 ("The struggle itself, in its unfolding, in its interior process, nurtures the diverse directions of culture and sketches out new ones").

[57] Gustavo Gutierrez, *Teología de la liberación* (Lima, 1971) p. 228 ("the historical, political, liberating event *is* increase of the kingdom, *is* salvific happening..."). Admittedly, the author adds: "but it is neither *the* coming of the kingdom nor *the whole* salvation."

[58] *Op. cit.*, pp. 339.

[59] *Op. cit.*, pp. 180–90.

[60] Judith Plastow Goldenberg, *The Coming of Lilith*, in Ruether, *Religion and Sexism*, p. 343.

can be dealt with at the superficial level of how we speak. The hypothesis that the male masters of the Church and of theology have adopted and maintained the sexist language that has prevailed in society since the fading away of a hypothetical matriarchal age reaches deeper levels. It touches on the fundamental structure of language. It touches also on the fundamental structure of theology, since the Church is accused of endorsing a male conception of God by excluding in practice the use of feminine pronouns to speak of the Divinity.

I have shown that this polemic rests largely on a series of misunderstandings: on the nature of language, which is not an ideology; on the nature of linguistic gender, which cannot be equated with sex; on analogical thinking, which cannot be identified with metaphors and comparisons; on Trinitarian theology, which cannot separate the Persons at the level of their essence designated by the pronouns. I have also found the true location of linguistic sexism in the language games that unconsciously have been and are played in society and in the Church. I have indicated that the solution does not lie in superficial reforms of manners of speech, but in a fundamental restructuration of Christian symbols. And I have suggested that both the theological and the mystical traditions contain steppingstones toward this restructuration, which requires an integration of the fulness of human experience, including its feminine dimension, in our relationship to God and in the thematization and formulation of this relationship. But, unlike political revolutions, theological renovations can be done only in serenity. They require, not the conflict of classes, sexes, or theologies, but the working together and, if need be, the reconciliation of all in the sorority-fraternity of the gospel.

VIII

TOWARD A RENEWED ANTHROPOLOGY

As indicated by the range of topics included in this issue of *TS*, the new feminism, popularly known as the women's liberation movement,[1] presents a serious challenge to the areas of language, interpersonal relationships, work in the world, and ministry in the Church. Beneath all these topics, however, lies a crucial issue for theology as a whole: an adequate understanding of what it is to be human. As the Dutch phenomenologist F. J. Buytendijk has correctly noted, "it is of the essence of human being always to be either man or woman."[2] This differentiation of the human race into two sexes, which most feminists take to be a primal and paradigmatic differentiation,[3] demands an adequate understanding of the distinct dimensions of female as well as male existence. Moreover, it demands that the perspective of each sex, with all the experience, history, insight, and imagination which is its own, contribute to the description of human being and of God which grounds a theological anthropology.

It is the contention of feminists that the prevailing ideas about what it means to be human have been male-oriented and male-shaped. This is what is meant by "sexism." Theology, no less than any other discipline, is being called to an examination of consciousness; for this reason, everyone engaged in the work of theology needs to listen to the rising chorus of feminist authors. To facilitate this encounter, we intend to survey here books and articles of the past ten years that have pushed forward the frontiers of consciousness about the mystery of humanity, male and female. My survey will deal with publications that do not have a consciously religious framework; Anne Patrick will concentrate on specifically religious publications, works which address more directly the question of an inclusive theological anthropology through interpretations of Scripture, tradition, and church practice.

Feminism itself is an elusive and much-disputed term.[4] Here it is used

---

[1] For an excellent overview of the movement, see Donald McDonald, "The Liberation of Woman," *Center Magazine* 5 (May-June 1972) 25-42. For a very different approach, see also Jo Freeman, "The Origins of the Women's Liberation Movement," in *Changing Women in a Changing Society*, ed. Joan Huber (Chicago, 1973) pp. 30-49.

[2] *Woman, A Contemporary View*, tr. Denis J. Barrett (New York, 1968) p. 34.

[3] See Simone de Beauvoir, *The Second Sex*, tr. H. M. Parshley (New York, 1952), and Shulamith Firestone, *The Dialectics of Sex* (New York, 1971).

[4] Beverly Harrison has recently developed a distinction between "hard" feminists (those who reject the two-human-natures theory) and "soft" feminists (those who recognize a special nature in women and want to "feminize" the public world). See "The New Consciousness of Women: A Socio-Political Resource," *Cross-Currents* 24, 4 (Winter 1975) 445-62.

in the broad sense articulated by Henrietta Rodman in 1915: "Feminism is the attempt of women to grow up, to accept the responsibilities of life, to outgrow those characteristics of childhood—selfishness and cowardliness—that we require our boys to outgrow, but that we permit and by our social system encourage our girls to retain."[5]

The work of feminist thinkers, then, is threefold: (1) to identify those specific traits of sexism that pervade the society within which we live and by which we are shaped; (2) to offer theories about the causes of sexism, in order (3) to formulate strategies for change. These attempts must be met with a critical response, so that we can see what is at stake in each formulation and what questions are posed to theology and theologians.

THE FEMINIST CRITIQUE

Ever since Betty Friedan debunked the "feminine mystique" in 1963,[6] feminist authors have been determined to lay bare the awesome gap between the rhetoric about women and the reality of attitudes embedded in societal structures. Marily Webb sums up her insight into how women are commonly viewed in her article "Woman as Secretary, Sexpot, Spender, Sow, Civic Actor, Sickie."[7] One of the best anthologies to date, *Woman in a Sexist Society*,[8] expands on this initial insight by offering articles which cut through the cult of beauty, the image of women in advertising, textbooks, and American fiction, the results of voluntarism, and the ways in which women are socialized into a sexist society through the psychotherapeutic relationship.[9]

Nothing has angered women more than the realization that the socialization processes have been based on a thoroughgoing double standard that has succeeded in keeping women from the centers of power, making of them perpetual outsiders.[10] Judith M. Bardwick and Elizabeth Douvan have carefully analyzed the patterns of child rearing that eventuate in preparing young boys for a life in the world while reinforcing in young girls those tendencies which are best suited for the private, interpersonal world.[11] Caroline Bird and Cynthia Fuchs Epstein

[5] June Sochen, ed., *The New Feminism in Twentieth-Century America* (Lexington, Mass., 1971) p. 50.

[6] Betty Friedan, *The Feminine Mystique* (New York, 1963).

[7] *Motive* 24, 6–7 (March-April 1969) 48–59.

[8] Ed. Vivian Gornick and Barbara K. Moran (New York, 1971).

[9] Una Stannard, "The Mask of Beauty," pp. 187–206; Lucy Komisar, "The Image of Woman in Advertising," pp. 304–17; Marjorie B. U'Ren, "The Image of Woman in Textbooks," pp. 318–28; Wendy Martin, "Seduced and Abandoned in the New World: The Image of Woman in American Fiction," pp. 329–46; Doris B. Gold, "Women and Voluntarism," pp. 533–54; Phyllis Chesler, "Patient and Patriarch: Women in the Psychotherapeutic Relationship," pp. 362–92.

[10] Vivian Gornick, "Woman as Outsider," in *Woman in Sexist Society*, pp. 126–44.

[11] Judith Bardwick and E. Douvan, "Ambivalence: The Socialization of Women," *ibid.*, pp. 225–41.

deepen this analysis in two works which concentrate on the debilitating effects of being born female and prepared for woman's place for anyone who aspires to a professional career and economic independence.[12]

The women's liberation movement, however, is interested in more than exposing the distorted images of women; it is committed to challenging and changing them. This cannot be done without facing the charge that it is "unnatural" for women to seek to be different. In one of the most widely quoted articles of the last eight years.[13] Naomi Weisstein has met the chief perpetrator of the "two natures" theory[14] on its own grounds. Weisstein argues that psychology has been a major force in limiting the potential of women, yet in truth it can tell us nothing about what women are really like, because (1) it has looked for inner traits when it should have taken into account the social context[15] and (2) it has operated out of theories that do not stand up when put to the test of empirical evidence. On this second point, she recounts an incident from her experience as a graduate student at Harvard.

. . .I was a member of a seminar which was asked to identify which of two piles of clinical tests, the TAT, had been written by males and which by females. Only four students out of twenty identified the piles correctly, and this was after one and a half months of intensively studying the differences between men and women. Since this result is below chance. . .we may conclude that there *is* finally a consistency here; students are judging knowledgeably within the context of psychological teaching about the differences between men and women; the teachings themselves are simply erroneous.[16]

It is not enough, however, to challenge the categories which keep women from developing those capacities which are encouraged and rewarded in men. An equally important aspect of the new feminism is the determination to call into question the very standards by which excellence and success in the public world are judged. An unusual and highly readable example of this is Nora Scott Kinzer's article on "Sexist Sociology."[17] It is basically a reflection on failure.[18] With the clarity of hindsight, the author confesses that her doctoral research on "Role

[12] Caroline Bird, *Born Female: The High Cost of Keeping Women Down* (New York, 1969); Cynthia F. Epstein, *Woman's Place* (Berkeley, 1971).

[13] Naomi Weisstein, "Psychology Constructs the Female," in *Woman in Sexist Society*, pp. 207–24.

[14] Weisstein is concerned chiefly with Erikson, Bettelheim, and Freud.

[15] See esp. R. Rosenthal and L. Jacobson, *Pygmalion in the Classroom: Teacher Expectation and Pupil's Intellectual Development* (New York, 1968).

[16] Weisstein, *art. cit.*, p. 185.

[17] *Center Magazine* 7, 3 (May-June 1974) 48–59. On the same theme, see Betty Richardson, *Sexism in Higher Education* (New York, 1974).

[18] It is interesting to note that when Kinzer outlined the paper to a male colleague, he cautioned her not to make such an admission.

Conflict of Professional Women in Buenos Aires" was more an imposition of North American role-theory on Latin American experience than an attempt to study the culture itself. She now sees that her acceptance of the ideals of objectivity and value-free research blinded her to reality because it prevented the operation of sympathy for the other. Kinzer questions the hegemony of these ideals:

. . .women social scientists seem doomed to follow the same false gods. Why must we make the same mistakes and do the same dreary research in the same pedantic way?. . .Caring, loving, being sympathetic to another person's feeling and respecting another nation's culture are eminently worth-while traits. If these are "feminine" traits, then the feminine eye is a humane perspective.[19]

Beverly Wildung Harrison has written a very important piece which touches the same theme. Arguing that the new consciousness of women is a valuable sociopolitical resource, Harrison gives clear expression to the tension experienced by contemporary feminists: that they must "stand and fight the hokum of the ideology of pedestalism, with its double-standard" in a public world which is alien to the values that women hold dear. The tragedy, she maintains, is that these values have lost their relevance to the public world, and she calls upon women to "translate their meaning in a direction which overcomes their privatism and personalistic overtones—in short, in a way which gives rise to community."[20]

Increasingly, then, women want more out of life than to be programed for one particular role; but some also want to be true to an ancient feminine skill: listening to experience, particularly their own. Elizabeth Janeway has noted that "for the first time in history, perhaps, it is women's experience which is changing faster and more radically than that of men. In itself, that bears witness to the profundity of the changes and it might alert men to the value of taking a look at them."[21] Jane Howard's A Different Woman[22] is an excellent place to begin. After the death of her mother, with whom she had never talked about the experience of being a woman, Howard decided to tour the country interviewing women from as many walks of life as possible. This is a work which transcribes living voices—a mountain artisan of West Virginia, a fisherwoman of the west coast, women in communes, women in the deep

[19] Kinzer, art. cit., p. 59. See also Jessie Bernard, "My Four Revolutions: An Autobiographical History of the ASA," in Huber, op. cit., pp. 11-29.

[20] Harrison, art. cit. This drive toward community is also noted in Bernard's discussion of the "agentic" and "communal" modes of sociological and psychological research; cf. art. cit., pp. 22-23.

[21] Elizabeth Janeway, "The Weak Are the Second Sex," Atlantic, December 1973, p. 104.

[22] New York, 1973.

South—and does much to counter a monolithic approach to feminine experience.[23]

A significant effect of the rising consciousness is that women are beginning to write about sex. In *Free and Female: The Sex Life of the Contemporary Female*[24] Barbara Seaman rejects the notion that women are less capable of enjoying sex and less interested in it than men. Instead, she argues, it is the female who has been endowed by nature with the greater capacity, and civilization has had to devise ways to rein her in for the good of the family and ultimately of the race.

The research done by Masters and Johnson has sparked a debate among women writers about Freudian sexual theories. In a widely reprinted article, Anne Koedt maintains that the definition of frigidity as the inability to attain a vaginal orgasm has been very destructive. Women who are perfectly healthy are thus taught that they are not, so that, in addition to being sexually deprived, they are told to blame themselves.[25]

It is impossible to report adequately on the growing body of literature about the sexist character of society in such a short survey. What we have given is but an indication of important areas of concern. Before leaving this topic, however, it should be noted that there is another way to try to subvert the sexism which permeates contemporary culture: in addition to argument, documentation, and persuasion, there is humor. No one has surpassed Dorothy Sayers' exercise in role reversal, originally written in 1947 but reprinted in recent years to the delight of feminists everywhere:

Probably no man has ever troubled to imagine how strange his life would appear to himself if it were unrelentingly assessed in terms of his maleness. . . . If he were vexed by continual advice how to add a rough male touch to his typing, how to be learned without losing his masculine appeal, how to combine chemical research with seduction, how to play bridge without incurring the suspicion of impotence. . . . If, after a few centuries of this kind of treatment, the male was a little self-conscious, a little on the defensive, and a little bewildered about what was required of him, I should not blame him. . . . It would be more surprising if he retained any rag of sanity and self-respect.[26]

[23] See also *Woman an Issue*, ed. Lee R. Edwards, Mary Heath, and Lisa Baskin (Boston, 1972), and *Growing Up Female in America: Ten Lives*, ed. Eve Merriam (New York, 1971).

[24] New York, 1972. See also Mary Jane Sherfey, *The Nature and Evolution of Female Sexuality* (New York, 1972).

[25] Anne Koedt, "The Myth of the Vaginal Orgasm," in *Radical Feminism*, ed. Anne Koedt, Ellen Levine, and Anita Rapone (New York, 1973) pp. 198–207. Germaine Greer differs from Koedt in *The Female Eunuch* (New York, 1970) pp. 304–5. See also Anselma dell'Olio, "The Sexual Revolution Wasn't Our War," *Ms.* Spring 1972, pp. 104–10; Susan Lydon, "The Politics of Orgasm," in *Sisterhood is Powerful*, ed. Robin Morgan (New York, 1970) pp. 197–205; Boston Women's Health Book Collective, *Our Bodies, Our Selves* (New York, 1971).

[26] Dorothy Sayers, *Are Women Human?* (Grand Rapids, 1971) pp. 39–42.

THREE FACES OF FEMINISM

The logic of the human imagination is such that one cannot come to such an awareness of the many ways in which women have been.sold short, kept down, convinced of their inferiority without seeking the cause of such a state of affairs. Since men are the ones who seem to be "on top," it should not be surprising that a great deal of feminist venom has been directed at men.[27] *The Redstockings Manifesto* of 1969 clearly identified the agents of oppression. Male supremacy is seen as the oldest, most basic form of domination, with all other forms of exploitation as extensions of it. *"All men* receive economic, sexual, and psychological benefits from male supremacy. *All men* have oppressed women."[28] Not all feminists of this persuasion conclude with Robin Morgan that the solution is to "kill your fathers, not your mothers,"[29] but a violent rhetoric is very much part of the tactics adopted by these authors. At a minimum, they have in common the determination to change men, being convinced that none of the blame for the current situation can be put on women themselves. For some radical feminists, this leads to a call for separatism, an exhortation that women refuse to sleep with the oppressor—or share his life in other ways. Lesbianism and celibacy, then, are seen by this group as political tactics.[30]

An interesting and very different version of the "men are to blame" face of feminism is proposed by Elaine Morgan in her book *The Descent of Woman.* She postulates that all the hostility between women and men can be traced back to that point in the evolutionary process when copulation changed from the dorsal position to the ventral. "For the first time in history," Morgan says, "the sex act had been accomplished by force in an atmosphere of hostility and fear and violence. The first tenuous mental connections had begun to be laid down between sex and ruthlessness on one side, and sex and suffering on the other." In Morgan's estimation, then, this was the event that led down the road to the sex war, to sadomasochism, and to the whole "contemporary snarl-up" of prostitu-

[27] See Susi Kaplow, "Getting Angry," and Pamela Kearon, "Man-Hating," in *Radical Feminism*, pp. 36–41 and 78–80.

[28] "The Redstockings Manifesto," in *Masculine/Feminine*, ed. Betty Roszak and Theodore Roszak (New York, 1969) p. 273. See also Valerie Solanas, "The SCUM Manifesto" *Masculine/Feminine*, pp. 262–68.

[29] Robin Morgan, "Goodbye to All That," *ibid.*, p. 245.

[30] See Judith Brown, "Towards a Female Liberation Movement," in *Voices from Women's Liberation*, ed. Leslie B. Tanner (New York, 1970) p. 363; Radicalesbians, "The Woman Identified Woman," in *Radical Feminism*, pp. 240–45; Anne Koedt, "Lesbianism and Feminism," *ibid.*, pp. 246–58; Sidney Abbott and Barbara Love, "Is Women's Liberation a Lesbian Plot?" in *Woman in Sexist Society*, pp. 601–21; Simone de Beauvoir's discussion of lesbianism as a response to the pressures of a male-dominated society in *The Second Sex*, pp. 379–99.

tion, prudery, Casanova, white slavery, women's liberation, *Playboy* magazine, *crimes passionels*, censorship, strip clubs, alimony, pornography, and a "dozen different brands of mania."[31] It is difficult to tell how seriously she intends her proposal to be taken, but, as women are beginning to learn, mythical thinking is a very powerful force in overcoming myths.[32]

A second approach is to place the blame for women's sense of inferiority and powerlessness on women themselves. Though by most standards hardly a feminist, Midge Decter does want women to grow up. In her important work *The New Chastity and Other Arguments against Women's Liberation*, Decter levels a stinging critique of the movement and of women—a critique which deserves serious attention. Decter examines the four areas of work (in the home and outside it), sex, marriage, and child-rearing from a single point of view. It is not opportunity for fulfilment that is lacking to American women, she argues; it is the willingness to accept responsibility for the individual decisions which rapid social change has forced on her. No longer can women depend on society's expectations to tell her what role in life to play, when to go to bed with a man, whether or not to take the risk of personal commitment to another, whether or not to have children and how to raise those that come. No single quotation can capture the complexity of this book's response to the women's movement, but a portion from the last chapter may give an indication of Decter's force as a writer and thinker:

. . .finally, for women to announce that their very womanliness results only from a bad and meretricious culture is the expression of a deep hatred for themselves. Such an expression of self-hatred is, indeed, exactly the primary emotion that informs Women's Liberation's diatribes against the impositions of motherhood. Neither society nor the current organization of the family but the womb itself—that "infirmity in the abdomen"—is ultimately the object of this movement's will to correct, to alter, to extirpate. There is no more radical nor desperately nihilistic statement to issue forth from the lips of humans than that there are no necessary differences between the sexes. For such differences do in themselves constitute the most fundamental principle of the continuation of life on earth.[33]

[31] Elaine Morgan, *The Descent of Woman* (New York, 1972).

[32] See Elizabeth Janeway, *Man's World, Woman's Place* (New York, 1971), for a detailed analysis of the way in which myths function in society.

[33] Midge Decter, *The New Chastity and Other Arguments against Women's Liberation* (New York, 1972) p. 180. For a much harsher (and less responsible) indictment of women, see Esther Vilar, *The Manipulated Man* (New York, 1972). For two responses by men, see Andy Hawley, "A Man's View," *Motive*, March-April 1969, pp. 145–50, and Warren Farrell, *The Liberated Man* (New York, 1974).

It must be noted, however, that Decter's views are frankly individualistic. Any woman can make her way if she will just shape up to the demands of the adult world. But Decter herself sees no need to call these demands into question. Despite vast differences in style and popular image, there is a strange similarity between Midge Decter and her nemesis, Germaine Greer. Greer's major work, *The Female Eunuch*,[34] is an exposé of the various ways in which women have been deprived of the rich possibilities of their bodily experiences (thus the title). More than any other writer to date, she has explored the particularities of women's experience, and has done so in a very personal way. Yet, for Greer too, everything comes down in the end to "a failure of nerves." Women, in her estimation, have not dared to win for themselves the spurs of freedom (primarily sexual freedom) because they are afraid. She, no less than Decter, fails to question the value of that liberty which men, it seems, have enjoyed.

The third face of feminism turns a critical eye toward the kind of society we have created. In one of the most balanced and objective works to date,[35] Elizabeth Janeway searches out the mythological roots of the ancient saying "It's a man's world—woman's place is in the home," in order to show the effects of this division on the structure of society. Myths, Janeway says, are psychic truths expressed symbolically. They are bound up with emotion, desires, wishes; and they try, by means of a description, to bring about what they declare to exist. Fundamental to the age-old division of the world are two myths about women: the myth of female weakness and the myth of female power. The first, which is older (and connected psychically to the shadow of the all-powerful mother), holds the second at bay. If we realize that myths help us to maintain order in the world, we will understand that the pressure on women to stay in their own sphere is based on a deep fear that failure to do so will overthrow the tenuous world order we have succeeded in establishing.

The social role that the society assigns to women, Janeway demonstrates, grows out of the twofold myth about women. Yet the idea that, for one sex, there is *a* role, *a* place—predetermined and fixed—puts women at odds with the whole long trend of Western civilization toward individual freedom and individual responsibility. This is especially critical for American women. Women's traditional role in itself is opposed to a deeply significant aspect of their culture and involves them

[34] Greer, *op. cit.* For very interesting reviews of the work from the point of view of radical feminists, see Arlyn Diamond, "Elizabeth Janeway and Germaine Greer," in *Woman an Issue*, pp. 275–79, and Claudia Dreifus, "The Selling of a Feminist," in *Radical Feminism*, pp. 358–67.

[35] *Man's World, Woman's Place* (n. 32 above).

in "the kind of conflict with their surroundings that no decision and no action open to them can be trusted to resolve."[36]

In a series of chapters, Janeway argues that it is isolation from the ideals of the society in which she lives, from the objective standard by which to measure herself and her actions, that has produced the being which we call "feminine." The drastic changes in what women now want to do are based on a profound longing to be different kinds of persons.

Women want to get out of a place that has become isolated from the mainstream of life and too narrow for them to use their abilities—that's very clear. . . . It seems to me quite remarkably hopeful; for in a time of disruption and uncertainty, women are refusing to sit passively by in their old protected place. Man's world is in trouble, and in spite of this, women are hell-bent to get out into it and go to work on its problems! One can, of course, see this as simply silly, as a badly timed and slightly hysterical decision to join the rat race. Or one can see it, more encouragingly, as a hardheaded refusal to put up any longer with vicarious living, a determination to find out what's going on out in the world even if the experience is not all rewarding.[37]

Shulamith Firestone, leading spokeswoman of the radical feminists, thinks the task cuts more deeply into the societal web than anything Janeway has envisioned. Not only must women question the kind of society we have created; they must challenge the created order that has been given to us: "Feminists have to question, not just all of *Western* culture, but the organization of culture itself, and further, even the very organization of nature."[38] Taking her cue from Simone de Beauvoir and her analysis of woman's status as "Other," Firestone argues that the deepest division in society is the distinction between the sexes and that all class distinction is based on that primal reality. There can be no good life for all, she maintains, until the fundamental biological inequality between men and women has been overcome. Thus she proposes that all the power of technology be used to offset the limitations imposed on woman by her body. This basic demand for artificial reproduction will result in the liberation of childhood, the destruction of the nuclear family, and economic independence and self-determination for all. If Janeway's vision is of one world where women and men co-operate in building the future, Firestone envisions a future in which there will be no women or men—or at least, in which "genital differences between human beings would no longer matter culturally."[39]

Although not all feminists in this last category go as far as Firestone, they are united in the effort to change the structures of society which oppress everyone, so that women as well as men may have more options

[36] *Ibid.*, p. 99.   [38] Firestone, *op. cit.*, p. 2.
[37] *Ibid.*, p. 301.   [39] *Ibid.*, p. 11.

open to them in the future. Women have begun to dream that things might be different. Alice Rossi has written one version of such a dream[40] and the fact that it has been included in so many recent anthologies is a tribute to the fact that it has touched the imaginations of many.

The imagination, powerful as it is, breaks no real bonds. If changes are to be effected, someone must design social policies that will embody the vision of enlarged opportunity for all. Constantina Safilios-Rothschild has written the most comprehensive work on the strategies for such social change.[41] There she offers specific proposals on how to liberate women, men, marriage, the institution of the family and family life, and tactics to free society itself from the sexism inherent in language, counseling, law, politics, and religion.

THREE VISIONS OF HUMANITY

Out of this cacophony of voices there emerge three basic ways of understanding the division of humanity into female and male. The first and more traditional position sees a polarity in which each sex embodies different possibilities of human being—possibilities which are denied the other.[42] The difficulties with this approach cannot be overlooked. (1) It entails an extrapolation of meanings from the male and female bodies (activity-passivity, reason-intuition, emotion-will, etc.) which runs counter to experience· and desire, especially the desires of women themselves.[43] (2) It limits the scope of human activity available to each of the sexes severely. (3) It involves an acceptance in some measure of the "anatomy is destiny" theory and results in a denial or diminishment of the specifically human capacity to exercise control over nature—even

[40] Alice S. Rossi, "Equality between the Sexes: An Immodest Proposal," in *The Woman in America*, ed. Robert Jay Lifton (Boston, 1967) pp. 98–143. It is increasingly clear that we need to pay more attention to the whole area of the imagination. For an excellent study of the way in which the female imagination has dealt with social problems, see Patricia Meyer Spacks, *The Female Imagination* (New York, 1975); Diana Trilling, "The Image of Women in Contemporary Literature," in *The Woman in America*, pp. 52–71. For examples of imaginative works by women with a new consciousness, see *Psyche*, ed. Barbara Segnitz and Carol Rainey (New York, 1973); *Rising Tides*, ed. Laura Chester and Sharon Barbra (New York, 1973); Barbara A. Wasserman, ed., *The Bold New Women* (Greenwich, Conn., 1970).

[41] Constantina Safilios-Rothschild, *Women and Social Policy* (Englewood Cliffs, N.J., 1974).

[42] The classic work is Gertrude von le Fort, *The Eternal Woman*, tr. Maria Cecilia Buehrle (Milwaukee, 1962). See also Karl Stern, *The Flight From Woman* (New York, 1965); Marie Robinson, *The Power of Sexual Surrender* (New York, 1962); Alan Watts, *Nature, Man and Woman* (New York, 1970).

[43] Buytendijk, *op. cit.*, attempts such an intepretation of meaning. I have been told that when his wife finally read the book she said: "So long a time we have lived together and you know so little about women!"

human nature—with a view to increasing the free exercise of judgment and decision. (4) It ignores the effects of cultural conditioning and social expectation on human behavior. (5) Neither sex can embody the fulness of humanity, nor can a person of one sex serve as a model for the other. The emphasis of this first position falls on difference and complementarity.

Though this way of understanding humanity has been seriously questioned by feminists (de Beauvoir, Rossi, Janeway, Firestone), there seems to be a curious rebirth of it in the insistence of some contemporary feminists that there is a female culture, long ignored or positively suppressed which must be rescued (Fourth World Manifesto), in the move toward separatism (Radical Feminists), and in the call for "sisterhood" and the proliferation of consciousness-raising sessions designed to heighten awareness of the specifically female experience.[44]

A second position sees the goal of human life as androgynous existence (Rossi, Janeway, Sayers, de Beauvoir, Safilios-Rothschild). While these thinkers admit that there are sexual differences, they will maintain that such differences are "purely biological" and affect only the reproductive functions of human beings. Otherwise women and men should be free to adopt a style of being which comprises the best of traditional masculine and feminine values and roles. The more one approximates this in one's life, the more human one becomes. According to this view, life increasingly requires that individuals know how to take the initiative and to be receptive, to be aggressive and sensitive, to nurture and discipline, to be strong and gentle, etc. Thinkers who hold androgynous existence as the ideal tend to emphasize the similarities between women and men much more than the differences. Indeed, the image of human existence is the same for both sexes. This position is also not without difficulties. At a time when philosophers (particularly of the phenomenological tradition) are discovering and defending the importance of embodiment to human existence,[45] it is difficult to accept or understand the assertion that the male or female body has "purely biological significance." Moreover, some research indicates that quite the opposite is true.[46] A second problem is that such an ideal of androgyny runs the risk of reducing the differ-

[44] See Barbara Burris, "The Fourth World Manifesto," in *Radical Feminism*, pp. 322–57; *Sisterhood is Powerful*, ed. Robin Morgan (New York, 1970); "Consciousness Raising," in *Radical Feminism*, pp. 280–81.

[45] See Alphonse de Walhaens, "Phenomenology of Body," in *Readings in Existential Phenomenology*, ed. Nathaniel Lawrence and Daniel O'Connor (Englewood Cliffs, 1967), and *Existence et signification* (Louvain, 1958).

[46] See Tom Alexander, "There Are Sex Differences in the Mind, Too," *Fortune*, February, 1971, pp. 76–134. One should keep in mind the criticisms of Weisstein and others about scientific investigation of sex differences.

ences which contribute to the "spice of life."[47] "Vive la différence," says the Frenchman, and many think he has a point. Though present experience indicates that there is still a difference between a woman who has learned to take up into her way of being some of the qualities which are admirable in men and vice versa, the specter of genetic manipulation can make one chary of adopting one ideal, even if it be a middle ground.[48]

The final way to approach the question is to adopt a unisex goal. Theoretically, it would be possible to envision a world in which that sex were female, but the most dramatic presentation of the unisex vision (Firestone) seeks to free women from the tyranny of the female body. Thus the sex is, to all intents and purposes, male. This is the ultimate denial of the goodness of sexual differentiation and the supreme victory of the "male" way of being—yet it has been espoused by a radical feminist. If the androgynous view seems to alter the spice of life, the unisex one robs it of all flavor save one. Yet this approach is extremely important because of its implications. Does it not mean that we have reached a stage where "male" characteristics are so highly valued and rewarded that (some) women are seriously considering a psychological and physiological alteration of the self in order to have a chance at the good life? It is a frightening prospect; yet this offbeat note in the feminist symphony may just be the desperate move needed to awaken people of reason to the realization that one cannot remain marginal forever.[49]

In a variety of ways, then, the new feminism presents challenges to any theological anthropology. What is the vision of the good life in the Christian revelation? Is it the same for men and women? Is it a sin to prefer one way of being in the world over another? If so, how does the salvation that Christians believe to have been begun in Christ Jesus touch concretely the age-old dominance of the male perspective? What does it offer—NOW—to women who feel defined out of the divine-human experience? Finally, what role does human desire play in the apprehension of God's will for us?

Loyola College, Baltimore   MARY AQUIN O'NEILL, R.S.M.

---

[47] See Simone de Beauvoir's rejection of such criticism in *The Second Sex*, p. 686.

[48] "Indeed, innate differences need not stand in the way even of the most homogenized androgyny that some radical feminists call for. If that were what society really wanted, it might one day be possible to use hormone pills to make males and females think and behave very much alike" (Alexander, *art. cit.*, p. 134).

[49] See Phyllis Chesler, *Women and Madness* (New York, 1972), for a description of the many ways in which women have protested this feeling of being marginal in the world.

IX

WOMEN AND RELIGION: A SURVEY OF SIGNIFICANT LITERATURE, 1965-1974[1]

In the past, THEOLOGICAL STUDIES articles surveying one sort or another of theological literature have sometimes included a disclaimer to the effect that the piece, for various reasons, cannot do justice to the immense body of recent items in print on the topic. The problem in the present case is staggering. Not only are bibliographies on women and religion expanding with great rapidity, but the time span from which to select examples is significantly larger than that ordinarily inspected by *TS* surveys. In the light of these limitations, what I shall endeavor to supply amounts to a rough guide to a vast and growing territory. Many books and articles will be omitted for lack of space or because they escaped my attention, but what will be mentioned is deemed of significance either because it provides a glimpse into how the women's movement is affecting religious institutions or because it deals with the specifically theological issues raised by the liberation experience.

The March 1972 issue of *TS* contains a useful discussion of literature on women's liberation, approached under the aspects of the oppression of women, its causes, and some proposed solutions. In that article Richard A. McCormick, S.J., rightly underscores the moral dimension of the issues raised by feminism, observing that the Church has contributed to the oppression of women by its theology and practice, and agreeing with Daniel Maguire that women's liberation is of prime importance for contemporary ethics because it is inherently concerned with the central question "What does human mean?" Without repeating McCormick's work, I will focus on four sorts of literature on women and religion: (1) general analyses of the current situation; (2) historical analyses; (3) works on selected issues: church law, liturgy, ministry, ordination, and models for Christian life; (4) constructive efforts and radical challenges.

GENERAL ANALYSES OF THE CURRENT SITUATION

The time span covered by this survey is framed at one end by the present, at the other by the period when Vatican II was drawing to a close. During this decade there has been a development of thinking with regard to women and religion, and to some extent an alteration in church practice concerning women. In view of this, analyses of the situation "current" at any point in the decade are likely to vary from those

---

[1] Where possible, relevant 1975 publications have been mentioned also. Bibliographic material on women and religion is included in many of the volumes cited in this survey. In addition, cf. *Genesis III* for Nov.–Dec. 1972; *Origins* for Feb. 24, 1972 and May 18, 1972; *Liturgy* for Dec. 1973, Nov. 1974, and May 1975.

"current" a bit earlier or later, and for this reason it is instructive to compare some of the earlier works with the more recent.

The conciliar documents themselves barely touch on the issue of women's equality. Indeed, the index to the Abbott edition[2] lists only five references under "women," four of which refer to the Pastoral Constitution on the Church in the Modern World (*Gaudium et spes*), and the other to the Decree on the Apostolate of the Laity (*Apostolicam actuositatem*). *Gaudium et spes* contains a strong passage against discrimination that has been cited often in more recent articles: "With respect to the fundamental rights of the person, every type of discrimination, whether social or cultural, whether based on sex, race, color, social condition, language, or religion, is to be overcome and eradicated as contrary to God's intent" (no. 29). This principle, however, is undercut by subsequent emphasis on the preservation of the "domestic role of women" (no. 52) and by the qualification "in accordance with their own nature," attached to the passage recommending that women assume "their full proper role" in cultural life (no. 60). Underlying this qualification seems to be the assumption that woman's nature is well defined and limiting. Finally, in a passage added during the reworking of *Apostolicam actuositatem* the Council fathers observe that "since in our times women have an ever more active share in the whole life of society, it is very important that they participate more widely in the various fields of the Church's apostolate" (no. 9).

Although the Council fathers had thus affirmed the equality of women and indicated some approval of the women's movement for social and legal equality, the Council on the whole does not appear to have dealt in a substantive way with the issues of women's liberation. In fact, the special closing message of the fathers to women indicates that past attitudes were still very much in the ascendancy. Even the existence of this message is telling, since there is no similar document addressed simply "to men," although there are messages addressed to "rulers," "men of thought and science," "artists," and "workers." This very arrangement of categories carries the implication that women are thought of primarily in sexual roles, while men are regarded in terms of diversified vocational contributions. Indeed, this is made clear in the opening sentence of the message to women: "And now it is to you that we address ourselves, women of all states—girls, wives, mothers, and widows, to you also, consecrated virgins and women living alone—you constitute half of the immense human family."[3] The message goes on to mention that "the vocation of woman" is in the present era "being

[2] Walter M. Abbott, S.J., ed., *The Documents of Vatican II* (New York, 1966). Subsequent references to conciliar documents are from this edition.

[3] *Ibid.*, pp. 732–33.

achieved in its fulness," a statement whose tone of assurance that the
Church already knows what this vocation is stands in marked contrast to
what is said in the message to workers ("very loved sons"): "The Church
is ever seeking to understand you better."[4]

For some, however, the time immediately following the Council was
regarded as a suitable one in which to raise the issues that follow from
accepting the principle of equality. A Zurich attorney, Gertrud Heinzelmann, collected statements of women addressed to Council fathers and
published them in 1965 under the title *Wir schweigen nicht länger!*,[5] and
in January of that year *Commonweal* ran her article "The Priesthood and
Women," along with Mary Daly's examination of Christian antifeminism, "A Built-in Bias."[6] The *Commonweal* piece was Daly's first article
on religion and sexism, and it was as a result of this article that she was
asked to write the book that eventually became *The Church and the
Second Sex*.[7] Another significant postconciliar book is Sally Cunneen's
Sex: Female; Religion: Catholic.[8] This 1968 volume contains the results
of a survey conducted by *Cross Currents* on attitudes of and toward

---

[4] *Ibid.*, pp. 735-36. Despite the fact that certain conciliar statements encourage
egalitarianism, subsequent official statements have not been consistent with the declaration in *Gaudium et spes* that discrimination based on sex is "to be overcome and eradicated
as contrary to God's intent." This is especially the case with regard to the 1972 *Motu
proprio* "On Laying down Certain Norms regarding the Sacred Order of the Diaconate"
(*Crux Special*, Sept. 29, 1972), which evinces a problematic selectivity in its affirmation of
tradition, at once dispensing with the traditional minor orders but reserving installation as
lector or acolyte to men "in accordance with the venerable tradition of the Church" (p. 1).
Several representatives to the 1971 Synod of Bishops addressed the issue of equal
participation by women in the ministerial life of the Church, but the Synod document
"Justice in the World" (Washington, D.C., 1972) states ambiguously that "women should
have their own share of responsibility and participation in the community life of society
and likewise of the Church" (p. 44). The international commission established after the
1971 Synod to study women in Church and society has not yet published any reports.
Finally, it must be observed that the statement issuing from the 1974 Synod on
evangelization seems weaker on this issue than the conciliar statements. Although
acknowledging the "intimate connection between human liberation and evangelization,"
the statement from the Synod is framed, for the most part, in sexually exclusive language,
and the bishops' condemnation of "the denial or abridgement of rights because of race"
stops short of any mention of discrimination on the basis of sex.

[5] Zurich, 1965. Heinzelmann has also edited a collection of interventions regarding
women by the Council fathers, *Die getrennten Schwestern: Frauen nach dem Konzil*
(Zurich, 1967). As far as the position of women is concerned, she claims in an introductory
passage that "'aggiornamento' has scarcely begun" (p. 9).

[6] *Commonweal* 81 (1965) 504-8 and 508-11.

[7] First published in 1968, this book has been reissued (with an extensive and critical
"new feminist postchristian introduction" by the author) by Harper and Row this year. It
will be considered in the final section of this essay, along with Daly's other works on the
subject.

[8] London, 1968.

American Catholic women. It reveals considerable diversity of opinion among the women, who were surveyed on such subjects as the Council, confession, education, sexuality, and church roles. In general, respondents favored women lectors and "deaconesses," but opposed the idea of women priests. Although the sample was not broadly representative and the results are dated, Cunneen's survey remains important; for it links an emerging feminism with the postconciliar climate of renewal, and thus presages the developments in Catholic feminism since the late 1960's.[9]

The title of Heinzelmann's second book, *Die getrennten Schwestern*, evokes associations with the ecumenical movement to which the Council gave considerable impetus. Indeed, it can be said in general that the ecumenical movement and the women's movement in the Church have been mutually influential. The spirit of ecumenism has encouraged Catholic women to notice similarities between their ecclesiastical situation and those of other denominations, and the sense of sharing a secondary status in the life and ministry of the religious community has contributed to a bonding process among Catholic, Protestant, and Jewish[10] feminists. Although the legal status of women varies from one denomination to another, women of all faiths have found they share similar concerns over issues such as committee representation, church employment,[11] theological education,[12] religious language, liturgical

---

[9] In *Today's Catholic Woman* (Notre Dame, 1971) Dolores Curran summarizes hundreds of interviews with the conclusion that "unless we change the role of today's Catholic woman and change it rapidly we may not have tomorrow's Catholic woman" (p. 10).

[10] The present survey focuses particularly on the Christian tradition. Significant recent articles on women and Judaism include Judith Hauptman, "Images of Women in the Talmud," *Religion and Sexism: Images of Woman in the Jewish and Christian Tradition*, ed. Rosemary Radford Ruether (New York, 1974) pp. 184–212; Paul E. Hyman, "The Other Half: Women in the Jewish Tradition," *Conservative Judaism* 26 (1972) 14–21; Barbara Krasner, "Endpoint: Where Torah and Family Touch," *Liturgy* 18 (Dec. 1973) 21–24. Especially useful is the extensively documented study by Gail B. Schulman, "View from the Back of the Synagogue: Women in Judaism." *Sexist Religion and Women in the Church*, ed. Alice L. Hageman (New York, 1974) pp. 143–66.

[11] Cf. Earl D. C. Brewer, "A Study of Employment of Women in Professional or Executive Positions in the Churches at a National Level," *Women's Liberation and the Church*, ed. Sarah Bentley Doely (New York, 1970) pp. 115–18. In reporting on a study of seventeen denominations, Brewer, Director of the Department of Research of the National Council of Churches, declares that "in summary, these data reflect adherence to the rhetoric of equality of opportunity for women on the one hand, and the factual conditions of considerable discrimination on the other" (p. 118).

[12] A report of the May 15–17, 1970 meeting of the National Conference on the Role of Women in Theological Education is also included in the Doely anthology, pp. 135–45. In addition, *Theological Education* has published two special issues: "Women in Theological Education: Past, Present, and Future" (Summer 1972) and "Women in Theological Education: An Issue Reexamined" (Winter 1975).

involvement, and educational patterns.[13] More than one writer has described the situation of women in churches where equality is legally recognized as analogous to that of blacks in this country. Sexism, they argue, is at least as pervasive as racism, which has not been overcome by a constitutional amendment or Supreme Court decision, the importance and necessity of these measures notwithstanding. "Like our black brethren," writes Norma Ramsey Jones, "we women ministers are rapidly discovering that the removal of legal barriers to the fullest expression of humanity and service is only the beginning of the fight. The years ahead will show whether we will be able to break out of the social and cultural straightjacket in which we have been bound up."[14]

Ecumenical solidarity on issues of women and religion is evident in the reports of certain formal interfaith conferences. For example, the report of the final meeting of the Worship and Mission section of the Roman Catholic/Presbyterian-Reformed Consultation (Richmond, October 1971) recommends the opening of seminaries to women, the ordination of qualified women, and the full and equal participation of women at all levels of ecclesiastical decision-making.[15] An ongoing ecumenical solidarity is demonstrated by the existence of such publications as *Genesis III*, newsletter of the Philadelphia Task Force on Women in Religion,[16] as well as by the fact that many books on the topic of women and religion expand their focus beyond the immediate context of the author's denomination.[17]

The moral component present in so many of the recent descriptive works on women and religion has been analyzed by Beverly Wildung Harrison in "Sexism and the Contemporary Church: When Evasion Becomes Complicity."[18] According to Harrison, sexism involves "an ethos and a value structure, and the formal and informal social patterns which support that ethos and value structure in our social world."[19] It is her claim that what makes this ethos and value structure wrong (and not simply a morally indifferent distinction of roles) is the "inequity of the human identity which that social differentiation between the sexes distributes."[20] Agreeing with Elizabeth Janeway's analysis of sexist

[13] Cf. Miriam Crist and Tilda Norberg, "Sex Role Stereotyping in the United Methodist Nursery Curriculum," Doely, pp. 119–24. *Momentum*, journal of the National Catholic Education Association, focuses on women and Catholic education in its Dec. 1972 issue.

[14] "Women in the Ministry," Doely, p. 69. Cf. Daniel H. Krichbaum, "Masculinity and Racism—Breaking out of the Illusion," *Christian Century*, Jan. 10, 1973.

[15] *Origins* 1 (1972) 793–98.

[16] P.O. Box 24003, Philadelphia, Pa. 19139.

[17] Cf. Margaret Sitler Ermath, *Adam's Fractured Rib* (Philadelphia, 1970), and Georgia Harkness, *Women in Church and Society* (Nashville, 1972).

[18] In Hageman, pp. 195–216.   [19] *Ibid.*, p. 196.   [20] *Ibid.*

structures in *Man's World, Woman's Place: A Study in Social Mythology*,[21] Harrison contends that the fact that the female is defined by a restricted "sphere" of activity within the larger world of the male society results in an "uneven distribution of identity." In other words, the development and sphere of activity of females is artificially circumscribed, whereas that of males extends to the limits of human possibilities. The sexist system thus functions to neutralize part of the human potential of women, and to the extent that this is the case, the system must be regarded as destructive and evil.

Among recent titles that indicate a perception of the problem similar to that of Janeway and Harrison are Elsie Thomas Culver's *Women in the World of Religion*[22] and Arlene Swidler's *Woman in a Man's Church*.[23] The subtitle of Swidler's book, "From Role to Person," and the title of her first chapter, "What's a Woman and Who Decides?" both point to the moral problem Harrison terms "inequity of identity distribution." Noting that the sexist culture has generally responded to the question "What's a woman?" by saying "Ask a man"—that is, consider the works of male theologians, psychologists, historians—Swidler observes that "men are extremely fortunate not to have all those books written about them," because the imposed definitions have "set limits and narrowed options."[24] Both Culver and Swidler are in agreement with the essence of Harrison's recommendation for remedying the oppressive situation, which involves not simply enlarging the boundary of woman's "sphere" within the "world" of man, but rather dissolving the boundary entirely.

To sum up the first section of this survey, it can be noted in general that literature analyzing the subject of women and religion has increased during the last decade,[25] and there is a greater frequency of books and articles by women, particularly by women with advanced theological degrees. With a number of good general surveys already in print, analysts have tended of late to concentrate in more depth on particular issues, and consequently the literature has grown more and more specialized. An ecumenical solidarity tends to characterize much of the literature, but there is also evidence of disagreement among feminists, though not about denominational concerns. At issue rather are such basic questions as whether, and to what extent, women should devote their energies to concerns involving traditional "patriarchal" religion. Most of the literature represents the position of those who value the religious tradition and seek in some measure to reform it, but an impor-

---

[21] New York, 1971.   [22] Garden City, N.Y., 1967.
[23] New York, 1972.   [24] *Ibid.*, p. 23.
[25] Cf. Marie Augusta Neal, S.N.D., "Women in Religion: A Sociological Perspective," scheduled for publication this year in *Sociological Inquiry*.

tant minority argues for a "separatist" or at least a "boundary" position for feminists vis-à-vis the established churches. Virtually all of the feminist literature on women and religion, however, is characterized by a tone of moral seriousness, even urgency. This sense of moral urgency has led many to search the tradition for clues to the causes of the oppression as well as for evidence that fragments of egalitarianism have been present from the beginnings of Christiantity.

HISTORICAL ANALYSES

Although nearly all the works mentioned in this survey touch in some way on Scripture or tradition, certain publications stand out as being particularly, though usually not exclusively, concerned with the historical aspects of the woman question. Under this general category of historical analyses it is possible to distinguish three principal types of literature: comprehensive surveys, works focusing on Scripture, and literature concerned with the history of Christianity after the apostolic age.

Comprehensive Surveys

Of works that attempt to convey a broad sweep of the picture the most comprehensive is Culver's *Women in the World of Religion*. In twenty chapters she discusses the tradition from pre-OT times through the present. To this survey she adds appendices on women in the major non-Christian religions, on religious careers, and on the "world picture" regarding ordination and representation in decision-making bodies in the various churches.

Although less comprehensive than Culver's work, George H. Tavard's *Woman in Christian Tradition*[26] is important for its close theological analyses of the historical periods treated. The first section ("The Old Tradition," which deals with OT times through Augustine) includes a particularly useful treatment of the ways the early Christians, and later the Greek and Latin Fathers, dealt with the issue of how the "new freedom in Christ" should be experienced in the relationship between men and women. Though somewhat irenic in tone, the section on the patristic age does not fail to discuss the tension evident in this literature between the spiritual appreciation of woman as redeemed Christian and the strong misogynism of so many of the Fathers. Tavard does not analyze medieval or early modern times, but rather focuses his second section ("The Recent Tradition") on nineteenth- and twentieth-century "models" and "reflections" in the Catholic, Orthodox, and Protestant traditions. It seems significant that this 1973 book shows him solidly in favor of admitting women "to all sacraments and to all positions of

[26] Notre Dame, 1973.

ministry and service," since "the freedom of the Christian, imparted to all in baptism, should remove all man-made barriers between human beings."[27] In an earlier essay, "Women in the Church: A Theological Problem?"[28] Tavard had minimized the ordination question (which he still regards as secondary to the anthropological question) in terms that seem to have skirted some of the concerns he deals with in the recent book.

A third notable comprehensive work is *What a Modern Catholic Believes about Women* by Albertus Magnus McGrath, O.P.[29] Less ambitious in scope than the Culver and Tavard volumes, McGrath's book provides a well-documented feminist analysis of sexism in the Catholic tradition, at the same time evincing the sort of ecumenical solidarity mentioned earlier in this survey. Of particular interest are her chapters relating the women's movement to sociocultural developments since the Enlightenment, especially the last chapter, "Women as the 'Nigger of the Church.'"

Biblical Studies

The works that focus primarily on Scripture include textual analyses, pieces dealing with hermeneutics, and attempts to relate new understandings of scriptural materials to "the person in the pew." A useful place to start the search for careful analyses of biblical materials in relation to the concerns of women's liberation is the anthology *Religion and Sexism: Images of Women in the Jewish and Christian Traditions*.[30] Phyllis Bird's "Images of Women in the Old Testament"[31] studies these images as they occur in legal writings, proverbs, historical writings, and creation accounts, and includes ample references for further study. Bernard P. Prusak's "Woman: Seductive Siren and Source of Sin?"[32] considers the pseudepigraphal materials and concludes that, although early religious writers had "created myths that flowed from and buttressed their prejudices," in the present era "it is no longer necessary for men to create theological reasons for excluding women from any active role in civil or religious society in order to preserve their own dominance and cope with their sexual drives."[33] A third helpful piece is Constance F. Parvey's examination of the attitudes of the early Church,

[27] *Ibid.*, p. 218.   [28] *Ecumenist* 4 (1965) 7–10.   [29] Chicago, 1972.

[30] Rosemary Radford Ruether, ed. (New York, 1974).

[31] *Ibid.*, pp. 41–88. Cf. also Phyllis Trible, "Depatriarchalizing in Biblical Interpretation," *Journal of the American Academy of Religion* 41 (1973) 31–34; J. S. Bailey, "Initiation and the Primal Woman in Gilgamesh and Genesis 2–3," *Journal of Biblical Literature* 89 (1970) 137–50; Martha M. Wilson, "Woman, Women, and the Bible," *Women and Religion: 1972*, ed. Judith Plaskow Goldenberg (Missoula, 1973) pp. 141–47.

[32] *Religion and Sexism*, pp. 89–116.

[33] *Ibid.*, pp. 106–7.

"The Theology and Leadership of Women in the New Testament."[34]
Parvey accounts for the religious egalitarianism of Gal 3:28 in terms of
the fact that the primitive community considered itself to be living at the
end of history and was in expectation of an imminent consummation of
the present order of reality. She implies that the societal applications of
this religious insight were not undertaken because believers expected the
present order to disappear soon. She then suggests that the fact that the
end did not come in the manner expected resulted in the prolongation of
a state of tension between "the theology of equivalence in Christ" on the
one hand and "the practice of women's subordination" on the other. In
its attempt to reconcile these factors the Church "maintained a
status-quo ethics on the social level through the subordination of women,
and it affirmed the vision of equivalence by projecting it as an other-
worldly reality."[35]

Here Parvey's analysis is particularly interesting when related to
Janeway's reading of the secular situation. If woman's essential sphere is
projected into "another world" beyond this temporal one, then the fact
that her this-worldly role is narrowly conceived (the situation Janeway
describes in *Man's World, Woman's Place*) appears to be less problematic than would be the case were there but "one world." At any rate,
this sort of reasoning appears to have been quite influential in Christian
thinking. As Parvey notes, the often confused and complex arguments
with which theologians have dealt with this tension between religious
equality and social subordination have tended to amount to a position
that men belong essentially to this world and are concerned with its
governance, while women "belong to the next world and act in the
Church only as hidden helpers and servants to men."[36] She concludes
that the subordination of women in Christianity is due not so much to
Paul as to the way subsequent generations of Christians have chosen to
interpret him.

Parvey's emphasis on the hermeneutical aspect of the problem is well
placed, and it suggests an affinity with the position presented earlier by
Krister Stendahl in an extremely important essay, *The Bible and the*

---

[34] *Ibid.*, pp. 117–49. Cf. also Robin Scroggs, "Paul and the Eschatological Woman,"
Journal of the American Academy of Religion 40 (1972) 283–303, and "Paul and the
Eschatological Woman: Revisited," *ibid.* 42 (1974) 532–37. This last issue also contains
Elaine H. Pagels' very useful essay "Paul and Women: A Response to Recent Discussion,"
pp. 538–49. Even more recent are William O. Walker, Jr., "1 Corinthians 11:2–16 and
Paul's Views regarding Women," *Journal of Biblical Literature* 94 (1975) 94–110, and A.
Feuillet, "La dignité et le rôle de la femme d'après quelques textes pauliniens: Comparai-
son avec l'Ancien Testament," *New Testament Studies* 21 (1975) 157–91. Feuillet
analyzes 1 Cor 11:7 and 14:33b–35, and Eph 5:22–23, and concludes that the attitudes of
Paul and Jesus toward women are complementary, not contradictory.

[35] *Religion and Sexism*, p. 146.   [36] *Ibid.*

Role of Women: A Case Study in Hermeneutics.[37] Undertaken in direct response to the debate over the ordination of women in the Church of Sweden, Stendahl's essay basically involves a three-stage exploration of the question "What is the significance of the NT view of the relationship between men and women for the contemporary Church?" He first identifies a present ecclesiastical issue (the ordination of women) as indicative of a deeper uncertainty: the nature of revelation and the meaning of Scripture. He then defines the essential "content" of revelation as a self-communication of God ("God and his mighty acts," he says, constitute the "center of revelation," a revelation which he describes as "anchored in the Christ event"), which he sees as something different from the anthropology that may derive from the human experience of revelation. "The understanding of man in the biblical view is valuable for our reading of the content of revelation, but it can hardly be the revelation itself."[38] The final and most fully developed stage of Stendahl's exploration involves a discussion of what results from the application of this distinction between revelation itself and the views ascendant in the community experiencing revelation.

Stendahl argues that it is an error automatically to apply the description, however accurate, of primitive Christianity as a norm for the Church in subsequent ages. "It is highly doubtful," he contends, that God wants us to play "First Century Semites."[39] He goes on to illustrate the principle that not even what was an "event" in the life of Jesus is necessarily normative for the Church, citing the example of Jesus' own consciousness (expressed in Mt 10:16) that his mission was limited to the house of Israel. This pattern has clearly not been regarded as binding "for all time," and this fact reinforces Stendahl's argument against automatically making NT descriptions normative for the Church. Stendahl nevertheless finds it important to understand the view of the relationship between men and women that obtained in the early Church; for such an understanding serves to illustrate the fundamental point that from the beginning of Christianity a tension has existed between the ideal (the "new" and "not yet" aspect of the Christian revelation) and its implementation in the community. Once one assumes that the religious ideals were not perfectly practiced in the early Church, there is no reason to insist that current practices replicate those of the primitive communities. This tension between the ideal and its implementation is illustrated in Stendahl's treatment of the "break-through" passage in Gal 3:28, which he sees as containing an unfolding agenda for the Church to

[37] Tr. Emilie Sander (Philadelphia, 1966). This edition is a revised and enlarged version of "Bibelsynen och Kvinnan," *Kvinnan-Samhället-Kyrkan* (Stockholm, 1958) pp. 138–67.
[38] Stendahl, p. 23.   [39] *Ibid.*, p. 34.

implement. He notes that just as the recognition of equality between Jew and Greek was not limited to an individualistic, *coram Deo* realm, but was actually applied in church practice, so too has it been necessary to carry the ideal of equality between slave and free, man and woman beyond the internal *coram Deo* dimension into the realm of ecclesiastical and social practice. The cogency of Stendahl's analysis has been demonstrated not only by the fact that the Swedish Church (despite its "ecumenical concern" over the possibility of losing its status as a "bridge" between Catholic and Protestant elements in Christendom) acted on these hermeneutical insights and began to ordain women, but also by reason of the fact that this article has been something of a "break-through" piece for persons in general concerned with the status of women in the Church.

Of works describing scriptural attitudes toward women with the nonspecialist in mind, Leonard Swidler's "Jesus Was a Feminist"[40] is especially noteworthy. Swidler's essay, which has been translated into at least a dozen languages, argues that the words and actions of Jesus in the Gospels give evidence that he "vigorously promoted the dignity of women in the midst of a very male-dominated society."[41] Other items designed to supply a general readership with scripturally-based discussions of feminist concerns include *All We're Meant to Be: A Biblical Approach to Women's Liberation* by Letha Scanzoni and Nancy Hardesty,[42] and *Women and Jesus* by Alicia Craig Faxon.[43]

Other Historical Studies

Works focusing on the situation of women in Christianity since the apostolic age differ not only according to the purposes of the authors, but also according to the extent to which they are informed by feminist questions.[44] Most supply some measure of documentation regarding the oppression of women within the tradition, but interpretations and emphases vary. Certain items mainly provide data about women that has not generally been emphasized in previous historical studies. For example, in *Women of the Church: Role and Renewal*[45] Mary Lawrence

[40] *Catholic World* 212 (1971) 177-83.   [41] *Ibid.*, p. 183.
[42] Waco, 1974.   [43] Philadelphia, 1973.

[44] Feminists have expressed their recognition of the masculine bias of most historical studies by attempting to supply "herstory." Examples of works that endeavor to bring the "hidden history" of women to light are Joan Morris, *The Lady was a Bishop* (Riverdale, N.J., 1973), and Roland Bainton, *Women of the Reformation in Germany and Italy* (Minneapolis, 1971) and *Women of the Reformation in France and England* (Minneapolis, 1973).

[45] New York, 1967. Cf. Roger Gryson, *Le ministère des femmes dans l'église ancienne* (Gembloux, 1972). An English translation of this study, prepared by Jean Laporte and Mary Hall, is scheduled for publication this year by St. John's University Press.

McKenna, S.C.M.M., offers a detailed study of the ancient orders of widows, deaconesses, and virgins. McKenna finds it paradoxical that the ecclesiastical status of women is lower today than it was ·in the "primitive" Church, although the status of women in society has risen. "What Christian women had then, and what is lacking today is the status of ecclesiastical *order*, and the attendant sense of having a definite place and function in the Church's official structure."[46]

Other works tend to emphasize theological analysis as well as reinterpretation of data. Of particular interest is Elinor L. McLaughlin's "The Christian Past: Does It Hold a Future for Women?" which combines useful methodological suggestions with historical illustrations of her thesis that within the dominant patriarchal tradition it is possible to recover "glimpses" of situations in the past where Christianity "fostered the being, experience, and authority of women."[47] McLaughlin contends that history should be both "responsible" and "usable," that is, it should deal with the past "on its own terms" and it should analyze the tradition in the light of "a new set of questions which arise out of commitments to wholeness for women and for all humanity."[48] The question at the base of McLaughlin's study is "whether in addition to the negative image of women and the male image of God, the tradition holds ideals or moments of realization of human wholeness which can call forth the *renovatio* in Christian history that has so often been a source of radical change, renewal, reformation."[49] She answers this question affirmatively, supporting her position with examples of spiritual leadership and egalitarianism from the biography of Christina of Markyate and from the writings of Julian of Norwich and St. Birgitta of Sweden. McLaughlin's approach is helpful and constructive, in this article as well as in her contribution to *Religion and Sexism*, "Equality of Souls, Inequality of Sexes: Women in Medieval Theology."[50] Other notable revisionist studies in this anthology include Rosemary Radford Ruether's "Misogynism and Virginal Feminism in the Fathers of the Church" and Jane Dempsey's "Women and the Continental Reformation."[51]

Finally, an aspect of history that is likely to receive greater attention as more and more revisionist analyses (particularly ones dealing with the modern period) become available is the resistance women have displayed over the centuries toward discriminatory religious structures. A recent example of this sort of focus is published in the 1973 proceedings of the working group on women and religion of the American Academy of

[46] McKenna, p. 147.
[47] *Anglican Theological Review* 57 (1975) 39.
[48] *Ibid.*, p. 38.   [49] *Ibid.*, p. 39.   [50] Pp. 213–66.
[51] *Ibid.*, pp. 150–83 and 292–318.

Religion[52] in the form of several essays on the nineteenth-century publication *The Woman's Bible*, a feminist commentary prepared by a committee led by Elizabeth Cady Stanton.

WORKS ON SELECTED ISSUES

The books and articles to be discussed below represent five issue areas that (*a*) tend to recur in the literature and (*b*) seem to be dependent upon theological advances in order for progress in liberation to occur. These include church law, liturgy, ministry, ordination, and models for Christian life.

Church Law

Although many recognize that the present code of canon law discriminates against women, literature on the specifically legal questions has not been abundant. The *Jurist* for Winter/Spring 1974 contains useful material on this subject. Of great importance is the address by Pope Paul VI on "Canonical Equity," in which he declares that "canon law is . . . not just a way of life and a series of pastoral regulations, but is also a school of justice, discretion, and charity in operation."[53] This principle of equity offers an ideal against which to measure the present code, a task undertaken by Lucy Vasquez in "The Position of Women according to the Code."[54] Vasquez' descriptive article concludes with the observation that the canons discussed "portray women as being less than full adults on a par with men. They are to be protected, separated, observed, supervised, and, at least on occasion, even mistrusted."[55] In the same issue Joan A. Range examines the history of canon law and finds precedent in Gratian for legislating on the basis of current theological understanding rather than in a spirit of blind adherence to tradition.[56] Range argues that essential to the reasoning behind laws prohibiting women from church office were Gratian's beliefs that woman is inferior and naturally subject to man, and that through woman sin entered the world. Pointing out that equality of the sexes is accepted by believers today and that the Church no longer blames Eve for original sin, she holds that there is no longer adequate theological reasoning to support

[52] Joan Arnold Romero, compiler, *Women and Religion: 1973 Proceedings* (Tallahassee, 1973) pp. 39–78. Stanton's work (with an introduction by Barbara Welter) has been reprinted as *The Original Feminist Attack on the Bible* (*The Woman's Bible*) (New York, 1974).

[53] Allocution, Feb. 8, 1973, to auditors and officials of the Sacred Roman Rota, *Jurist* 34 (1974) 2.

[54] *Ibid.*, pp. 128–42.   [55] *Ibid.*, p. 142.

[56] "Legal Exclusion of Women from Church Office," pp. 112-27. Cf. Ida Ramig, *Der Ausschluss der Frau vom priesterlichen Amt* (Cologne, 1973).

the discriminatory laws. The contemporary political factors involved in eliminating discrimination from church law are not discussed in these articles, and subsequent analysts would probably do well to link considerations related to removing sexual discrimination with broader questions about what sort of over-all revision is desirable. For example, the impetus for equal recognition of both sexes in church law might profitably be aligned with that favoring a pluralistic or regional approach to the question, since it seems more likely that certain reforms can be implemented sooner in some cultures than in others.[57] In "Canon Law and the Battle of the Sexes,"[58] Clara Henning depicts the current code as essentially a power tool designed to reinforce the dominant position of a male clerical caste, and expresses pessimism with regard to the forthcoming revision. "We are confronted with a system that will in every likelihood continue to write discriminatory new laws on the basis of discriminatory old laws."[59] Henning feels that only pressure from concerned women can result in the removal of discriminatory laws. Pressure is no doubt required, but it seems inadequate unless complemented by support of the principle of equity on the part of those preparing the revision.

Liturgy

In 1969 Paul Vanbergen observed in *Studia liturgica* that "every cultural mutation mediates new values, and these values must be integrated into the liturgy if the liturgy is not to run the risk of being completely out of touch."[60] Vanbergen's article does not deal directly with the profound cultural mutation involved in the women's movement, but he is aware that the crisis facing the churches is a "crisis of humanity" that calls for a "modern anthropology." Since 1970, however, a number of articles and at least two books on the relationship between worship and new understandings of woman have been published. Uniting this literature is a common insistence that the growing cultural recognition of woman's equality should be integrated into liturgical celebrations and a recurring cry for consistency between what the Church teaches about justice and equality and what it practices in liturgical life.

The Liturgical Conference, which has assumed considerable leadership in keeping the woman question before its members, devoted the October 1970 issue of *Liturgy* to articles related to the women's movement, of which Mary Catherine Bateson's "Where? Lydia's. On Liturgy and Its Need for Women," and Edward J. Foye's "The

---

[57] Cf. Martin J. McManus, "Canon Law: Justice by Variety," *America* 125 (1971) 257–59.

[58] *Religion and Sexism*, pp. 267–91.   [59] *Ibid.*, p. 286.

[60] "Liturgy in Crisis," *Studia liturgica* 6 (1969) 91.

Androgynous Church"[61] are especially important because they illustrate the tension between two main positions regarding woman's involvement in the Church. Bateson feels that worship should allow both men and women their "full expression" and "full contribution," and emphasizes a "complementarity" of roles between the sexes. "If the presidency of the eucharist is to remain a male prerogative, we need to search out ways of counterpointing this role,"[62] she observes, suggesting that if a man consecrates, perhaps a woman should convene the worshiping community and pronounce the final blessing. Foye, on the other hand, stresses the theological principle that the image of God is both male and female, and recommends the ideal of an "androgynous" worshiping community. He opposes prescribed sex-role definitions for worship because in the past these have entailed the "rejection of the feminine," which he sees as detrimental to both men and women: "If we reduce the feminine to silence, we are rejecting ourselves and defining in advance the graces God may give and to whom he may give them."[63] Both Bateson and Foye note that in many countries the fact that the sanctuary has been men's territory has meant that the nave has largely contained women, children, and the elderly. Whereas Bateson advocates remedying this by developing a "contrapuntal" role for women, Foye is unwilling to assume that a liturgical role should be assigned simply on the basis of sex, and maintains that fidelity to the Spirit in our times requires the ordination of women.

In a similar vein, Janet Walton, S.N.J.M., states in "Women, Worship, and the Church" that "as long as the church continues to differentiate according to sex rather than according to the gifts of each person, it is openly impoverishing the people of God."[64] Walton analyzes recent statements on women from three administrative levels of the Church—Rome, the National Conference of Catholic Bishops, and a diocesan priests' senate—and questions the inconsistency between these statements and other general statements. The lack of official support for the full involvement of women in ecclesiastical life is indeed problematic, but the problem is larger than this. As Sally Cunneen observed as early as 1971,[65] regulations at that time allowed considerably more liturgical involvement for women than had been permitted in the past, but

[61] *Liturgy* 15 (Oct. 1970) 6–8 and 16–19. Another special issue of *Liturgy* on women appeared in Dec. 1973 and a third is scheduled for Nov. 1975. *Living Worship*, also published by the Liturgical Conference, has focused occasionally on women; cf. Robert W. Hovda, "Women in a Sign-Church: Do We Lead or Follow in Human Liberation?" Sept. 1973, pp. 1–4.

[62] *Liturgy* 15 (Oct. 1970) p. 7.   [63] *Ibid.*, p. 19.   [64] *Liturgy* 18 (Dec. 1973) 4.

[65] "Women and the Liturgy: The Present Paradox," *American Ecclesiastical Review* 165 (1971) 167–74. Cunneen reports here on a survey conducted by a task force from the National Council of Catholic Women to measure the involvement of women in various

nevertheless participation was low despite the apparent willingness of many women to serve. She accounts for this "paradoxical" situation in terms of the laity's conditioned passivity and lack of knowledge of new regulations, and the lack of issue awareness on the part of church administrators. More recently, positive efforts to remedy the situation have been published in the form of books that include theoretical discussions as well as practical illustrations of nonsexist prayers and worship services. Arlene Swidler, who headed the task force conducting the survey mentioned by Cunneen, has edited *Sistercelebrations: Nine Worship Experiences*,[66] and Sharon and Thomas Neufer Emswiler have collaborated on *Women and Worship: A Guide to Non-Sexist Hymns, Prayers, and Liturgies.*[67]

Ministry

The action, experimentation, and reflection of American sisters and laywomen since the Council has resulted in a considerable body of literature regarding women in ministry. *The Changing Sister*, edited by M. Charles Borromeo Muckinhern, C.S.C.,[68] had indicated some of the directions renewal was taking among women religious in the mid-1960's, and by the early 1970's enough data was in for the National Assembly of Women Religious to publish two books based on the experiences of sisters who had taken seriously the challenge to examine their lives and works in the light of the gospel, the spirit of the founder, and the needs of the times. In the foreword to the first of these volumes, *Women in Ministry: A Sister's View*, editor Ethne Kennedy, S.H., notes that two significant trends of contemporary religious experience include "the phenomenon of sisters coming together in national groups designed to direct church action toward renewal and service" and "the discovery and sharing of professional competence of sisters in intercommunity fashion."[69] A second anthology, *Gospel Dimensions of Ministry*,[70] reports on new approaches to traditional apostolates of education and health care, as well as on such areas as campus ministry, pastoral ministry, ministry to the aging and to migrants, and involvement in housing, legal justice, and politics. Of significance also is M. Thomas Aquinas Carroll, R.S.M., *The Experience of Women Re-*

---

liturgical roles. The task force heard from 345 parishes in 71 dioceses and from 65 diocesan liturgical commissions. Of the latter, only 7 responded with an unqualified "yes" to the question "Does your diocese intend to promote the use of women as lectors and commentators in the parishes?" while 13 responded "yes" with unspecified limitations, 27 did not answer or did not know, and 18 responded "no."
[66] Philadelphia, 1974.   [67] New York, 1974.
[68] Notre Dame, 1965.   [69] Chicago, 1972, p. 12.
[70] Ethne Kennedy, S.H., ed. (Chicago, 1973).

ligious in the Ministry of the Church.[71] Carroll concludes that many of the difficulties experienced by those seeking to respond in new ministries are due to inadequate relations between men and women in the Church, and she is convinced that "one of the prime ministries must be a healing of the man-woman situation in the Church and in society."[72] Kennedy, Carroll, and others[73] have noted the relationship between developments among sisters and among contemporary women in general, a subject treated by Lora Ann Quinonez, C.D.P., in "The Women's Movement and Women Religious."[74] Quinonez finds affinities between the search of women religious and other women in terms of "a desire to experience ourselves as persons, not as symbols or mythic figures; a critical examination of old roles and an urge to shape new ones in which we can make our gifts available to others; a sense of the huge need for the liberation of all peoples and groups."[75]

Not surprisingly, the diversification of ministerial roles for women has met with some resistance. Kennedy observes that "resistance to woman's mature entrance to Church and civil societies is not limited to men and clerics alone," but is also due to the fact that women have been conditioned to mistrust one another" and "to underestimate feminine abilities."[76] Among others, Thomas Franklin O'Meara has noted that the assumption of leadership roles by women poses some threat to "clerical culture," a fact he interprets as ultimately beneficial for the Church. "In the midst of these changes," he claims, "women are initiating not a

[71] Chicago, 1974. Carroll reports that generally "as of today the Church in its prescriptions is not taking women seriously" (p. 17), although she regards as encouraging the fact that the Bishops' Committee on the Permanent Diaconate had mentioned in its 1972 *Guidelines* that a "critical question concerns the ordination of women as deacons" and reported that "among deacon candidates themselves and leaders of training programs, there is growing conviction that women would strengthen the diaconal ministry immeasurably" (Washington, D.C., 1971, p. 54).

[72] Carroll, p. 16.

[73] In "Religious Life Yesterday and Tomorrow," *New Catholic World* 312 (1972) 74–77, Annette Walters, C.S.J., describes the efforts of American sisters to liberate themselves from oppressive structures in order to serve more effectively. Cf. also my "Creative Ministry: Apostolic Women Today," *Sister Formation Bulletin* 19 (1972) 8–14.

[74] *Origins* 4 (1974) 337–43. In "Follow-up/The Liberation of Women," *Center Magazine* 5 (July-Aug. 1972), Anita Caspary, I.H.M., describes her work as superior general of the California Immaculate Heart community (a group that chose to lose canonical religious status rather than rescind the decisions of its chapter of renewal) in terms of a "struggle for the liberation of a specific group of women dedicated to the service of the church" (p. 19).

[75] Quinonez, p. 343.

[76] *Gospel Dimensions of Ministry*, p. 10. This conditioning for self-mistrust among women is analyzed by Susanne Breckel, R.S.M., in "Women and Ministry in the 1970's: A Psychologist Reflects," *Women in Ministry*, pp. 83–93, and by Letitia Brennan, O.S.U., in "How Women Can Break the Power Barrier," *America* 128 (1973) 552–55.

power play for ordination to the solitary pastorate as it is now, but a movement towards the liberation of the ministry itself."[77]

Ordination

Literature on this issue has appeared from time to time since 1965, but has increased dramatically within the last five years. In general, early works served to establish the import of the question. Subsequently writers have analyzed scriptural and traditional materials and focused on the pastoral dimensions of the issue. In 1965 Heinzelmann raised the question of ordination in relation to what the traditional practice of excluding women from priesthood may imply about the baptism of women. She cites the doctrine of the spiritual character imparted by baptism, which makes the recipient capable of receiving the other sacraments and grounds the Christian in the rights and duties of church membership, and asserts that "the exclusion of women from priestly ordination, a sacrament, quite obviously runs counter to this doctrine of the full effect of Baptism."[78] In another 1965 article, Charles R. Meyer urges a "careful" and "unprejudiced" re-examination of the question of the ordination of women in the early Church, and states that "to push the argument against the sacramentality of the ordination of deaconesses too far would be in fact to deny the sacramentality of the order of deacons."[79]

The most substantial Roman Catholic contribution to the ordination discussion currently available in English is Haye van der Meer, S.J., *Women Priests in the Catholic Church?*[80] He investigates the arguments from Scripture, tradition, the magisterium, and speculative theology

[77] "Feminine Ministry and Clerical Culture." *Commonweal* 98 (1973) 523–26.

[78] "The Priesthood and Women," *Commonweal* 81 (1965) 507.

[79] "Ordained Women in the Early Church," *Chicago Studies* 4 (1965) 301. A substantial part of this article is included in Meyer's *Man of God* (Garden City, N.Y., 1974) pp. 58–85.

[80] Tr. Arlene and Leonard Swidler (Philadelphia, 1973). This work, a doctoral thesis which van der Meer completed under Karl Rahner, S.J., in 1962, was first published as *Priestertum der Frau?* (Freiburg, 1969). The English edition is enhanced by a useful bibliographic survey in the "Translators' Foreword," and by the translators' concluding observations on developments that have occurred since the thesis was written. A notable Anglican contribution is Emily C. Hewitt and Suzanne R. Hiatt, *Women Priests: Yes or No?* (New York, 1973), which explores the issue in terms of popular feelings about priesthood, attitudes toward women, theological arguments, and ecumenical and "practical" considerations. This volume also contains official documentation and a selected bibliography. Odette d'Ursel's "Women's Accession to the Pastoral Ministry in the Churches Stemming from the Reformation," *Lumen vitae* 29 (1974) 554–82, cites the main events in the gradual opening of pastoral responsibilities to women from 1832 to 1974, and quotes from principal documents of Protestant churches and ecumenical conferences. D'Ursel attaches much importance to exegetical and theological studies, noting that such examination "has nearly always resulted in women obtaining to the pastoral ministry on an equal footing with men, despite the weight of the past" (p. 582).

that have been offered by dogmatic theologians to affirm the practice of excluding women from orders, and concludes that "Catholic dogmatic theologians may not hold that according to the present position of theology it is already (or still) established on a scholarly basis that 'office' should, by divine law, remain closed to women."[81] John J. Begley, S.J., and Carl J. Armbruster, S.J., likewise find the traditional material inconclusive and thus suggest that the issue of ordaining women is "pre-eminently a pastoral question."[82]

Pastoral arguments for and against ordination tend to emphasize two interrelated aspects of priesthood, the functional and the symbolic. Mary Angela Harper inquires in an early article whether woman's contribution might be destroyed by being forced into "the existing structure of ecclesiastical functions and offices,"[83] and J. Galot, S.J., has argued that the priestly tasks related to cult, government, and preaching are "specifically masculine." Women, he notes, are divinely destined to co-operate with these tasks but not to share them. He considers woman's natural "feminine docility" to be in accord with the "masculine pastoral function of government" and holds that, with regard to preaching,

[81] Van der Meer, p. 9. In 1973 the Committee on Pastoral Research and Practices of the National Conference of Catholic Bishops called for "exhaustive study" of the reasons for and against women's ordination. The Committee's report, "Theological Reflections on the Ordination of Women," is reprinted in the *Journal of Ecumenical Studies* 10 (1973) 695-99. It focuses on traditional arguments against ordaining women and does not give evidence of having taken into account the work of van der Meer. In "Will Women Be Ordained?" *Origins* 2 (1973) 743-44, Ann Gillen, S.H.C.J., objects to the negative emphasis of the report and predicts that a growing sense of rejection by the Roman Church will lead Catholic women to seek ordination in other Christian churches or to evolve an independent priesthood according to their sense of vocation. In "Biblical Material Relevant to the Ordination of Women," *Journal of Ecumenical Studies* 10 (1973) 669-94, J. Massyngberde Ford observes that "the bishops' report, while remaining open, has tended to overlook the evolution and diversity of thought and practice from the Old Testament to the New and also within the early Church itself" (p. 690). Ford sees no scriptural reasons for denying ordination to women, and underscores the statement of the 1968 Lambeth Conference: "The New Testament does not encourage us to believe that nothing should ever be done for the first time" (p. 693).

[82] "Women and Office in the Church," *American Ecclesiastical Review* 165 (1971) 145-57. Others stressing a pastoral approach include Meyer, *Man of God;* Gerald O'Collins, S.J., "An Argument for Women Priests," *America* 129 (1973) 122-23; George R. Evans, "Ordination of Women," *Homiletic and Pastoral Review* 73 (1972) 29-32; Agnes Cunningham, S.S.C.M., "Women and the Diaconate," *American Ecclesiastical Review* 165 (1971) 158-66; Carroll Stuhlmueller, C.P., "Women Priests: Today's Theology and Yesterday's Sociology," *America* 131 (Dec. 14, 1974) 383-87. Observes Stuhlmueller: "We of the Catholic Church must seriously ponder the consequences of endorsing women as lectors and teachers of theology and yet denying them the sacred orders of the diaconate and priesthood. Without realizing it, we may be producing a 'Protestant' form of Catholicism— a religion emphasizing the Word over the Eucharist, especially over the liturgical sacrifice of the Mass" (p. 387).

[83] "Women's Role in the Church," *America* 115 (1966) 93.

woman performs the indispensable function of assimilating the truth as proclaimed by male preachers and then transmitting it in unofficial situations, chiefly to the young.[84] Still others have suggested that the ordination of women at this time could have the negative effect of perpetuating a hierarchical "caste structure."[85] Gregory Baum, on the other hand, maintains that "the ordination of women to the priesthood would restore a prophetic quality to the Church's ministry, educating people to discern the injustices in present society and presenting them with an ideal for participation of women in the life of society."[86] Literature on women and the diaconate has particularly emphasized pastoral considerations. In 1971 the U.S. Bishops' Committee on the Permanent Diaconate released a "Report on the Permanent Diaconate" which states that "the current discussion of the theological dimensions of ministry should be pursued in terms of the Christian and not only in terms of the Christian male. Actual services being performed by women, both secular and religious, could often be rendered more effectively if they were performed within the office of deacon. The witness of history tells in favor of such practice, not against it" (no. 34).[87] Ford, Cunningham, Hünermann, and others have indicated that the ordination of women deacons is more immediately feasible than the introduction of women priests.[88] Nevertheless, most of the pastoral arguments advanced regarding diaconate can be extended to the areas of priesthood and episcopacy. As Begley and Armbruster have observed, "Because of the underlying unity of Church office, admission to one office implicitly affirms the theological possibility of admission to any of them."[89]

[84] L'Eglise et la femme (Gembloux, 1965) p. 203.

[85] Elizabeth Gössman, "Women as Priests," tr. Simon King, in Apostolic Succession: Rethinking a Barrier to Unity, ed. Hans Küng (Concilium 34) pp. 115–25; Ann Kelley and Anne Walsh, "Ordination: A Questionable Goal for Women," Heyer, Women and Orders, pp. 67–73.

[86] "Ministry in the Church," Women and Orders, pp. 57–66.

[87] Prepared by a committee of eleven members of the Catholic Theological Society of America, the report is published in the American Ecclesiastical Review 164 (1971) 190–204, as well as in Crux and Worship.

[88] Ford, art. cit.; Cunningham, art. cit., and "The Ministry of Women in the Church," Review for Religious 28 (1969) 124–41; Peter Hünermann, "Conclusions regarding the Female Diaconate," THEOLOGICAL STUDIES 36 (1975) 325–33.

[89] Art. cit., p. 151. The CTSA report cited above (n. 87) does not limit its conclusions regarding women to diaconal ministry, but rather states in general that the Catholic Church must be open to the Holy Spirit on the question of women's ministry; "for many women experience a desire to serve in capacities of spiritual leadership and sacramental service not available to them in the present structures and institutions of the Church" (no. 32). Noting that female leadership is a growing contemporary phenomenon, Karl Rahner observes in The Shape of the Church to Come (New York, 1974) that in the Christian community leadership should be linked with sacramental and liturgical life, which will entail women's serving in priestly roles in communities where they are leaders (p. 114).

Symbolic considerations have received much attention in the discussion about priesthood. Frederick P. Chenderlin, S.J., acknowledges that ontologically God could "work the miracle" that would empower a woman to "fulfil the task of consecration," but argues that the maleness of Christ is important because at the Last Supper he was "playing a particularly masculine role"[90] in undoing the harm caused by Adam. As Chenderlin interprets Paul, the maleness of Adam is essential to his headship and authority, and analogously, Christ's redemptive activity must involve maleness, since "man has a precedence in authority over woman."[91] Evans, Price, and Barnhouse, on the other hand, maintain that including women in ordained ministry could enhance the representational power of priestly service.[92] They are basically in agreement with Begley and Armbruster, who hold that "it is extrinsic and accidental to the incarnation that the specific human nature assumed by the Son was masculine."[93] Evans maintains that "men and women redeemed in Christ's friendship might be better symbolized by male and female priests, not the one sex voiding half the meaning of the symbol,"[94] and Cunningham points out that the ordination of women at this juncture of history might well serve to guarantee and express orthodoxy of faith, since to exclude woman from priesthood on the basis of sex amounts to "a new mode of neo-Arianism."[95] Recently, arguments for ordination have emphasized the need to symbolize the fact that the image of God is both male and female,[96] and this approach entails an important shift in the discussion. Rather than asking whether it is right to *include* women in official ministry, these writers are inquiring, at least implicitly, whether it is wrong to continue *excluding* them.

[90] Frederick P. Chenderlin, S.J., "Women as Ordained Priests," *Homiletic and Pastoral Review* 72 (1972) 27.

[91] *Ibid.*, p. 31.

[92] Evans, *art. cit.;* Charles P. Price, *Ordination of Women in Theological Perspective* (Cincinnati, 1975); Ruth Tiffany Barnhouse, "An Examination of the Ordination of Women to the Priesthood in Terms of the Symbolism of the Eucharist," *Women and Orders*, pp. 15–37.

[93] *Art. cit.*, p. 154. Nor does van der Meer find difficulty with the notion of females representing Christ. There is "something significantly feminine," he observes, "not only in the Church as bride as receiving, but in the Church as imparting, as dispensing life" (p. 149). He argues that to claim that women cannot administer sacraments because of their femininity logically entails that one must find it problematic for men to receive sacraments.

[94] *Art. cit.*, p. 30.

[95] "The Ministry of Women in the Church," p. 138. In this 1969 article, however, Cunningham did not recommend the immediate ordination of women to priesthood, but suggested instead that women become deacons "in preparation for the moment when the ordination of women will be a reality" (p. 140).

[96] Cf. Hewitt and Hiatt, *op. cit.;* Price, *op. cit.;* Eric Doyle, O.F.M., "God and the Feminine," *Clergy Review*, 1971, pp. 866–77.

Models for Christian Life

That the basic acceptance of an egalitarian approach to human relationships—in contrast to a model of domination-subordination—carries ramifications for Mariology as well as for Christian ethics and moral education is evident in the writings of Sidney Cornelia Callahan, Janice Raymond, Beverly Wildung Harrison, and others.[97] In *The Illusion of Eve: Modern Woman's Quest for Identity*,[98] Callahan explores the results of the emphasis on sexual polarities in Christian thinking, and notes that although the concept of Mary as the New Eve contributed to the theological appreciation of woman's dignity, adulation of Mary has not necessarily helped women in society. "The New Eve may be exalted, and even woman in the abstract glorified, but all other women living here and now must be kept away from business, education, the professions, government, and (heaven forbid) the altar."[99] Callahan comments on the effectiveness of imprisonment upon a pedestal and criticizes past emphasis upon a piety of silence and submission in "imitation" of Mary. Interestingly enough, Paul VI's recent Apostolic Exhortation "Devotion to the Blessed Virgin Mary" gives evidence of recognizing this problem. The document acknowledges that the Marian image characterizing much devotional literature can hardly be reconciled with the way women live today, and insists that the "permanent" and "universal" exemplary value of Mary's life cannot be located in the time-bound conditions of her background. It also asserts that the qualities of Mary's discipleship are to be imitated by men as well as by women. Mary's strength and courageous involvement, it points out, "cannot escape the attention of those who wish to support, with the Gospel spirit, the liberating energies of man and of society" (no. 37).[100] Callahan argues against a "feminine" spirituality, insisting that sex should not restrict the Christian freedom of women. She finds that despite the Gospel demand for a "single high standard of Christian behavior for both sexes," emphasis on presumed

[97] Cf. Roger Ruston, O.P., "Theology and Equality," *New Blackfriars* 55 (1974) 52-60; Joyce Trebilcot, "Sex Roles: The Argument from Nature," *Ethics* 85 (1975) 249-55; Penelope Washbourn, "Differentiation and Difference—Reflections on the Ethical Implications of Women's Liberation," *Women and Religion: 1972 Proceedings*, pp. 95-105; Rita Gross, "Methodological Remarks on the Study of Women in Religion: Review, Criticism, and Redefinition," *ibid.*, pp. 121-30; Gwen Kennedy Neville, "Religious Socialization of Women within U.S. Subcultures," Hageman, *op. cit.*, pp. 77-92; Harriet Goldman, "Women and a New Spirituality," *Cross Currents* 24 (1974) 51-54; Margaret A. Farley, R.S.M., "Liberation, Abortion, and Responsibility," *Reflection* 71 (1974) 9-13. Farley's piece is an especially useful contribution on the subject, since it takes both the tradition and the feminist perspective seriously, and challenges both proabortionists and antiabortionists to greater honesty in dealing with the problem.
[98] New York, 1965.
[99] *Ibid.*, p. 66.
[100] *The Pope Speaks* 19 (1974) 75.

sexual differences has often led in practice to tolerance for double standards.[101]

Raymond would overcome the problem of double standards and other shortcomings of "patriarchal" morality by replacing it with "androgynous morality." Using Tillichian terms, she asserts that androgynous morality would employ "ontological" rather than "technical" reason, that is, it would enable persons "to combine cognition with intuition, experience, feeling, and action, i.e., 'reason rejoined with its depth.'"[102] Raymond suggests that whereas polarized notions of masculinity and femininity have fostered an unrealistic sameness, androgyny would allow for the acceptance of diversity. "It is ironic," she comments, "that the biological argument which attempted to ground sex role definitions in nature did not take our biological differences seriously enough. That is, such an argument failed to recognize the range of biological differences between individuals of the same sex."[103] In Raymond's view of androgyny, "what we have traditionally regarded as opposites (masculinity-femininity) are not static states of being, encompassed in a male or female body, but rather processes of becoming, each defining the other, within each human person."[104] She thus describes the human project in terms of recovering the part of one's humanity that has been stereotyped as alien, and growing toward wholeness of being.

Harrison also emphasizes the problems inherent in the popular acceptance of the theory of a "special" feminine nature.[105] By accepting this theory, women have enjoyed the limited benefits of "pedestalism," which, according to Harrison's analysis, attributes to women a superior ability to live out the values that are losing ground in the "public" sector of society, values that "can no longer be effectually expressed in the lives of men."[106] Agreeing with Habermas that the deepest crisis of

[101] *Op. cit.*, p. 107. Cf. Dorothy D. Burlage, "Judaeo-Christian Influences on Female Sexuality," Hageman, *op. cit.*, pp. 93–116.

[102] "Beyond Male Morality," *Women and Religion: 1972 Proceedings*, p. 92. In this article Raymond illustrates the application of "androgynous ethics" with a discussion of homosexuality.

[103] *Ibid.*, p. 88.

[104] *Ibid.*, p. 87.

[105] "The New Consciousness of Women: A Socio-Political Resource," *Cross Currents* 24 (1975) 445–62.

[106] *Ibid.*, p. 449. The negative effects of accepting a subordinate role are treated by Nancy van Vuuren in *The Subversion of Women* (Philadelphia, 1973). Building on Gordon Allport's analysis of the ego defenses he terms "traits due to victimization," van Vuuren suggests that historically women who have identified with the religious institutions have tended to adopt "intropunitive traits," while "extropunitive traits" have been especially manifested by rebellious women, particularly those involved in witchcraft and prostitution. Cf. also Barbara Yoshioka, "Whoring after Strange Gods: A Narrative of Women and Witches," *Radical Religion* 1 (Summer/Fall 1974) 6–11.

contemporary society is "the almost total erosion of the interpersonal interface of lived-world communication from the 'public' sector of our life,"[107] Harrison defines the ethical task of feminists as one of simultaneously overcoming pedestalism and promoting in the public sphere the values previously confined to "woman's place."

CONSTRUCTIVE EFFORTS AND RADICAL CHALLENGES

Constructive efforts to incorporate feminist insights into Christian theology tend to be based on liberation-theology models. Noteworthy contributors in this area include Rosemary Radford Ruether and Letty M. Russell, both of whom treat the subjugation of women as part of an interlocking structure of oppression that also involves classism, racism, and colonialism. As a consequence, they emphasize the danger of advocating the feminist cause exclusively, although they recognize the necessity of overcoming sexual oppression because of its universality and because it supplies a "psychic model" for other oppressor-oppressed relationships. Both regard their work as only a beginning of the task demanded of theology today. Russell concludes her *Human Liberation in a Feminist Perspective—A Theology*[108] with a "Prologue" calling for a never-ending process of experimentation, action, and reflection, and Ruether has observed that "multidisciplinary teamwork" integrating the human sciences is required "before we can begin to speak of the basis for a theology of liberation adequate to the present situation."[109]

Russell's extensively documented volume relates themes of traditional theology—such as salvation, conversion, justification, incarnation, communion—to the liberation experience. She emphasizes the need to reinterpret traditional words and concepts, observing, e.g., that *diakonia* for women today will involve claiming authentic power and authority. The ministerial model she advocates stresses pluralism and the recognition that every Christian is called to action and reflection. She opposes the stratification of Christians into clergy and laity, and suggests that ideally "the 'laying on of hands' would not set apart only those with certain degrees, but whatever members of a congregation who have a particular calling and ability to perform the service or mission needed in the life and mission of that witnessing community."[110]

[107] Harrison, p. 455.

[108] Philadelphia, 1974. Cf. also Russell, "Women's Liberation in a Biblical Perspective," *Concern* 13 (May–June 1971); Monika Hellwig, "Hope and Liberation: The Task of Sexual Complementarity," *Liturgy* 15 (October 1972) 13–15.

[109] *Liberation Theology: Human Hope Confronts Christian History and American Power* (New York, 1972) p. 2.

[110] Russell, *Human Liberation*, p. 180.

Ruether approaches the subject of women and religion from the perspective of historian and "radical" theologian. Her articles have stressed the cultural factors involved historically in the subjugation of women and other oppressed groups, and her ideas have influenced other writers considerably. In an early article, "The Becoming of Women in Church and Society,"[111] she builds upon Jung's analysis of psychological growth and observes that the classical epoch of history can be likened to the stage of individual development when consciousness separates itself off from the subconscious. "Just as the rise of the ego in the individual is the origin of the dualism of the self, so the rise of the self-consciousness in history is the origin of the dualisms in both society and the cultural images of society."[112] Whereas primitive society had been characterized by psychic and sexual integration, the emergence of consciousness in the race led to a split between a "thinking elite" and the "mass of humanity" subject to this elite. The dominant elite then attempted to "canonize its seizure of power through the myth of fixed natures and states of life."[113] She goes on to suggest that the rise of socialism in our times is analogous to what Jung termed "individuation" in human development, i.e., "the stage of the emergence of the mature self when the ego integrates itself with its subconscious and out of that integration rises the mature whole self which no longer lives on antagonisms and projections."[114] This new stage in history can lead to a "new communal society," a realization of the "kingdom of God," in which social roles will be based on function rather than on caste, and will be temporary and contextual rather than "ontologized into fixed characters and states of life."[115]

More recently Ruether has modified this analysis somewhat by characterizing preclassical society as an earlier stage in the oppression of women rather than a time of integration in relationships. In *Liberation Theology* she points out that the emergence of classical civilizations provided an opportunity for the overcoming of taboos based on woman's physical characteristics and for the recognition of her mental abilities. What occurred instead, however, was an intensification of misogyny: "The prejudice against woman was translated into the intellectual sphere, and men reconfirmed their right to be the stronger by declaring that they alone possessed genuine mental power and all the spiritual

[111] *Cross Currents* 17 (1967) 418-26.

[112] *Ibid.*, p. 421. Ruether has favored Jung's approach over those of Freud and Erikson, whose writings on women she criticizes in "Male Chauvinist Theology and the Anger of Women," *Cross Currents* 21 (1971) 173-85.

[113] *Ibid.*, p. 422.

[114] *Ibid.*, p. 423.

[115] *Ibid.*, p. 424.

values that went with it, while women were identified with the body and what was seen as the 'lower psyche.'"[116] Ruether attributes classical sexism to "misappropriated dualisms," which resulted from the fact that such dialectical elements of human existence as carnality and spirituality were symbolized as sexual polarities, which were then "projected" socially as the essential "natures" of women and men. Consequently, she notes, in classical culture "autonomous spiritual selfhood is imaged (by men, the cultural creators of this view) as intrinsically 'male,' while the 'feminine' becomes the symbol of the repressed, subjugated and dreaded 'abysmal side of man.'"[117] Ruether has traced the effects of this dualism in the history of Christian thought, emphasizing the tensions in patristic theology[118] and the effects of residual dualism on the contemporary Church. Moreover, she attributes the dehumanization experienced in technological society and the dichotomization of ethics into private and public spheres to the limited God-concepts resulting from a dualistic understanding of reality.

A recurring theme in Ruether's writing is her opposition to dualism and encapsulation of thought. She sees humanity on the edge of an era when classical polarities can be transcended by "dynamic unities" between "the historical and the transcendent; the spiritual and the somatic; the holy and the worldly."[119] In her advocacy of social change she rejects "apocalyptic dualism" (typified in the language of "children of light" and "children of darkness") in favor of an emphasis on the need for greater humanization of both oppressor and oppressed. In "Crisis in Sex and Race: Black Theology vs. Feminist Theology" she cautions against the danger of elitism in the women's movement, and stresses the importance of recognizing the "primordial power of the mother symbol as Ground of Being to restore an ontological foundation to the 'wholly other' God of patriarchy."[120] She views the ordination of women as neither simply a question of women's rights nor a capitulation to clericalism, but rather a step toward a "psychological revolution in the way we relate to God, to leadership, to each other, to 'nature' and to the relation of the Church to 'the world.'"[121] The challenge she sees before the women's revolution in general is to transcend the "masculine ethic of competitive-

[116] *Liberation Theology*, p. 98.

[117] "Male Clericalism and the Dread of Women," *Ecumenist* 11 (1973) 66.

[118] Cf. "Misogynism and Virginal Feminism in the Fathers of the Church," *Religion and Sexism*, pp. 150–83.

[119] *Liberation Theology*, p. 7.

[120] *Christianity and Crisis* 34 (1974) 73. For critical responses to this article (with a reply by Ruether) see "Continuing the Discussion: A Further Look at Feminist Theology," *Christianity and Crisis* 34 (1974) 139–143. Cf. also Theressa Hoover, "Black Women and the Churches: Triple Jeopardy," Hageman, *op. cit.*, pp. 63–76.

[121] "Male Clericalism and the Dread of Women," p. 68.

ness that sees the triumph of the self as predicated upon the subjugation of the other" and to contribute to the building of a new "cooperative social order out beyond the principles of hierarchy, rule, and competitiveness."[122]

Whereas Ruether writes from within the Roman Catholic Christian tradition with a view toward reconstructing its symbolism so as to integrate transcendence with the historical struggle for liberation, Mary Daly's pursuit of the question of transcendence has led her to a "postchristian feminist" rejection of the tradition. Daly's writings span the decade covered in this survey, and deserve the careful analysis of theologians not only because she articulates the anger of growing numbers of women who are alienated from institutional religion, but also because she raises in a particularly forceful way the question of whether the oppression of women is intrinsically bound up in the symbol structure of Christianity. Daly's progressive radicalization is somewhat analogous to that of Luther, and possibly as consequential for the churches. In a spirit of postconciliar optimism, the "early Daly" had supplied some "modest proposals" toward achieving partnership in the Church. She had advocated "radical surgery" for overcoming "theological misogynism," but was basically confident that the Church could eventually be freed of the "'demon' of sexual prejudice."[123] Indeed, she held that "the seeds of the eschatological community, of the liberating, humanizing Church of the future, are already present, however submerged and neutralized they may be."[124] More recently, however, Daly describes her earlier hopes as "misplaced," and states that "the entire conceptual system of theology and ethics, developed under the conditions of patriarchy, have been the products of males and tend to serve the interests of sexist society."[125] She cautions against "cooptable reformism that nourishes the oppressive system,"[126] and looks to women to rename reality in ways that affirm the dynamism inherent in the process of being and becoming. "The freedom-becoming-survival of our species will require a continual, communal striving in be-ing," she comments. "This means forging the great chain of be-ing in sister-

[122] *Liberation Theology*, pp. 124–25.

[123] *The Church and the Second Sex* (New York, 1975) p. 193. The edition cited here includes a "new feminist postchristian introduction by the author" in addition to the unrevised text of the 1968 edition.

[124] *Ibid.*, p. 221.

[125] *Beyond God the Father: Toward a Philosophy of Women's Liberation* (Boston, 1973) p. 4. Cf. also "Theology after the Death of God the Father: A Call for the Castration of Sexist Religion," Hageman, *op. cit.*, pp. 125–42; "Post-Christian Theology: Some Connections between Idolatry and Methodolatry, between Deicide and Methodicide," *Women and Religion: 1973 Proceedings*, pp. 33–38.

[126] *Beyond God the Father*, p. 6.

hood that can surround nonbeing, forcing it to shrink back into itself."[127] Daly describes her method as one of asking "nonquestions," that is, pursuing areas of inquiry that are "invisible" to traditional methods because these areas do not fit into accepted categories of thought. This involves especially the analysis of "nondata," the experience of women, which has largely been ignored by patriarchal systems of thought. Daly insists on the need to affirm freedom and to reject the "false dichotomy" between good and evil inherent in the myth of the Fall (which has functioned to reinforce the myth of feminine evil), as well as on the need to reconceptualize God as an active principle of "ultimate meaning and reality."[128] Regarding Christology, she suggests that "as a uniquely masculine image and language for divinity loses credibility, so also the idea of a single divine incarnation in a human being of the male sex may give way in the religious consciousness to an increased awareness of the power of Being in all persons."[129] She finds Tillich's Christological concept of "New Being" of some use because it is "to some extent free of strictly 'biblical' thought and of hellenic formulas" and because "it stresses the humanity of Jesus (as opposed to a 'high' Christology) and recognizes the Christ as a symbol."[130] Nevertheless, she faults Tillich for failing to deal with the fact that the symbol has been used oppressively, and states that the "long history" of such use may indicate "some inherent deficiency in the symbol itself."[131]

In a recent *Horizons* symposium Daly observes that the context or "sense of reality" of Christian theologians is so at variance with her feminist perspective that real "hearing" and constructive exchange of thought between the two contexts is unlikely.[132] She is reluctant to spend energy mediating between her futurist position and the tradition; this mediating function, however, is lately being assumed by others. In the same symposium June O'Connor describes *Beyond God the Father* as "brilliant and profoundly provocative," but disagrees with Daly's insistence that sexism is the basic cause of other forms of oppression.[133] This criticism points to a need for further analysis of what is at the root of sexism, and of how sexism is related to other structures

[127] *Ibid.*, p. 198.
[128] *Ibid.*, p. 6.
[129] *Ibid.*, p. 71.
[130] *Ibid.*, p. 72.
[131] *Ibid.*

[132] "A Short Essay on Hearing and the Qualitative Leap of Radical Feminism," *Horizons* 2 (1975) 120–24. This essay is Daly's response to a series of brief critiques of *Beyond God the Father* in "Symposium: Toward a Theology of Feminism?", pp. 103–20. Introducing the critiques is an extremely helpful essay by June O'Connor, "Liberation Theologies and the Women's Movement: Points of Comparison and Contrast," pp. 103–13.

[133] *Ibid.*, p. 108 and p. 115.

of injustice and to traditional concepts of sin. Another contributor to the *Horizons* symposium, Elisabeth Schüssler Fiorenza, describes *Beyond God the Father* as "political theology at its best," but challenges Daly to move beyond the necessarily derivative writing of polemics and to develop her constructive insights in more detail and with greater attention to the "androgynous goal or ideal."[134] Although Daly states that "it matters more where we are going than where we started from,"[135] she still focuses on the intermediate goal of bonding in sisterhood rather than on the long-range goal of achieving androgyny. Fiorenza, on the other hand, advances the discussion by stressing the need to "recast eschatology not only in female but also in androgynous symbols pronouncing full human integrity."[136]

To date, the most thorough attempt at mediation is Sheila D. Collins' *A Different Heaven and Earth*,[137] a volume describing the process that has led over the past several years to the articulation of feminist theology. Collins discusses such areas as history, God-language, ethics, worship, and communal "theologizing." Although she argues for a more or less radical feminist position vis-à-vis the established churches, Collins is reluctant to "destroy the deeply emotional psychic bases upon which we have erected our systems of truth and the symbols which unite us with universal meaning."[138] As a result, she is particularly conscious of the need to remythologize religious truths "in a way that has personal and communal depth of meaning for us."[139] This task mainly lies ahead, along with the task of developing original systems of thought based on feminist insights and that of mediating further between these insights and other contemporary approaches to religious thought.

Divinity School   ANNE E. PATRICK, S.N.J.M.
University of Chicago

[134] *Ibid.*, p. 118. Fiorenza, who finds Daly's phrase "sisterhood of man" an "excellent critical formulation" but one that "still communicates sex divisions and dependence upon a parental figure," offers as an androgynous substitute the category of "friend/friendship" to symbolize a "community of equals."

[135] *Ibid.*, p. 123.

[136] *Ibid.*, p. 118.

[137] Valley Forge, Pa., 1974.

[138] *Ibid.*, p. 21.

[139] *Ibid.*